Black Dog, Blue Sea

Also by Danforth Slater

This is Not a Holiday
March of the Warmdüschers

Black Dog, Blue Sea

Circumnavigating the Caribbean with a Grumpy Old Man

DANFORTH SLATER

Blmph!

First published in Australia by Blmph! in 2022

Cover design by Claire Smith, BookSmith Design, Sydney, Australia
Typeset by Andrew Tennant, Edinburgh, Scotland
Editing by Write My Wrongs, USA
Route map by jimxon, France
Blmph! logo by Nils van der Werf

www.thisisnotaholiday.com

ISBN 978-0-6456172-0-7

For my grumpy old man. Don’t go a-changing!

Contents

Circu
Havana
Start
/ End
Cancún
Tulum
Santiago de
Cuba
Caye Caulker
Santa Marta
Panama City
San José
Cartagena
Méri
N

navigating The Caribbean 2013

Introduction

Monachopsis

"I spent my youth and early adulthood desperately trying to be human and to mix with you people. And I failed, so I was forced to re-evaluate. If I'm not human, I must be extra-terrestrial. Since I was unable to integrate with the indigenous population here, I have been obliged to study them objectively, and what a strange species you are. You have this wonderful method of communication called speech—a fairly good, though not excellent, way of relaying useful information, giving instruction, and expressing ideas. And what do you use it for? Two of you sit down together and begin to make comments about topics of which neither of you are really interested, i.e., the weather, then you give personal information about yourselves that is of no interest to the other party, desperately searching for common experiences so you can form a relationship. I have attended such meetings and noted that everyone is anxious to talk about themselves, wanting to have their say, but not listening and absorbing what the other participants are saying.

I have to conclude that this activity is not to exchange information but is purely a social activity, which is the equivalent of apes grooming each other. I have tried talking to men, whose main interests are football, motor cars, and women. The former two, I find, are not worthy of discussion. I am more successful discussing with ladies, though with them, it is difficult to track the rapid changes in subject material. If one listens to two females in full flow, the changes in topic are so swift that I believe some sort of telepathy must be in use, since even if they use the wrong words, the meaning still seems to be transmitted. I myself, of course, have to rely solely on the words themselves to understand the content of the conversation. I have to listen and filter through the various meanings of each word in order to find the appropriate intended meaning. I often choose the wrong one."

– Peter Slater

Part I

Song Sung Blue

Chapter 1

Dysphoria

Tulum, Mexico. February 2013

What would you see if you could shine a beam of darkness through a prism? Infinite shades of black? A greyscale rainbow? I often imagine him in black and white, the colours of childhood memories, so when the low sun refracts through a crack in the window pane, it's a monochrome spectrum that illuminates his shuffle up the hallway. The ashen light washes his face with a bleak pallor, which for a second seems all too real, until my thoughts clear and the colour returns to the warm amber glow of dusk.

"Are you ready then, Dad?" The rhythm of my foot tapping on the terracotta tiles increases in tempo as I hold the door open in a passive-aggressive gesture designed to hurry him up. "Let's go see Tulum!" I guide him down the path of our hostel, the poorly lit passage an obstacle course of garden detritus and lush pot plants. I fumble for my torch to light the ground at his feet. I wouldn't want him to hurt himself so early into a three-month trip.

"Isn't this great?" I gush once we reach the street. I'm not generally a person who brims outwardly with enthusiasm, but this evening, I'm practically skipping with excitement—as much as someone still jetlagged from twenty-four hours in economy class can be, anyway. I'm in Mexico—with my father! After half a lifetime of following my

N.B. Find the chapter glossary at the end of the book.

adventures through postcards, emails, and photos, he's finally joined me on one. At last I get to show him my world, to share my passion for travel and chaperone him through this unstable and complex region. I'm buzzing like a dog on its way to the park after a week locked indoors.

The one-horse Tulum of my memory is now a sizeable town on the east coast of the Yucatan Peninsula, a winding string of perfect beaches squeezed between emerald jungle and turquoise sea, known as the Mayan Riviera. My previous visit comprised a wonderful few days lounging in a hammock on a quiet beach, drinking beer in the sun with fellow travellers, and carousing all night. I treasure the recollections of a perfect morning routine: awoken at dawn by the first fingers of the sun poking through the cracks in the woven palm walls of my *cabaña*, I'd heave myself from my swinging bed and pad down the still-cool sand to the water's edge. There, I'd throw myself face first into the bathtub-warm Caribbean, slapping away the thickness of the previous night. Agatha Christie said, "Never go back to a place where you have been happy. Until you do it remains alive for you. If you go back it will be destroyed."[1] I generally observe that axiom, but Tulum is a convenient stop on the way to Belize, and I'm interested to see if I recognise the paradise it had been.

Fragments of those halcyon days returned when the harsh sun found its way onto my sleeping eyelids that morning, although, sadly, our twin room is in town, far from the beach and the sparkling cure for morning yawns. I sat up and stretched, pausing for a moment to examine my father's sleeping form. He was face up, hair thrown chaotically around his pillow like a native headdress, his breathing deep and wheezy. How long had it been since I saw him sleeping, I wondered. Decades, probably. How long should I leave him to sleep? How much sleep did he need? I'm grateful, at least, he doesn't sleep naked anymore, although maybe he's retaining his modesty purely for my benefit.

So, who is this pseudo-stranger with whom I've agreed to go travelling? Physically, he could be mistaken for a late-vintage Willie Nelson

1 From her autobiography, *Agatha Christie: An Autobiography*

(and indeed he has been) with his head of long white hair, tinged slightly yellow by minerals in his local well water and tied back in an almost waist-length ponytail. The full, neatly trimmed beard is whiter still yet sports a little black fringe at the top of his cheeks, matched by the rogue follicles sprouting wiry tufts from dark crevices. He was an attractive man in his youth, so I'm told, and now his strong features have softened into a gentle cragginess. His waistline has expanded somewhat, and his nose, never small, seems to be taking over his face. He tries not to smile in photographs because one of his front teeth is dead and rotten, but when he does, it's a full-face effect: his eyes crease up, and his mouth widens halfway to his ears in an infectious grin. It's hard not to join him when he cracks a genuine beamer.

I picked up the travel bug (among others, mainly intestinal) in India, but that wasn't where it really started. My first proper, parent-free holiday was a month-long Interrail journey through Europe when I was eighteen, after which I couldn't wait to tell my dad about all the amazing things I'd seen and done. I was naïve enough to imagine he'd be as interested in my trip as I was, whereas it likely would have bored him to tears. He wouldn't have let on, hopefully, but as it happened, I didn't see him for months after I got back to the UK, and when I did, the grand narrative I had prepared seemed a trifle overblown, and I dispensed with the trip in a few awkward sentences.

Now could be my chance, though. We have months of conversation ahead of us. I can go into as much detail as I want, and he won't be able to get away! Unfortunately, that European odyssey was twenty-two years ago now, and I can barely remember which countries I visited, never mind the nitty-gritty details. Was that the time I went to Prague? Or was it Budapest? It doesn't matter. After eighty-odd countries, mostly in the developing world, I have a lot of other stories to tell which I *can* remember.

I link my arm in his as he grunts an affirmative, staring at nothing in particular. I'm not sure what to say next, but I'm satisfied just being within his orbit. Since leaving home to study chemical engineering at university, I haven't seen near as much of either of my parents as I would have liked. Despite living only four hours' drive away, I saw them roughly three times a year when I caught the bus home for the holidays. Occasionally, one or both would come to visit, but I wasn't one of those students whose parents routinely dropped by with a box of food and/or money. I stayed on in my adopted city after graduation, and with the constraints of a full-time job, our meetings became even less frequent. I remember once being shocked when I calculated I hadn't seen my dad for over a year, even though he was essentially just down the M5 motorway.

We didn't speak on the phone that often, either. I've never really liked telephone conversations and can go for weeks without talking to those I consider my closest friends. It's something about the impersonality of a disembodied voice. I knew what he was doing anyway: working seven days a week in his plastic injection moulding business. I figured if anything drastic had happened, someone would have told me. Things didn't improve when I moved to London or subsequently Cape Town, South Africa. We barely spoke at all after that, and the next thing I knew, I was in Sydney, Australia, and Dad was living in a small mountain village in Spain, over fifteen-thousand kilometres away, with a woman who wasn't my mother.

"So, what do you fancy eating? Do you like tacos? They're the only real Mexican street food anyway. Well, them and tamales," I babble as we reach the main street. "Fajitas and burritos and all that, they're Tex-Mex, American. Mind the kerb." I know he enjoys his food, but beyond that, I've no idea of his preferences. "I mean, what do you feel like? We'll find pizza if you want. It's totally up to you." I look around, mentally cataloguing every option, from street-side barbecues to teeming restaurants. The dusty street is lit by the orange wash spilling from every doorway, illuminating tourists strolling about in the stern holiday business of post-beach dining and drinking. I wasn't expecting this US seaside town vibe. Tulum is very different from how I left it twelve years ago.

It's a few seconds before I register his lack of reply. Maybe he didn't hear me. I turn to face him and, for the first time, notice his dour expression, brow furrowed like a rumpled tapestry, eyes downcast. "Are you alright?"

Finally, he takes a deep breath and speaks. "I'm clinically depressed," he says. I have no time to process this information before he continues in his clear baritone, each word measured and exact. "I don't take pleasure in anything. All pleasure I have had in the past has been erased, and I look forward to nothing."

I'm stunned. These words, essentially a bold statement of intent, aren't the first I'd choose to hear from any travelling companion, let alone one whose company I've been anticipating for so long. My lips flap uselessly as we continue walking in silence. I was vaguely aware he had a history of depression, but it's been so long since we spent any real time together that I'd pretty much forgotten about it. Wasn't all that over and done with? Apparently, depressed people stay depressed, and now that I'm confronted directly with his illness, a small void opens up inside my chest. A human being, one of my favourite human beings, in fact, one of the three I've known my entire life, is effectively dead inside. In one succinct sentence, he has unerringly expressed to me the pointlessness of his existence, and I have no idea how to handle it. I consider brushing it off with a glib remark, unwilling to enter into a discussion that will likely drag me into a deep well of despair, but eventually concede it's an issue I'll have to face head-on if this trip is going to be any kind of success at all.

It's a warm spring night, mild enough for shorts and a t-shirt, and Tulum's main street resonates with an indistinct hum of low chatter, chirping insects, and the pleasant crunching of vehicles driving slowly over gravel. I steer Dad into a wooden building, a roughly scrawled menu on the door the only clue to its function as a taco restaurant. I'd noticed he'd been very quiet since we met up in Cancún yesterday, but I was so excited to finally be away that I didn't think too much about it.

And now this: clinical depression. He must have hidden it well for the last forty years because I had no idea the gravity of the situation. Perhaps it's not as bad as he's making out? Maybe he's just in a rare trough of despondency, I tell myself, hoping by some miracle that's the case. Either way, I can't think of any acceptable reply, witty or sympathetic, so I escape to the counter to select my tacos, one of each flavour of the three available. I fetch him the same, as his slumped posture is practically begging me to protect him from having to talk to anyone.

"When you asked me at Christmas if I was looking forward to the trip," he begins on my return, thankfully breaking the strained silence, "it reminded me that I should start some anti-depressants."

I think for a moment while I finish a mouthful of spicy chicken and flour tortilla. "If you're clinically depressed, and have been for so long, then why aren't you on them already?" I ask. It comes out more bluntly than I'd intended.

He takes a weary breath. "Well, I did take some in the 1970s. The fact is that for a long-term depressive, the depression becomes the norm and, consequently, the familiar and, therefore, the comfortable. One then has no real desire to leave. Like being institutionalised in prison, there's a reluctance to reenter the world. One can be happy to be unhappy, as it were, so there's no great desire to take the medication."

This reminds me of some lengthy bus journeys I've endured while travelling the larger expanses of the globe. After twenty-four hours or so, even the nicest vehicle feels like a cramped, filthy box you yearn to escape from, yet the thought of disembarking in a strange, vast city in the dark of night, with its attendant risks and smells and jabbering touts, is enough to make you want to sink deeper into your stiff, nylon seat and refuse to leave.

I allow him time to devour a taco before asking, "Then why are you thinking about starting now?"

"I'm anxious to protect you from my moods for the duration of our time together," he explains, speaking slowly and deliberately as though he has rehearsed the sentence beforehand. And maybe he has. This is not a man who stumbles over dialogue, taking wrong turns, filling gaps with "ums" and "ahs," or stopping abruptly, half-finished words hanging in the air. His utterances are measured, never polluted by contractions or slang. In fact, he speaks like I would write a paper for a scientific journal, almost like an android character from a science fiction novel. As someone who allows his brain to race far ahead of his mouth, my speech is a garbled morass of mashed-up words and missing links. Not for the first time, I wish I could replicate his delivery.

"I actually did go to a clinic to get a prescription for an antidepressant called sertraline, but the doctor I saw refused to prescribe it."

"But why?" I ask, over the gentle hubbub of cheerier conversations.

"I didn't act sad enough." He shrugs. His face is a cliff, rough and expressionless. "I didn't say the right things."

"Were you having a good day?" I drag up what little I know of so-called "manic" depression, hoping for a feeble ray of light to penetrate this otherwise dark alley I have blundered into. "Do you have good days?"

"Bipolar is a fashionable new term, but no, I wouldn't say I experience regular highs," he replies, killing my newfound optimism. "Perhaps on two occasions, whilst driving my car, I have felt an inexplicable surge of joy, but who knows what is going on in the subconscious mind?"

I watch the light wind whip up dust from the street outside. "So why come on this trip if you knew you'd get no pleasure from it?"

"Well, I was flattered you invited me," he admits. "It was an opportunity to spend time with you. Plus, I would be travelling to places I hadn't visited before, an adventure, and one in which you took all the responsibility of leadership."

I guess that makes sense, but then, he always does. I take it as a massive compliment he's willing to step outside his "comfort zone" of daily depression to avoid negatively impacting me, even though he's convinced he'll get no pleasure from it himself. It sounds like a monumental stride forward.

So here we are, a middle-aged man and his father strolling around a small Mexican town on a warm February night, full of tacos. Across the street, a wandering mariachi trio is trying to entice tourists into their aural orbit, their once-grand, matching outfits now faded and patched. To my despondent ears, the lightly plucked guitar and weeping violin are augmented in their melancholia by the trumpet's plaintive waning and the soft crooning of the singer. I don't know what the song is about, but it clearly doesn't end well for somebody. It's an appropriate soundtrack to the evening's revelations.

The playfulness of vacationing families taunts me further. Every laugh, casual embrace, and even rebuke is amplified, a stark contrast to our weighted silence. I have to remind myself that it wasn't always like this. I fondly recall a road trip the family took to France when I was in single digits. We'd stopped for the night in some small town, falling into bed after the long drive.

From a deep sleep, I was gently nudged awake, a gruff voice whispering in my ear, "Get up." It was still night outside, the glow from the streetlights playing on the walls and illuminating the drab furnishings of our cheap hotel. The sounds of music and garbled language filtered through the faded curtains as I struggled free of a sleep that felt too fresh to be more than an hour old. It wasn't.

Dad hurried my brother and me into our clothes and tip-toed us out of the twin room. As we crept down the hallway, careful not to wake our mother and sister in the next room, an atmosphere of collusion filled the air, heady and exciting. We made our way carefully down the stairs towards the front door. There was only one explanation: he was taking us on a boys-only, night-time adventure, possibly some sort of espionage in the streets of rural France. He didn't actually say the words "Don't tell your mother," but he may as well have.

It was late, well past the bedtimes of eight- and nine-year-old children, yet there we were, approaching the brightly lit town square where a funfair was in full swing. The amusement rides that accompanied Bonfire Night in our local park formed one of the pinnacles of my calendar, and yet here were the same rides seemingly sprung from nowhere. Even without the requisite month of anticipation that would normally precede such a momentous occasion, the excitement was immense. Our first overseas holiday in years, only a day old, had already heralded amazement when Dad revealed over £100 in cash hidden in one of his boots, ready to be changed into francs. I'd never fully imagined such a sum, let alone seen it. A hundred pounds! Could it be real? Surely, we were rich!

We kept close to his shielding presence, staring out at the townsfolk: middle-aged ride operators, carefree adolescents sneaking drinks, rotund parents, and squealing children. Surely the demographic of any funfair in the world, yet to me, there, they looked different. Skin was darker, faces more angular, more . . . *French*, somehow, was the only way I could explain it to my innocent self. Equally curious local children stared back, captivated by eyes bluer than glacial melt water and hair bleached white in the summer sun. Living in Spain, years before, they'd called me *El Rubio*—Blondie—and given me sweets while tousling my hair. I was a superstar. I'm sure my radiant locks also inspired Dad's nickname for me: Sunshine.

Matt and I didn't know where to start, so Dad took control and purchased tokens for the dodgems, or bumper cars as we called them. When the wailing siren signalled the end of the session, we raced to the nearest car and jumped in, inserting our first token into the slot on its bonnet. When the siren shrieked a second time, we shot off. It could have been my goaded imagination, but surely these cars were far faster and more powerful than those back home. The speed was hair-raising and the collisions hefty. I watched in amazement as one car broadsided another against the guardrail, knocking it so far over that the passenger was thrown out onto the cobblestones of the square. No one took a blind bit of notice; the riders continued smashing, and the ejected youth jumped up, laughing. We turned back into the maelstrom, having so much fun I even forgot to argue for my share of the driving. And then there was Dad, beckoning us over to the rail, mid-ride, to thrust more tokens into our hands.

He was my hero that night, and I refuse to believe he was depressed then, despite his claims to have been so since the year I was born. I can recall plenty of other instances when he was apparently happy, maybe not the ever-jolly, sitcom father figure of legend, but cheerful enough that our home wasn't a black pit of despair. He liked taking us to the pictures, the Odeon Cinema in nearby Sutton Coldfield, and playing I Spy in the car on the way. We'd go to the park on Sundays to play Cowboys and Indians, maybe get fish and chips on the way home. Every child deserves the opportunity to see their parents as heroes. I was in awe when he wrote to the manufacturer of my favourite toy soldiers to procure replacements for the badly moulded ones I'd bought. Such power, I thought. Was there nothing this man couldn't do? The dark, frowning figure by my side little resembles the father of my childhood memories. But then, if I'd taken the time to connect the dots, I wouldn't have been so surprised. After all, Asperger Syndrome in adults is often linked to depression.

We find a pharmacy and easily pick up some sertraline, which in Mexico doesn't require a prescription, but the bad news is the pills could take six weeks to have any effect. Back at the hostel, he apologises for his gloominess. "I'm sorry I mentioned it. I don't want you to dwell on it." Well, that might be a little difficult now that I'm asking myself, for the first time in my stupid, selfish life, how my father became depressed in the first place. The truth is, I hoped if I pretended the problem didn't exist then I wouldn't have to deal with it, and until now, I haven't. But if our journey of reconnection is going to be anything more than just a shallow excuse for me to feel better about the last two decades of distance, I'm going to have to find out.

Chapter 2

Farouche

The Yucatan Peninsula is the heartland of the ancient Mayan civilisation that thrived for a couple of thousand years before mysteriously imploding around the tenth century CE.[2] On my first visit, I'd seen most of the classic Mayan ruins: Tikal, Palenque, Copán, Uxmal, and nearby Chichen Itzá, as well as numerous other small, rarely visited sites. Indeed, the initial reason for my presence in Central America was an archaeological dig deep in the Guatemalan jungle. A professional archaeologist, for five weeks I'd lived in a tent on site, excavating tombs, intricately carved stelae, and even full-sized pyramids. I was suffering temple fatigue by the time I reached Tulum and could never quite rouse myself from my hammock long enough to visit the local ruins, despite them lying only a stone's throw away.

I consider it an excellent idea to complete my Mayan education today, but Dad isn't so sure. "Is there much walking involved?" he asks, transferring a forkful of pancake into his mouth. I consider refined flour smothered in high-fructose corn syrup to be a ridiculous breakfast choice, but they're included in the price of our accommodation, and so, as our budget dictates, we must avail ourselves of them. "I can't keep up with you anymore, you know."

"We'll go slowly, I promise." I pat him on the arm.

"It's very hot out there. I'm afraid I might overheat," he persists. I can't tell if this is a genuine concern or if he's making excuses because

2 Common Era, an areligious equivalent of AD, or *Anno Domini*

he doesn't want to face the world. It's a boiling cauldron of a day, true, but we'll find him some shade.

Ignoring his protests, I usher him outside into the glare of a cloudless tropical day to await the bus to the site, where we join a tour group being led slowly around the handsome ruins by a garrulous Mexican guide. Tulum was one of the later sites of the Mayan civilisation, built after the collapse of the Classic Period and persevering until the Spanish conquest in the fifteenth century and, as such, is very well preserved. The white limestone buildings are spread around a flat, rocky headland, the grounds meticulously kept with lush lawns and manicured flower beds. I'm surprised how busy the place is, small groups continuously sliding between the main structures like blobs of human mercury. This is clearly the standard day of culture to break up every tourist's week of golden sand and cheap tequila.

Sadly, I find it hard to summon the enthusiasm with which I used to greet archaeological ruins. I'm not sure if this is due to the package-tour feeling of Tulum or just that the passing of years has somehow diminished the reverence I always felt when absorbing the architecture of such a grand age. Still, even without my previous passion, I can appreciate the site, but Dad doesn't even feign interest. He mooches along at the back of the group, looking like he's enduring a lecture on medieval farming techniques. Clearly, he only allowed himself to be dragged along to appease me, but I try to put that out of my mind and enjoy myself.

The picturesque beach below the site is packed with day-trippers cooling off in the sea, and I can't resist joining them. On my return, I discover Dad crouching under the shade of a small bush, reading his Kindle. He looks incongruous amid the overweight, Hawaiian-shirted hordes, like a gnarled old hermit hiding at the entrance to his cave. He doesn't seem bothered by either his appearance or location, but guilt envelops me, making me feel like a bad son who's abandoned his helpless parent to the mercy of the elements. I finally admit to myself this was a bad idea, and we head home for lunch.

Unable to contain myself to the hostel, I arrange another outing in the afternoon. I bundle Dad into a minibus bound for the town beach, a crowded and unsightly place, its natural beauty besmirched by scruffy amenities and brightly coloured detritus. The sand is a threadbare carpet of muscled and tattooed Americans, the sort of beautiful people who seem a different species to pale, skinny Englishmen like me. I swear I'm genealogically closer to a birch tree than to these hunks, but I thread self-consciously between them anyway and bathe in the gorgeous water. Dad sits at a cocktail shack with a margarita and a frown, studiously avoiding any social contact.

"Nice spot, eh?" I ask as I hop back to him, trying to minimise contact with the foot-melting sand.

"I'm sorry, pardon?" He blinks over at me, roused from whatever pessimistic reverie he'd been enjoying.

"I said 'nice spot,'" I repeat, at the same time politely nodding at a face I recognise from breakfast, who nods back.

"Who was that?" Dad asks, his face rearranging itself into a picture of amazement that I should apparently have a passing acquaintance so far from home.

I shrug. "Just someone from the hostel."

"I tell you, my facial recognition is getting worse and worse." He sighs with a slight shake of the head. "I don't recognise anyone walking past me in the street. 'Who's this?' I have to ask myself. 'Do I know this person walking towards me? Because he looks as though he's going to speak to me!' Then I worry I'm going to cause offence by ignoring them or creep them out by looking at them as if I do know them when, in fact, I don't. It's a lose-lose situation, so I prefer to just keep my head down or cross the street to avoid people.

"It also amazes me how people are always waving at each other in cars as they go past," he continues, warming to the subject. "Apparently, when people drive along, they look at the drivers of other cars! Do you do that?"

I start making a non-committal noise, but it was clearly a rhetorical question.

"I look at the road. I don't look at the cars; I don't look at the shops. I look at the road. People honk their horns as they go past, and I'm thinking, 'What's going on?'"

"Not to worry," I say. I suppose I ought to be grateful he recognises *me* every morning. "You probably didn't see him. He was behind you at breakfast. Relax and enjoy the beach."

"Oh, yes," he replies sarcastically. "I love the beach. You get to wade into cold water, avoiding sharp stones and jellyfish, and take a nice mouthful of diluted sewage. Then you drag yourself out and roll your wet body in sand, which manages to get into every crevice and wrinkle and hangs around for days. What's not to like?"

Hypersensitive to any negativity after the previous day's revelation, I first interpret this as the classic rambling of a depressed individual, but I soon recognise he's actually just being a plain-old misery guts, an important distinction. Even so, it's not exactly the outlook I was hoping for on a tour of the Caribbean, home to some of the most spectacular beaches in the world. I raise my eyebrow as he begins to explain his theory that male circumcision was clearly invented by desert tribes to remove the irritation of sand caught under the foreskin, but I take this as a signal that his black mood of last night has passed and he might be receptive to a little conversation.

Despite my eagerness to unload travel anecdotes, from the inception of this trip I have been harbouring a vague worry about the possible dearth of conversational topics. While part of me eagerly imagined deep and meaningful dialogues, reminiscences, and verbal sparring, my realistic self was remembering all too well the shallow exchanges that would result in a phone call home being inadvertently answered by my father. These were of the typically limited cave man variety:

"How are you, son?"

"Fine, you?"

"Fine."

"Did you want to speak to your mother?"

That sort of thing. When he came to visit me, the chat flowed more freely but would eventually dry up, and he would saunter about my bedroom, looking at my belongings and asking irrelevant questions clearly of no interest to either of us. Looking back now, I'm not sure if that was an Asperger thing or just a regular father/teenage son thing.

"Peter was very parsimonious with words," my mum once told me. "He wouldn't use two when one would do."

The same adjective could apply to me. I remember one incident when I was sixteen. Dad, Matt, and I were sharing a healthy salad for lunch. Gaily decorated with balusters and aprons, the wooden dining table and matching chairs were far better suited to our previous suburban semi-detached than the slate flags and exposed stone walls of this old Cornish farmhouse. I was shovelling down food like the teenager I was, hardly bothering to chew, pondering the optimum division of pocket money between girls, CDs, and beer. With my mind focused on that very serious business, I neglected to chew one mouthful properly and inhaled a slice of carrot. In a heartbeat, the morsel lodged in my windpipe, and my brain experienced the sudden and devastating loss of the oxygen supply on which it had come to rely. I panicked. I jerked to my feet, face red, and proceeded to spasm uncontrollably in a frantic quest for air.

I've seen people choke in films and on television. They always appear to be overacting, panicking too soon, clawing at their throat in desperation. Surely, a healthy person can hold their breath for a minute or more, or at least thirty seconds. "Slow down," I'd think at the screen. "Go and find somebody, or dial the emergency services, then you can panic knowing help is on the way." That's what I'd do.

No way. My instantaneous reaction to the closure of my trachea was batshit-crazy hysteria. Forget calling an ambulance, forget trying to drop myself on my stomach to dislodge the obstruction, forget trying to do anything other than feeding my screaming brain with O_2. The natural instinct is to attempt to force air past the blockage, but, of course, this actively sucks the foreign object further in. When that didn't work, I tried again, harder. That was all I could think about, and I didn't have long.

Enter my father. Through a blurry veil of tears, I saw the outline of movement as he rushed towards me. I don't know if he was aware of the proper procedure or if he just instinctively knew what to do, but he gave me several powerful whacks in the small of my back. On about the third strike, the carrot trying to kill me flew out of my mouth onto the floor, along with a fair amount of drool. I sucked in air like an industrial extractor fan until my legs ceased shaking and I returned to my normal pallor. "All over," said my brain. "Nothing to see here."

"Thanks," I exhaled. We sat back down and resumed eating, my immediate thoughts of mortality and promises to eat more slowly soon giving way once more to financial calculations. None of us felt the need to discuss the incident further, or indeed ever again. We could have shouted things like: "Sheesh, that was close!" or "Chew your food properly next time!" but these things were obvious to all of us. What else needed to be said?

I don't even know if my mother ever heard about my near-death experience.

Two years ago, I married my fiancée of five years. We chose the Indian Ocean nation of Mauritius for our ceremony and honeymoon as a location roughly equidistant from both our families and Australia (and also, admittedly, as an excuse to see a part of the world I would probably otherwise never have afforded). To our great pleasure and surprise, over forty friends and family members made the journey to be with us, and the event was a perfect, magical day that ranks up there with the best in my life.

Of my own relatives, only my immediate family attended. We've never been a particularly close-knit bunch, but I knew of no rifts, no secret shame, or explosive fights with one side disowning the other. I prefer to socialise with my friends, anyway. They're more fun, for one thing. Also, it's not like I have a large extended family model to follow: Dad has one brother he speaks to only infrequently and Mum one sister, and their families were only a peripheral presence in my youth.

This was the first occasion that my parents, brother, sister, and I had all been in the same room since my sister's nuptials ten years previously. High on emotion, and not a little alcohol, the sight struck a chord, and I decided enough was enough. Clearly, I had to do something, or I would waste one of the most amazing gifts that life bestows—one's relationship with one's father. I didn't want to be a son whose constant intention to spend more quality time with his dad endured right up to the day I travelled halfway around the globe to attend his funeral. At seventy-two, he was showing his age, not decrepit by any means, but slow and creaky like a . . . well, like an old man, really, so I seized the day and set things in motion.

He claimed to be both flattered and mystified by my invitation. "Why," he asked, "would you want to spend your valuable holiday with a moody old curmudgeon like me?"

It was hard to formulate a reply. Just . . . because. He didn't seem to understand that, selfishly, I wanted more memories of him. They don't have to be rose-tinted recollections of the two of us riding a tandem bicycle or sipping cocktails on the beach at sunset. It doesn't matter what constitutes these new memories—they just have to exist. I'll be logging them for later. Of course, I now know he doesn't like the beach or the sea. I doubt he'll like the jungle either, and he's definitely not interested in meeting any new people. An inability to socialise is one of the main problems people with Asperger Syndrome face throughout their lives, but I knew that beforehand. The memories will come, though. I have no doubt of that.

We colluded by email and Skype, plotting our reconnection, a chance to catch up on the last twenty years, to get to know the more mature us. I didn't think too hard about what we would actually do together. Most of the activities I would normally pack into my travels would be beyond him, but we would no doubt find a happy compromise. We would tell each other stories, discuss the state of the world, dissect the past, and plot the future.

The premise of the trip was a circuit of the Caribbean Sea, starting and ending in Cancún. We'd head south through Central America, east across the top of South America, then island hop north and west through the Caribbean islands to Cuba and complete the loop back in Cancún. I knew nobody who'd done such a journey, and I eagerly anticipated the gratifying sense of closure that returning to our start point would bring. Mapping our route would bring me almost as much pleasure as travelling it, and it was also a way to fill in some gaps from my previous visits to the region, covering countries I'd missed. Dad agreed to any plan I put forward. I initially assumed he was being easygoing, but now I was beginning to see the truth: he didn't care where we went, as he wouldn't be enjoying it anyway.

Securing months off work isn't a simple proposition, not if one wants to return to the same job. It helped that mine was within the travel sphere—a shop selling clothing and equipment for hikers and globe-trotters. The more well-travelled I was, the more I could impress customers with first-hand advice on any far-flung destination from Bhutan to Djibouti. I don't mean to be callous, but I had another stroke of fortune—my boss's mother had died the previous year, so I deliberately played on this fact when I applied for extended leave, stating that this adventure "might well be the last chance I get to spend significant time with my dad before, well, you know . . ."

That thought had actually been swirling in the mists at the back of my brain for a while. Could this really be the last holiday we would ever take together? The idea seemed appalling yet all too plausible. He was reasonably healthy, but even should he reach his century, he wouldn't be undertaking lengthy trips in developing countries for much longer. I pushed such thoughts from my mind. Nothing was to be gained by dwelling on the inevitable; better to focus on the positive and concentrate on having the best time together we possibly could. In the end, I applied for four months leave and my boss pulled me back to three, which is what I wanted all along.

So, now that we're here, will the conversation flow forth like a burst dam or trickle out like sewage from a cracked pipe? I test the waters that evening by telling him about my previous visits to Latin America, and soon discover he's also been to Mexico before, which is the sort of thing one should really know about one's father. We chat about Acapulco and how we both disliked the city, a tacky place he dismisses as a 'Mexican Benidorm.' I found its corners dingy and foetid and the atmosphere menacing. As I was walking down the street one evening, a Jeep full of armed police screeched to a halt beside me, the cops leaping out and pointing their automatic rifles at my belly in mute intimidation. After a second's awkward silence from all parties, they dropped their barrels, mumbled, "*Lo siento*" (Sorry), hopped back in their vehicle, and took off, leaving me agape.

This prompts a story from him about a near miss he had while driving through Spain. "I was attempting to follow my GPS instructions without the benefit of sound," he recounts in his curiously exact speech. "I had somehow offended the well-spoken lady inside, probably because of my language on a previous occasion on which she had misled me. Now, she was refusing to speak to me at all, and so I was obliged to keep one eye on the GPS screen while driving. I was approaching a motorway feeder road but couldn't clearly see which fork to take until I was committed to take what transpired to be the wrong one. I huffed and puffed and cursed the lady anew while approaching the T junction at which I could correct my course. In my agitated state, like any good English driver, I arrived at the junction, looked to the right and turned left on the left-hand side of the road, only to find myself playing chicken with a fuel tanker. I was lucky I had time to swerve sharply into the centre lane. If I had turned ten seconds later, it would have been curtains."

It's good to know he can still make me chuckle, and I sense that maybe we're going to be okay on the conversation front.

Beads of sweat trickle between my shoulder blades, and dark spots on the chest of my t-shirt meld to create a tell-tale damp patch. We're trudging along the shore, me peering between the low dunes, trying to identify anything that might jolt loose a memory. A tragic victim of nostalgia, I'm keen to find the *cabañas* of my memory, though the place was little more than a reception area and bar with a few thatched shelters where we hung our hammocks. We pass property after identical property, cheap resorts set back from the beach, protected by flaking wooden fence posts, but I recognise nothing. Dad hasn't said a word, but I belatedly realise the old man must be exhausted, so I send him home in a taxi while I take another look, still convinced the place must be around here somewhere. I succeed on my second pass, but the bleached wooden shacks seem all but abandoned, and the harsh afternoon sun renders the plot flat and lifeless. I sigh wistfully. Just as Agatha said, this place is not living up to my memory.

Within this resort had stood a mean little shack owned by a scuba instructor named Fernando, a bit of a cowboy by my reckoning, who seemed to cobble together equipment from odds and ends lying about the office. "Oh, wait, I think this valve leaky," he'd say while preparing my compressed air tank. "Don't worry, I have spare one somewhere." Nevertheless, he talked a good talk, so I trusted him, resulting in one of my most memorable dives. Cenotes are natural limestone sinkholes, generally circular and filled with groundwater, and are magical places due to a combination of crystal-clear water and shafts of sunlight piercing the shadows like helicopter searchlights from above. The rough limestone is a haven of twisted formations, dark corners, and exciting swim-throughs. You never stray too far from open water, but if something goes wrong in a cavern, the usual emergency escape route (i.e. swim straight-up) is barred and, well, complications may ensue.

I'm desperate to dive another cenote, but, of course, Fernando's shack is no longer there. I'm standing, lost in recollection, when a young Mexican man saunters past, and I optimistically stop him to ask if he happens to remember Fernando and his shack. In a ridiculous fluke, he laughs and introduces himself as Fernando, son of the very Fernando I seek! It takes a few seconds to get over this coincidence before he informs me his father is currently out of town. However, it's a twist of fate too crazy to ignore, and so although there are many dive shops in Tulum, most of which are undoubtedly more sensible options than hiring a perfect stranger on the beach, I capitulate to chance and commission Fernando Jr. to take me diving in the morning.

I call into Dive Tulum's town office at the appointed time. It's just as chaotic as I remember it, the tables cluttered with seals, valves, and other bits of apparatus. Fernando Jr. turns out to be every bit as sketchy as his old man and seems completely unprepared for this gig. Obviously, he wasn't expecting to pick up some extra pocket money from a gormless gringo this weekend. Come to think of it, maybe I should ask to see his Dive Master credentials?

Looking like he might have spent some portion of the previous night in a disreputable drinking establishment, he hurriedly assembles some Self-Contained Underwater Breathing Apparatus (SCUBA) as if throwing together a packed lunch from whatever leftovers he can find in the fridge. Seeing his father's idiosyncrasies in Fernando makes me wonder if they still dive together. Do they get along, or are they drifting apart fraction by imperceptible fraction? I feel the urge to grab him and shake him like some scenery chewing, kitchen-sink character actor, shouting into his confused face, "Don't waste these precious moments with your father!"

There are over six thousand cenotes dotted around the Yucatan Peninsula, many located in sparse jungle. Fernando Jr. takes me to Cenote Angelita, a straight-sided, circular fissure that drops about seventy metres into the earth. He somehow forgets to mention the hole is on private property and I'll have to pay the owners an entrance fee on top of the cash I'm dropping for his services, but he laughs off my protests and sets about bargaining the price down on my behalf.

A short walk through a dappled stand of skinny trees and tangled roots brings us to a calm forest pool, its deep cobalt surface scattered with fallen leaves but still as a floor of polished tanzanite. Plunging through the looking glass, we sink through clear water to a depth of about twenty-five metres, where I become aware of the rare phenomenon Angelita is famous for. At this level sits the tip of a mountain of vegetation: leaves, branches, and whole tree trunks that have fallen in over hundreds of years. The slowly rotting vegetation produces a gas called hydrogen sulphide (common in the breakdown of organic material in the absence of oxygen) which, instead of escaping to the surface, floats around the edges of the debris as a thick, white cloud layer, exactly resembling a nebulous liquid pooling around a geographical feature. The astonishing clarity of the water makes it easy to forget one is submerged, and I imagine myself gliding above a river in a phantasmagorical dream, turbid milk eddying around the log-strewn bank. The hydrogen sulphide cloud is four metres thick, and while I'd love to descend through the opalescent fog to something like the next level of hell, Fernando won't allow it. It would get dark fast, and disorientation would quickly follow; far safer to float above and enjoy the trippy view.

Our second cenote, Calavera, is more of a traditional cavern dive with walls that flare out beneath the skull-like triple entrance. This pool is popular with swimmers and snorkelers, so we must negotiate curious day-trippers in board shorts, somewhat surprised at a couple of neoprene frogmen clomping among them. After an ungainly leap from the lip of the roof into the water, an array of bulbous limestone formations come into focus, submerged stalactites and stalagmites looking even more beautiful underwater than they do in a regular cave. As part of a larger system, Calavera has numerous dark passages leading beyond the rim of daylight, with eerie STOP signs warning that death lies beyond for insufficiently experienced divers.

Ten metres down, freshwater and saltwater meet at a floating horizontal layer called a halocline. Descending through this layer is another bizarre experience: the saltwater is several degrees colder than the freshwater, and though both fluids are transparent, the mixing that occurs when the halocline is disturbed creates a blurry muddle that's hard to see through until it re-establishes itself. The effect is suddenly having the world defocus, like removing a pair of strong prescription spectacles. With practice though, it's possible to make minute adjustments to one's depth simply by breathing in and out, and thus experience the transfer smoothly. By the time we resurface, my brain is scrambled with the effort of processing these new experiences. All in all, this is a day I am never going to forget.

"I can't ever remember seeing my parents happy," announces Dad suddenly over dinner that night. Usually we eat in silence. He's a very serious eater. He'll lay down his cutlery and chew thoughtfully, staring into the middle distance, as if ingesting food is work that needs to be done properly. It doesn't show on his face, but he does take pleasure in eating. I know this because he refuses to eat pudding straight after dinner, claiming he's still enjoying the former and doesn't want to mix the flavours. It makes sense and has influenced me to do the same. "I've never understood the popularity of going out to dinner and watching other people mash food up in their mouth," he told me when we sat down. "It's not a pleasant thing to see. It's a bit like sex, and that's something people do in private." I'm with him on that one—open-mouth chewing is one of my pet hates.

"I wonder if they ever were," he continues. "I suppose they must have been once, as they had three children." Their firstborn, John, died of meningitis as a baby, and their second, Michael, is Dad's older brother. "My father was never affectionate," he goes on, dispassionately. Walter, my paternal grandfather, was a toolmaker and partner in a company which manufactured collets for machine tools, a collet being a type of chuck to clamp the tool. The business was successful during the Second World War, and when peacetime arrived, Walter sold his share for a handsome sum, took the money, and left my grandmother after seven years of marriage to become some sort of playboy. Dad was three years old at the time. "There was no hand-holding, no sitting on laps, no playing. He was a distant figure, closer to the traditional Victorian father, which you must remember was only a generation before."

I never met the man, or any of my grandparents, but such failure of affection for one so close to me is difficult to hear. Having grown up in a household with all those expressions of love, I feel a distant loss in his words and, perhaps, for a moment, in his tone, too, although the sentence is delivered as emotionless fact. How easy it would have been for him to copy the fathering techniques he was subjected to, and how tragic for me. I feel a new surge of appreciation for his strength of character in overcoming these obstacles to become the father he did.

"I always thought of my father as a villain," he says next, his mouth set in a firm line. He never refers to him as *Dad*. "He was rich for a while," he remembers, "but he hardly sent any money back to us. He gave my mother two pounds a week, and I only remember one Christmas we got presents from him; mine was a metal crane. Yet he had four cars at one stage, and he couldn't even drive." This seems so implausible that I have to check I heard correctly, but it seems I did.

"He did invest some money back into a chain of dry-cleaning businesses, one of which my mother ran briefly. I remember it cost a penny to catch a tram to the shop, which was about a mile from where we lived, but if I got off one stop earlier, it was only a ha'penny."

When Dad started school, he was a latchkey child. With his mother working as a typist and stenographer, he had to let himself into the house when he got home from school. On one occasion, he lifted the sash window of the front room and climbed through, but the window closed on his trailing leg, so he couldn't turn around to lift it again. He was trapped but, luckily, rescued by a passing stranger.

Another way to enter the house was to walk down a steep slope to the cellar level, pass under the house through an entryway, then surface at the other end. Once, while descending, his foot slipped and he fell backwards, bumping his head and knocking himself unconscious. It may have been this accident which persuaded his mother to give up her office job and take in lodgers.

This was a much more difficult life. She'd work all day cleaning the men's rooms, making their lunch and doing their laundry, then cook their dinner at night and wash up, after which she and the two boys had to sleep in the living room, as all the other rooms were let. I remember him telling me long ago, in one of his you-don't-know-how-lucky-you-are lectures, that he only had one set of clothes, his school uniform, which he had to wear all the time, including weekends. My boyhood-self found this hilarious, of course, assumed he was joking, and never thought about it again. Now I know he wasn't.

Chapter 3

Alexithymia

Noisy, cold, and uncomfortable, night buses are the bane of the long-term traveller. Our first is south to Belize, an eight-hour drive. Journeying by road is unnecessarily lengthy, but this trip is essentially a low-budget undertaking. We are backpackers and will be staying in hostels not hotels, travelling mostly by bus not aeroplane, and eating street food not restaurant fare. In twenty years of travel this has always, out of necessity, been my way, and I thoroughly enjoy it. While the depredations can sometimes be tiresome, the rewards are manifold. Sitting on a clanking bus for a whole day next to a toothless old crone with three children and a fistful of chickens is, for me, a much more enjoyable travel experience than taking a photograph of a famous monument then going back to the hotel for a nap. There's also the obvious consequence that less money spent each day means more time on the road.

My companion is apparently content to adhere to my low-budget travel philosophy. It was necessary to set some expectations beforehand, but I'd been unsure how to broach the subject or how he'd react. Would he consider me a skinflint? Would he demand air-conditioning every night and maid service? It reminded me of meeting a new housemate for the first time and gently sussing out how much noise you can get away with making or how much cleaning they expected you to do. I needn't have worried.

"You're the captain," he'd told me. "Do it the way you normally would." Although he's genuinely determined I shouldn't outlay more than usual, it's not just magnanimity; he has an ulterior motive. Like me, he finds it very difficult to spend money and has all his life. An addiction to travel has rendered me career-less and used to having limited funds, but he doesn't have that excuse. He worked hard for forty-five years and, on retirement, sold his business for a worthy sum, which he shrewdly invested.

"I want to be able to enjoy the money I've spent my life accumulating," he'd added, a note of frustration creeping into his voice, "but I can't bring myself to do it. I find no pleasure in splurging on things. I tried to talk myself into a cruise recently, but I knew I would feel trapped. I don't want to meet new people and avoiding them would be too much effort. And a meal is temporary, as is a bed for the night, so why take the more expensive option?" I have to agree with him. Why spend a hundred dollars on a room where you will lie unconscious for eight hours when you can do the same thing in a ten-dollar room? In essence, we should be the perfect travel companions: an eternal pauper and a joyless miser.

While I appreciate his dedication to stinginess, it does present me with a dilemma. To wit, I'm fortunate to be fit and healthy enough to put up with cheap hotels and transport. Him? Not so much. He won't be able to physically endure some of my routine money saving methods, e.g. walking miles, fully loaded, to a bus station to avoid paying for a taxi. I'll have to be gentle with him yet avoid being patronising. One thing he has insisted on is a private bathroom, a perfectly reasonable concession, but should we upgrade from basic fan to air-conditioning? I normally wouldn't, but surely, he should be more comfortable if he can afford it. It's something we're going to have to play by ear.

Packed and ready, we arrive at Tulum's small bus depot for our 12:45 a.m. departure. The vehicle sits idling under the incandescent strip lights while a host of winged beasties buzz aimlessly around their unnatural glow. I leave Dad to guard the bags while I join the shuffling ticket queue. Despite living in Spain for the last nine years, his grasp of the language is rudimentary, whereas I learnt it while travelling through Latin America and find I can dredge it up quite comprehensively whenever I return. Consequently, I'm doing most of the talking: I make transport enquiries, buy supplies, check out accommodation, etc. He's comfortable ordering food and drink, perhaps because that's something he also does at home, but casual conversation with strangers doesn't happen. When he does communicate, he uses European Spanish pronunciation, with a soft, lisping C and slang local to his home province of Valencia. I try to teach him Latin American usage and pronunciation, and in return, he schools me in technicalities like verb declensions I tend to ignore or stumble over.

Dad is travelling with a thirty-two-litre backpack, concerned he won't be able to carry more. He's not a snappy dresser, generally happy in a t-shirt and suit trousers or cords, sometimes a collared shirt. I've forced him to buy a decent pair of sturdy shoes, but he's still carrying his old pair in case the new ones turn out to be uncomfortable on his involuted toenail. In addition to his pack, he wears one of those fishing vests with a ludicrous number of pockets.[3] He's literally carrying everything of value on his person at all times, secreted somewhere in this voluminous vest: passport, money, iPod, reading glasses, sunglasses, phone, Kindle, and reams of paperwork. He has a pen in there somewhere, but when he actually needs one, it can take several minutes to locate.

He even carries a digital voice recorder, and has a recording of my wife, Gerda, saying, "Don't do anything stupid!" that he was instructed to play to me whenever I'm considering undertaking a dangerous activity. Yes, Aletta Gertruida Opperman, to give her full name, knows me too well. It's a great pity she couldn't have joined us for this voyage, but as a hairdresser with her own business, she simply couldn't spare the time. I'm assured she's a brilliant stylist, though I usually have to cut my own hair as she is no mood to work when she gets home. The cobbler's children and all that. She's sometimes too tired even to speak English. No, I won't be doing anything stupid. She'd never let me forget it.

3 Thirteen

In his vest, Dad also carries several days' worth of tablets. As well as the sertraline, he needs daily doses of doxycycline (an anti-malarial), magnesium (for restless leg syndrome) and ibuprofen for his enlarged prostate. He's been suffering from this prostate problem for a couple of years now, despite the existence of a routine operation which would fix it. He says he's afraid of the surgery leaving him either incontinent or impotent, although I rather think he's just having trouble spending the money. He needs to urinate often because the enlarged gland presses on his bladder, not the best problem to have while travelling through the developing world. It's marginally possible the symptoms could worsen to the point of requiring immediate medical attention.

"It's the only thing that could possibly interrupt our trip," he admits. Well, that's comforting.

The lateness of the hour and quality of the coach make it easy to relax as we coast along the smooth highway, dry bushes and sand verges visible in a blur beyond the yellow beam of the headlights. At least we're saving the expense of a night's accommodation, although for one who is terrible at sleeping on buses, that's little consolation. I keep an eye on the old man throughout the night. He claims to get car sick if not driving, and, indeed, I have very few memories of him in a vehicle while not at the wheel, but he dozes off easily, his restless legs twitching sporadically like live electrical cables.

Our first view of Belize is cast in the light of dawn and filtered through bleary eyes. It's very green. Belize is a curious little country settled by British loggers in the late 18th century. Their industry, primarily based on mahogany, was underpinned by slave labour, and many thousands of Africans were imported to work the jungles. By the time the British Empire abolished slavery in 1833, the white, native, and Spanish population was vastly outnumbered by those of African descent, giving the country, and the rest of the isthmus' east coast, a much more Caribbean feel than the rest of Central America.

Fully half of the country is dense rainforest which forms a wall of foliage outside the bus window, at least until the grimy, grey smudge of Belize City intrudes. This workaday port, comprising the entirety of a bulbous peninsula jutting east into the Caribbean Sea, holds no interest for us. Like most tourists we'll head straight for the cayes, a group of idyllic islands an hour offshore. Ambergris Caye is the country's main tourist destination while the smaller Caye Caulker, a five-mile-long sandbar covering a limestone shelf, is unofficially reserved for backpackers. I couldn't fully appreciate Caulker on my last trip due to a nasty bout of tropical giardia picked up in the jungle, so I'm looking forward to giving the place another shot.

Transport is a large speedboat with seating for ten or fifteen passengers and, fortunately, a canopy to protect us from the sun. It's while we're sitting on the waiting room's cheap plastic chairs that Dad mentions he also gets seasick. I sigh. What kind of motion-challenged landlubber am I dealing with here? To prove the point, he sits unmoving, slumped over and eyes closed, throughout the crossing, either concentrating on fighting nausea or sound asleep. A dusting of beard dandruff flecks the chest of his dark t-shirt like the ash thrown out by some minor, chin-based volcanic eruption. He's obviously shattered but has not uttered a peep of complaint all night. What a trooper.

It's a breezy morning, the blue sky decorated with a smattering of drifting clouds. Caulker village is just beginning to show signs of life when we arrive, breakfast bars serving the odd sleepy-faced gringo, and a few residents cycling back and forth on errands along the sandy main street. There are no cars on the island, just bicycles and electric golf carts to dodge, and the prevailing atmosphere is one of unhurried tranquillity. Caulker seems like a place it will be impossible not to relax in; raising one's voice is probably illegal. The national language of Belize is English, and the national music, by the sounds of the beats emanating from every open door, is reggae.

Strolling between the gaily painted wooden buildings, each complete with a sandwich board advertising dive trips, tattoos, or tonight's entertainment, we are hailed from the balcony of a two-storey house by a hearty American voice. "Hey, guys, looking for somewhere to stay?" it twangs enthusiastically. "The Miramar is the best hotel on Caulker!" Though outward appearances would dictate this is neither the newest, cleanest, or most expensive place, it's certainly the friendliest so far and that translates as "best" by my standards. The American on the balcony seems to be the ringleader of a rabble of bemused travellers who have also been corralled by his boisterous recommendation. The tattoo on his arm declaring "You'd better Belize it!" in large, cheerful letters marks him out as a regular, although the young man checking us in rolls his eyes at the guy's exuberant grandstanding. It's as good a way as any to gather a social crowd, so while Dad has a lie down, I go outside and make friends.

And there it is—I make friends with a group of total strangers based on the slightest of introductions. Most people wouldn't think twice about doing the same thing, but for Dad, this would be totally inconceivable. When most people hear the words Asperger Syndrome, they think of a particular stereotype—an outsider who is hopelessly socially inadequate, doesn't have any friends nor really wants any, a person who prefers the company of books or computers and is good at using them. I'd been aware for some time that my father may have Asperger's, although he's never been officially diagnosed, but until recently, I'd never taken the time to investigate exactly what that meant. After all, he is who he is, and no new-fangled syndrome is going to alter how I feel about him one iota.

The basic facts are these: Asperger Syndrome (AS) is defined as a mild developmental disorder somewhere on the autism spectrum. Think of the spectrum as a two-dimensional line running from left to right, with 0 representing "normal" and 100 representing full autism. The latter is typically characterised by severe impairment in four major areas: social interaction, communication, sensory systems, and behaviour. Sufferers may be completely non-verbal and display self-injurious behaviour, but may be highly gifted in art, music, or mathematics.

High-functioning autism, with which people can function in society but are often regarded as socially awkward, became known in 1994 as Asperger Syndrome. Hans Asperger was an Austrian paediatrician who had studied psychological disorders in children. Asperger Syndrome has since been relabelled in the US as Autism Spectrum Disorder (ASD), but neither term carries a neat checklist of symptoms. In very simple terms, Aspergians exhibit a lack of empathy coupled with an abiding interest in systems. These two traits contribute to a range of behaviours on the low end of the spectrum, with each sufferer displaying a unique profile of characteristics, some more socially acceptable than others. Common examples include social awkwardness, difficulty making eye contact, misunderstanding situations, an obsession with very specific interests, being very routine-oriented, an above-average intellect, mild sensory issues, lack of interest in others, and clumsiness. Most people will be familiar with different forms of autism from modern portrayals in films, television, and books.

Right off the bat, I was unimpressed by the labelling of AS as a "disorder" and those born with it as "sufferers." In the words of John Elder Robison, author and proud Aspergian, "Asperger's is not a disease. It's a way of being. There is no cure, nor is there a need for one."[4] My mother knew from very early on that her husband was not a "normal" person, and when she became aware of the existence of AS, after they had been married for twenty-three years, she was convinced it applied to him. Knowing he wouldn't respond well if she brought it up, she took a test on his behalf and the results were, in her words, "off the scale."

For my entire childhood and early adulthood, I simply thought of him as a bit of a loner, and I hadn't spent enough time with him since then to analyse his behaviour in light of this new label. However, with our trip pending, I'd picked up one of the best known and most respected works on the condition, a book called *The Essential Difference* by Professor Simon Baron-Cohen of Cambridge University. First published in 2003, the book expounds Baron-Cohen's own theory on the difference between male and female brains, sometimes called the empathising-systemising (E-S) theory. The central tenet of Baron-Cohen's theory is this: The female brain is predominantly hardwired for empathy, and the male brain is predominantly hardwired for understanding and building systems.[5]

4 Robison, *Look Me in the Eye*, 5.

5 Baron-Cohen, *The Essential Difference.*

It's important to understand that the terms "male brain" and "female brain" are based on generalisations, and it's quite possible for females to have male brains and vice-versa. Even so, no one can deny males and females are physically different, and generally speaking, I think it reasonable to assume there are also psychological differences, such as those that Baron-Cohen suggests. He defines empathy as "the drive to identify another person's emotions and thoughts, and to respond to them with an appropriate emotion of our own. It occurs when we feel a reaction that is triggered by the other person's emotion and is done in order to understand that person and connect with them." Systemising is "the drive to analyse, explore, and construct a system, figure out how it works, or extract the underlying rules that govern its behaviour. This is done in order to understand and predict the system or to invent a new one."[6] In this case, systemising does not just refer to mechanical or mathematical systems but could refer to music, climate, gardening, sport, or almost anything in which the result changes predictably with a change in input.

The second, crucial part of Baron-Cohen's theory is the existence of people who display "extreme male behaviour." He defines this as an over predilection for systemising and an under abundance of empathy, a behavioural combination which accurately describes individuals on the autistic spectrum. Systemising and empathising depend on independent sets of regions in the human brain, and people like my father are gifted with understanding, designing, and using systems while having difficulty in sensing other people's emotions. Baron-Cohen describes this as being "mind blind" to some extent to the 412 distinct human emotions his team has identified.[7] E-S theory only accounts for some of the symptoms of AS, and now that we've embarked on this journey together, I'm curious to discover the subtle nuances of my father's condition.

6 Baron-Cohen, The Essential Difference, 7.

7 For more scientific background on AS, see Appendix I: Further Notes on Asperger Syndrome

Difficulty interacting socially may well be the most noticeable aspect of his AS. My mum remembers his awkwardness with a mixture of fondness and scientific interest: "He'd put his foot in it sometimes," she'd told me once, a smile flirting with her lips. "We'd be in a social situation and somebody would say something, and he'd give completely the wrong response. He'd show an absolute lack of understanding as to how what he said would be taken." Asperger Syndrome people have no inborn sense of how to deal with a situation, but are intelligent enough to analyse other people's reactions and file them away, ready to pull out and use themselves in similar circumstances.

"Many of them struggle to work out a huge set of rules, by trial and error," concurs Baron-Cohen, "concerning how to behave in each and every situation, and they expend enormous effort in consulting a sort of mental table of how to behave and what to say, from minute to minute. It is as if they are trying to write a manual for social interaction, or to systemise social behaviour when the natural approach to socialising should be via empathising."[8]

"I remember a couple of times," she continued, "he shuffled through the list of appropriate responses in his head, picked out the wrong one and jumped in with both feet, saying something so off the page that everyone just looked up and said, 'What?' I know he was aware of it and worked hard on it, and that's why he was in such inner turmoil."

Nowadays he's well aware of his condition and comfortable with it, although he rarely mentions it by name, but whether it be the AS, depression, or just plain introversion, Dad shows zero desire to talk to strangers. As well as the social awkwardness, he has certain intellectual parameters for a conversation partner that he isn't willing to compromise. However, unlike him, I relish making new friends. At home, I get tired of talking to the same people all the time. I crave fresh perspectives and novel verbal collisions, both of which are easy to find in fellow travellers.

Unfortunately, I'm terrible at approaching people. My teenage years were riddled with crippling shyness. I was actually delighted the

8 Baron-Cohen, The Essential Difference, 141.

guy on the Miramar balcony gave me such an easy invitation into his group, and I jumped on it like a stray cat on a fishbone. Without such an intro I would have hung around their periphery awaiting a wayward comment or question, which I could then use to insinuate myself into the conversation without looking too desperate. This strategy also allows me to listen to the group chat for a while and judge better how to make my conversational gambit. This is apparently a strategy more commonly employed by females; male newcomers tend to barge in and attempt to steal the attention.[9]

At age fourteen, I attended a school camp, one week of outdoor activities in the Brecon Beacons National Park in Wales. One evening, all the boys were gathered in the common area having a raucous time, joking, and shouting. I'd somehow contrived to be late and could hear through the door the buzz and clatter of voices raised in laughter and argument. They were playing some sort of word game which sounded like tremendous fun, but I just could not bring myself to walk through the door. I knew everyone would look at me when I did, albeit momentarily, and the threat of that brief attention paralysed me. I skulked outside like a guilty interloper for half an hour until a teacher arrived and asked why I wasn't inside. I lied, pretending I was feeling unwell to cover my embarrassment, and then had to endure an inquisition from the duty first-aider. It took years to conquer that feeling of being a gunslinger pushing open the swing doors of the saloon in a strange town, and I still find it hard to walk up to strangers and introduce myself. Even so, I'm a social magnet compared to my old man.

Initially confused on what I expect him to do on a small island of palm trees and sand, Dad soon relaxes into a routine of drinking coffee, reading, and taking the occasional stroll. It's a pleasant walk down to the Split, where a channel has been dredged between the two halves of the sandbar to allow east-west passage by fishing boats. On

9 Baron-Cohen, *The Essential Difference*, 45.

my last visit, I searched for manatees with one Captain Chocolate (at least that's what he called himself) who had developed a special relationship with the gentle cows of the sea. It was a remarkable experience to see them swim up to his boat and murmur their hellos like old friends, and I've had a soft spot for manatees ever since.

Gradually, I can sense Dad beginning to feel more at ease in my presence. He resumes his old habit of singing to himself, either humming ancient tunes, the words long forgotten, or unashamedly crooning snatches of old songs from his childhood. Post-war show ditties, music hall classics, I've no idea where he dredges them up, but he has a surprisingly steady voice, even when lapsing into "la-da-dee, la-la-la" lyric substitutions. "I Just Blew in from the Windy City, and the Windy City is Mighty Pretty," by Doris Day is a popular one at the moment. I use these melodies as a crude barometer to gauge his mood, which seems to be improving.

I don't want to push him for conversation, but there is much I want to learn, both about him and things that happened in our past. I want to know why we suddenly moved to Cornwall when I was twelve. I'd been born and raised in Birmingham, like generations of our family before me, and I'd never got over my dismay at being forced to leave. I want to know what happened with his business partner and why their successful company all but collapsed. At one stage, he bought a huge, formally trained guard dog and applied for a shotgun licence, things I accepted as a child without question but have since caused me some concern.

Ultimately, I need to understand the absolute truth about why my parents got divorced. Was it related to his depression, his AS, or just the usual reasons—money, boredom, infidelity? I was an adult by then but was so disappointed in what I saw as their joint failure that I didn't ask either of them much about it. My mother ranted constantly but mostly in the form of bitter accusations, a stream of vitriol derived from her deep shock at what she saw as his betrayal and her subsequent depression. I blanked out her harsh words because they caused me too much pain, both to hear such hatefulness from the mouth of my beloved mother and for any attack on my father. Typically, he remained mute on the subject.

Fortunately, for someone who generally keeps to himself, he seems content to engage me in conversation. "So, what shall we talk about?" is his opening gambit when we sit down to eat, and I know whatever topic I propose will be met with intelligent debate, or informed conjecture should he have no passing knowledge of the subject matter. However, it doesn't take long to be reminded of his favourite theme: he can talk for hours on finance and speculation. He's constantly seeking new investment opportunities for his savings, and he checks the gold price daily, sometimes making small online purchases or sales. He's totally on the ball financially, yet he can't remember what he had for breakfast or even if he had breakfast at all, or his pills with it.

His personal anathema is the evils of government, particularly taxation and the misuse of public funds, wasted through inefficiency or stolen via corruption. The usual tirade encompasses tax loopholes, teachers' holidays, overpopulation, the UK National Health Service, a single property tax, unemployed loafers, etc. Aspergians' views of the world are often black and white.[10] They are typically convinced their opinions or beliefs are correct and that any differing ones are wrong, and they will spend a long time trying to convince others of the fact. They don't understand how these things can be a matter of subjectivity. Dad isn't actually too bad in this regard. Sure, he can fairly rattle along when his blood is up, not giving much opportunity for rebuttal, but I wouldn't call it ranting; he's carefully thought through all his favourite problems and devised solutions to them, most of which sound feasible. His intelligence and thoroughness are such that I can't fault his thinking, although I try my best. The trouble is that some of his views are, shall we say, contrary to contemporary opinion.

A good example of one of his more unfashionable beliefs is his total opposition to the UK laws of equality. "You can't legislate equality," he insists one afternoon. We're sitting on plastic chairs in the shade of some palm trees in front of the Mirador, doing nothing but chewing the fat. "You can't force an employer to employ certain people; it comes naturally. And I don't agree with the idea that you must have a

10 Baron-Cohen, *The Essential Difference*, 147.

minimum percentage of women in your employ and a minimum percentage of ethnic minorities. Women will make their place in the world with their ability. If you force society into equal employment you risk putting the wrong people in the job." While his initial statement sounds like a call-to-arms at a right-wing rally, it comes from purely logical thinking, not sexism or racism. Even so, there are many who would disagree with him. That's when he'll follow up with the sucker punch.

"The most disadvantaged group in society, in my opinion, is ugly people." He's in his element now, leaning forward as if to drill his opinion into me. "How are you going to legislate for equality for ugly people? In terms of getting a job, a good-looking, attractive person is much more likely to be successful in an interview than someone with a big nose and long hair whose eyebrows meet in the middle." His tone is serious, but a faint sparkle in his eyes betrays the self-deprecating humour. I indulge him with a grin as he continues. "You can't make it a level playing field. It's an absolute load of nonsense! Equality will make its own way. Women will be equal to men and maybe even superior, but it will happen naturally over time, as will multiculturalism. Things have changed a lot over the last hundred years, and it may take a few more generations, but forcing it creates resentment. It has to be done slowly so people can get used to it gradually."

Whilst there are hundreds of arguments for instituting pro-equality policies, I can't fault the evolution of his logic, despite how much I want to disagree with his original statement. It's always been known that affirmative action or positive action programs can result in the wrong people being employed, and that's just accepted as a policy casualty in the fight for the greater good. With this in mind, and his insistence that equality will prevail over time (except for ugly people), he's almost converted me to his viewpoint. I'm convinced he would have made a great orator had he the confidence for public speaking, yet he left school at the age of fifteen.

"Grammar school was one long nightmare," he recalls matter-of-factly. This is not a man given to casual exaggeration—as far as I can tell, he doesn't lie at all—so I take this account seriously. "I did not have the confidence to speak out in class. I arrived late most mornings. I served detentions most evenings. My grades fell consistently each year. I was always perceived as the 'weirdo,' that guy you speak to once and from his responses you know to move on." I feel my cheeks flush, reminded of the times I'd done that exact thing to some other poor 'weirdo.' "I was invisible, a loner. I needed help, counselling, sympathy, friendship, understanding . . . anything from anybody. I made not one friend at school . . . ever."

When I try to recall memories of him hanging out with friends, in the evenings or at weekends, they just aren't there. He would work late most weekdays at his factory, often arriving home after dinner but in time to tuck us into bed. He never went out to the pub, he wasn't interested in sports, and strangers rarely visited the house. He mostly worked, watched television, or embarked on ambitious projects, large and small. I can only think of a handful of names I would associate as 'mates,' most from a short period when we lived overseas for his job, and a single, solitary one in Birmingham. I can't imagine how lonely life must be with nobody to discuss tough times or celebrate successes, to laugh with, joke with, or even just share some basic human interaction. In fact, he might consider me one of his closest friends and I hardly ever see him!

His description of school life resonates with that of Temple Grandin, an autistic American woman who has become a professor of animal science and spokesperson for the condition. According to her, "Some of the bright, socially awkward teenagers need to be removed from the torture chamber of high school and enrolled in technical classes at a community college."[11] Contemporary autism experts agree it is common for AS patients to pursue their own intellectual interests to high levels while failing in academic subjects.

Initially, Dad just stopped going to school. He used to leave the house every morning and stay out until he was due back. At that time, you had to be sixteen to leave school, but he persuaded his mother to sign the papers, allowing him to leave a year early and find a job. She

11 Grandin, *The Way I See It*, 225.

must have been sorely disappointed, as she had dreams of him becoming a doctor when he first passed the school's entrance exam.

He left school on a Thursday, went to the Youth Employment Exchange, and found a position as an electrician's mate, starting work the following Tuesday. Electronics in those days were limited to valves, capacitors, and resistors, and the transistor radio was still barely known. His interest was piqued by the intricate systems produced by the components, and he took another job as a trainee electrician in a television repair shop.

"I remember the week I started that job," he muses, squinting slightly as the sun begins to peek between the fronds of the palm tree shading him. "Since two of us worked alternate Saturday mornings, I was alone on the first Saturday and managed to repair a television to the amazement of my boss. I can't remember that I ever repaired another, though, as he put me on radios if I was lucky and record decks and irons if I wasn't."

Dawn sees a lazy bustle of activity around the wooden jetty as dive instructors and bleary-eyed clients mingle, moving tanks and equipment and filling out paperwork. The glow of the day's sun tinges the calm sea to the east with a rim of red to match my eyes, and everyone is glad when the boat is loaded, and we can resume our interrupted sleep. It's a two-hour crossing to Lighthouse Reef, a small atoll which forms part of the Mesoamerican Barrier Reef, one of the largest coral reef systems in the world.

On my last visit to Belize, I was in no financial state to afford the area's big underwater draw, the infamous Great Blue Hole. The Blue Hole is a perfectly circular submarine sinkhole about three-hundred metres across and plunging over a hundred metres down through the coral of Lighthouse Reef. Spectacular from above, the intense blue of the deep water resembles the limpid gaze of some submerged monocular beast lying in the gentle turquoise of the shallow reef. This time, I booked my place as soon as I arrived.

The clients are mostly couples, so I end up sharing space with a lithe, blonde German backpacker and one of the dive masters (DMs), whose enthusiasm for her conversation is matched only by his apathy for mine. The first dive of the day will be in the Blue Hole itself, and the atmosphere aboard is buzzing with anticipation as we approach. I pull on my wetsuit while listening to the briefing. In the 1970s, oceanographer Jacques Cousteau acclaimed this as one of the top ten dive sites in the world, but I never thought to research exactly why. I just assumed there would be huge pelagic species down there, all teeth and tentacles, with maybe some gorgeous coral fringing the vertiginous walls. The reality is very different.

As a large group, we require two DMs, one each at the front and back to keep us in line as we descend to forty metres. I'm third from last, followed by the German girl and her Belizean admirer. It's a cloudy day so visibility is not especially good, and by the time we level off, we're enveloped in gloomy darkness, floating silently among the vague shadows of the other divers. If it weren't for the limestone wall to position us, we would be hopelessly disoriented. But what a wall it is! At this depth it suddenly juts inwards, creating a gaping overhang, before curving back ten metres down to continue its straight plunge into the deep. The resultant grotto is filled with impressive stalactites and stalagmites, evidence that this section of the sinkhole was once above sea level (actually some twelve-thousand years ago). With jagged columns dripping from the roof of the yawning crack, the concavity resembles the gaping maw of some gigantic, petrified, deep-sea anglerfish, and I spend our precious few minutes of bottom time swimming between and around its monstrous teeth.

Too soon it is time to ascend, and I dutifully pursue the fins of the swimmer in front, turning briefly to check that Blondie is following. Instead, I see a curious sight—she and the DM are disappearing back under the overhang. Instinct tells me he is probably showing her a really cool, secret spot in an attempt to impress his way into her bikini later, and I make the split-second decision to kick back and join them, invited or not. If there's something extra exciting down there, I want in!

When I reach the place I last saw them, I find only a dark recess, just wide enough to pass into without bumping my tank. I fin forwards, expecting some sort of swim-through, but the hole deepens, narrowing to a tunnel and getting darker with every kick. They must have gone this way, though, so I continue exploring. It's soon too constricted to turn around and I realise with a start that if I reach a junction, I won't know which way they've gone and might have difficulty reversing. As the dull glow of daylight fades, I spy a faint luminescence in front—the DM's flashlight, I presume. I pray they don't accelerate too far ahead, or turn a sharp corner, or that I don't fall victim to any number of misfortunes that can occur when one swims through a tight underwater passage forty metres below the reef with no light and no map. How on earth did this happen?

I think of Dad and his voice recorder. I imagine him floating beside me, his arm thrust out and the strident, disembodied sound of Gerda repeating, "Don't do anything stupid!" from the machine, over and over again. Would he be alright if I never returned from my day out? Of course, he would. I almost emit a bubbly giggle when I draw a parallel between my situation and his. Blundering around in the dark, alone, hitting dead ends. Is this what depression feels like? Helpless, panicky, unable to move, close to drowning, while other people are enjoying themselves a short distance away? My nascent laugh dies as the air bubbles hit the ceiling of the cave and slide around, unable to find a way out. My morning could almost be a clumsy metaphor for his whole life, except that I expect to escape from this, and he never will.

The light stops up ahead, and to my relief, I catch up with my quarry where the passage widens at a dead end. There's a look of genuine shock in the eyes of the DM when he sees me; he knows he's been caught out. He recovers quickly, but there's no room for him to pass me and light the way out, so he motions me to shuffle around and plunge back into the inky darkness of the tunnel. I feel my way along the bottom until the ambient light bleeds back in, and I can see out of the monster's throat to a place we can safely ascend.

Back at the surface, I am all adrenaline and serotonin. I share a conspiratorial wink with Blondie, but she seems to be passing the experience off as nothing special, like she swims into dark, dead-end caves every day before breakfast. Were it not for our horny DM, I'd be regretting having blown ten days' budget on what was basically a deep, dark swim. No, the Blue Hole was definitely not what I expected, but our unplanned detour was without doubt the highlight. I take solace from the fact and decide that while the mood of our trip so far has not been as congenial as I'd expected, there may be pleasure to be had in the most surprising of places if I seek it out.

The beer flows freely that evening, as do the jokes, and hearty laughter rolls across the Mirador balcony like staccato claps of thunder. It's tremendous fun, or so it appears to me, stuck way over in the opposite corner. The balcony crew are ramping up for the night, and I can't help wishing I could join their conversation instead of the one I'm currently engaged in. One of the great pleasures of the road is interaction with other travellers. There's no time to waste getting acquainted; strangers are thrown together in outlandish situations and more or less forced into company. Chit-chat and small talk are jettisoned in favour of a few establishing questions (Where are you from? Where are you going?), then drinks, jokes, and bonding. What could be better?

In trying to balance Dad time with friend time, I need to find a happy equilibrium. I've reconciled myself to the fact that evening escapades will be tricky with an old man in tow, but I'm keen to let loose a little on my last night on Caye Caulker. Yet here I am debating the merits of various post-war music hall entertainers. I slump in my seat. Can't this wait? I generally enjoy our conversations, but right now, that group of wisecracking guys is my first taste of on-the-road camaraderie and I'd like to take advantage of it. I can't even share a beer with my father. He's always favoured wine, I know, but now he reveals that he physically cannot drink beer. It's not that he doesn't like the taste, but rather he can't burp.

"One day, about fifty years ago," he explains, raising his voice to compensate for the excited chattering behind him, "I escorted my mother and yours to a concert by Michael Holiday.[12] In those days, I was still trying to be a regular guy, as it were, and I used to drink beer even though it made me severely bloated. At this venue, beer was only served by the quart (almost a litre) but the ladies with me did not drink beer. In those days, no lady did, so I attempted to drink it all myself. I became so uncomfortable, in pain in fact, that I was obliged to go outside and stagger around the car park. I wasn't drunk, mind you, just bloated. Eventually there was an enormous rumbling noise as something bubbled up from my gut." He pauses for effect, clearly enjoying the retelling of an incident he probably hasn't thought about for decades.

"The foundations of the building clearly vibrated." He chuckles, his ribcage imitating them. "Slates rained down from the roof, passing traffic stopped in its tracks. Had there been alarms on cars, they would all have been triggered. And the discomfort ceased. How I wish I could burp again, but alas, the pressure required to trigger the event has not since occurred."

I laugh. Now, this is exactly the sort of thing I want to be learning about my old man! He's even beginning to display signs of a sense of humour! I shouldn't have been so quick to write him off. As entertaining as he is, though, I haven't been able to stop myself throwing conspicuous glances at the opposite corner of the balcony, and I'm sure my face falls comically when the guys all rise to leave.

One common symptom of AS is an inability to read facial expressions. Aspergians hear people speak but don't pick up any meaning beyond that of the actual words. This makes them bad at reading emotions, understanding hints or suggestive body language, or perceiving what would be, to most of us, obvious signs of distress. They can't tell when people are getting angry with them, bored, frustrated, or sending out romantic signals. Some might talk in great detail about their chosen pastime without realising the listener has absolutely no interest in the subject. Much of human interaction is contained within subtle eye movements that occur during

12 a popular British crooner of the '50s and '60s

conversation, but Aspergians sometimes struggle to follow eye movements, especially rapid ones, and thus remain unaware of this whole level of communication. The ability to attribute mental states to others and read them is called Theory of Mind.

According to Temple Grandin, "These are social thinking skills that develop without formal instruction in neurotypical individuals at a very early age. These are also skills that most people assume exist in all people to a greater or lesser degree of development, but this is not the case within the autism population. Without a fully-functioning social system, individuals with AS stumble along through social situations missing valuable bits of verbal nuance or nonverbal body messages that are woven into typical conversation."[13]

Lacking this Theory of Mind often leads Aspergians to misunderstand humour, and endeavouring to replicate it in conversation can be a minefield. My brother told me of the awkwardness he felt once when the two of them went to visit Dad's lawyer in Spain, and an attempt to be jovial came across as very rude.

"How are you?" the lawyer had politely asked.

"I'd be a lot better if I hadn't had to come back into town to see you," Dad had replied, as the office had been closed the day before.

"He could've just said, 'Fine, thank you,' but he was trying to be amusing and it fell extremely flat," related my brother. "Anyone else, even me, would have known it wouldn't work."

Dad really only discovered how much he'd been missing his whole life after reading about the psychology of human relationships. "This is what happens with ordinary people," he'd explain to me, as if I shared his confusion. "You go into work and pass a particular person every day, and initially you just nod to them, then later on you might say good morning to them, and later on ask about the weather, and apparently you get this gradual development of a relationship. When I read that I just thought, 'Wow! Is that how it works?' I never knew."

The progression was obvious to me, but how? I learned by observing others and copying them, responding to their signals: a raised

13 Grandin, *The Way I See It*, 167.

eyebrow, a pause, a smile. When I actually stop and consider how much of communication is unspoken, it's a huge proportion. "It's like a foreign language," he'd concluded. "I have to try to translate what people mean from what they have said, and then formulate a reply calculated not to cause offence." Aspergians' conversational replies are often thought too honest or direct. "And why do people get offended when they are criticised?" he'd ask, sincerely curious. "Surely the appropriate reaction would be to question oneself on how the criticism arose."

Apparently, his recognition of emotion isn't as bad as all that because he finally notices my agitation. "Oh, do you want to go with your friends?" he asks abruptly, his face transformed into a mask of concern. "I don't mind! Please do."

I'm too surprised to hide my relief, and after a second's pause to admire his powers of observation, I spring from my chair and bid him goodnight. He's not such a bad old goat after all.

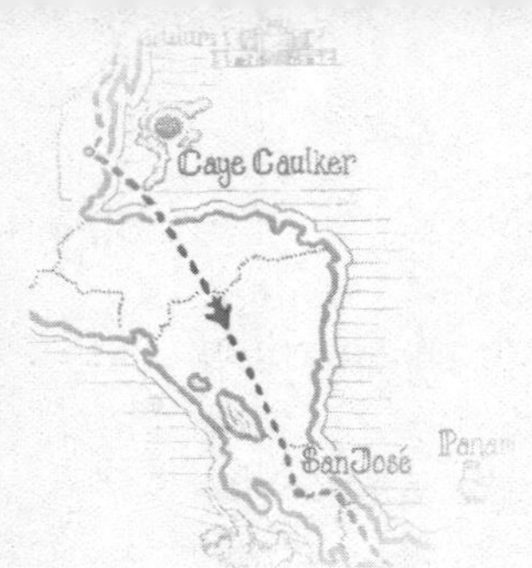

Chapter 4

Sophronise

I let out a contented sigh as the small craft pulls away from the bobbing jetty the next morning, its twin outboard motors gradually accelerating away from the churning water and into the choppy blue waves. Having completed my underwater business here, I'm happy to fast-forward to pastures new rather than re-tread the paths of Guatemala, Honduras, and Nicaragua. This, however, brings us to an unfortunate reality.

Ordinarily at this point, I'd board a long-distance bus in Belize City and stay in my seat until San José, Costa Rica some thirty-five hours later (if I'm lucky). No stranger to ridiculous bus journeys, I once chose a gruelling ninety-four-hour epic between Lima, Peru, and Asuncion, Paraguay through the hot, dusty Gran Chaco with no air-conditioning and only a single Harry Potter book for entertainment. It was a bona fide contender for Worst Journey in the World, but I'd do the same thing again because I always prefer to go overland if possible. This isn't due to a fear of flying, but because sticking to the surface of the planet, by land or by sea, just seems to me an infinitely purer method of travel. Unfortunately, with a septuagenarian in tow, an aeroplane is our only realistic option.

Well aware of my ideals, and of being the cause of the increased expense (by a factor of almost three), Dad had assumed I would ask him to pay for both our flights to San José. He'd actually been girding his loins for the bus journey instead; it's that hard for him to spend money! Of course, I would never take such advantage of him, and for that, I get his most heartfelt thanks so far. Our flight isn't until 5:00 p.m. so we've been lounging in the sun until taking the early afternoon boat back to the mainland. However, one can never fully relax while waiting to leave somewhere, particularly for the airport, and doubly so when the journey might at any moment be delayed by bad weather and/or operator lethargy.

My contentment at our successful departure is short lived when Dad claps a hand to his chest with a hearty slapping noise, a fraught expression vivid on his face. My stomach drops to my knees as I automatically fear some serious medical emergency might be upon us. Relief that this isn't the case thus tempers my annoyance when the real reason for his performance comes to light: he's left his money belt in the desk drawer in our room.

Gah, I almost say out loud. Finally, the punishment for travelling with a scatter-brained old fool is revealed. My overactive brain flashes a series of images before my eyes: his creased maroon passport peeking out of the cream-coloured fabric, grubby banknotes in the fingers of the cleaning lady, the plane taking off without us, myself hailing a passing speedboat and being extorted for a lightning return trip. I force myself to breathe, calculate rough timings, and consider all the options. It's my fault, obviously. My sweep of the room should've been more thorough. I checked under the beds but didn't consider the furniture, even though I saw him put it in the drawer three days ago.

Personally, I never take my money belt off except to sleep or swim. It's part of me for the duration of my trip. No matter how sweaty, smelly, and ragged it becomes, it stays on. He was quite happy with his many-pocketed fishing vest, but I insisted a money belt was the absolute number one essential item for long-term travel and made him buy one. Years of experience have taught me this is the safest place for your valuables—as long as you hang on to the bloody thing, that is! I need to up my game, be more vigilant.

"It's a good job I've still got this," he says brightly, as all these thoughts are colliding between my ears. I look up to see him clutching his passport. "It lives in my vest."

I exhale noisily as my muscles relax, then a second later jerk up again, this time in confusion. "So, what is in the money belt?"

Frustratingly, he can't remember. "Maybe some English money?" he shrugs. "I keep most of it right here." He pats one of his pockets, completely unfazed.

"Is that it? How much?" I'm frightened to hear the answer.

"I really don't know. Maybe just some coins?" he says, dismissively. "I think I put something else in the drawer as well, but I can't remember what. I didn't check my packing list, you see."

"You have a packing list?" I ask, nonplussed. "Don't you just pack, like, everything, every time we leave somewhere?"

"Don't you have one?" he asks, equally surprised. "It's a very useful thing if you spend a lot of time away from home, although admittedly not so useful once you've left." In the end we decide there's nothing worth an expensive and potentially flight-missing return journey. As for the mystery item, we never do find out what it was.

It takes just over an hour for our aeroplane to traverse the jungles and beaches of Central America, without doubt the setting for maybe the most enjoyable few months of my life. After finishing the archaeological excavation I was working on, I was free to roam the region until my money ran out. I went south through Guatemala to the Bay Islands of Honduras, where I met a lot of cool people. I stuck with a Swedish guy for a while, and in Nicaragua, we met up with a couple of Austrians with whom we forged an inseparable bond within just a few hours. We hung out in the old colonial city of Grenada for several days, absorbing other travellers within our field of easy fellowship. We organised day trips, discussed the world, laughed endlessly, and drank a lot of rum.

At the end of the week we parted ways. I needed to head north to Mexico where, after a couple of weeks, I reached *San Cristobal de Chiapas*. There I met an American guy, and together we travelled to Oaxaca, gathering a Namibian girl on the way and a couple more good sorts in the hostel there. By the simple expedient of sitting in the town plaza with a bottle of mescal and a bag of chilli grasshoppers, our numbers grew, and it was a multinational group of seven that caught a night bus to the sleepy Pacific beach town of Mazunte.

Mazunte was the culmination of two solid months of the best kind of travelling, a sun-soaked, ocean-washed wonderland that passed in a blur of cold beer, fireside dancing, swimming, and sleeping. Every minute we spent together was epoxy resin, setting friendships that would never come loose. On the point of exhaustion, we finally parted ways. The American bought a shack in *Puerto Escondido* that he planned to turn into a beach bar, the Namibian went back to London, where she'd been living for years, and I escaped with another Englishman to Mexico City, where I flew back to the UK.

Acquaintances forged between single travellers on the road become tremendously strong in a very short time, and I have such circumstances to thank for many of my long-lasting friendships. For the following few years, the group from Nicaragua would periodically reconvene in one another's cities, be it Vienna, London, or Stockholm. Within London, where I was also living by then, I'd frequently meet up with some of the Oaxaca crew. As the years stretched out, I sadly lost touch with some of them, but not all. I still see the Englishman from time to time. I'm meeting one of the Austrians in Cuba on the last leg of this trip. And the Namibian? Well, to paraphrase Charlotte Brontë's *Jane Eyre*: Reader, I married her. After ten years of living, travelling, and sharing adventures together, that flame-haired, white-skinned African became my wife. Like I say, it was one of the best times of my life.

My first job was working for the old man. I suppose it's a common enough scenario, but for most people, it doesn't start at the age of eight. Dad's injection moulding factory was on an industrial estate in north Birmingham, about half an hour's drive from our home. A lofty warehouse with high ceilings, concrete floors, and sacks of raw plastic piled up the walls—it was a messy and exciting wonderland of hot metal, hammering hydraulic plates, and sharp, twisted debris. The acrid stink of burnt nylon filled the air, and bright sunlight filtered through the cracked windows far above my head. A few lackadaisical staff worked the huge moulding machines that pumped out sheets of car badges or cable ties, combs, and soap dishes. This was certainly not a place for children, yet on the occasions I was allowed to visit *the factory*, as my mother would refer to my father's work—usually with some distaste—I was thrilled, eager to discover the legendary location where so much of his time was spent.

One of the unavoidable by-products of the injection moulding process is the sprue, the small skeleton of plastic to which the useful items are attached when they are ejected from the mould. These sprues must be sorted from the sellable product. It's a tedious and repetitive task ideally suited to excited young children with small hands, with the additional benefit that it keeps them from wandering off and climbing all over the teetering plastic sacks. As a reward for this illegal child labour, I'd get a crisp, green one-pound note. That was certainly exciting, but the Queen's beatific face smiling up from my dirty palm was less of an incentive than the pleasure of being allowed to help Dad at *the factory*.

Although the occasional hour of sorting sprues was a lark, I got the opportunity to earn real money a few years later. Dad won a contract to make cable tie bases, small square mounts through which a cable tie could be threaded and affixed to a flat surface. The moulding of the bases was easy, but they required an adhesive backing which had to be applied by hand—work which could be done at home in our spare time at a piecework rate. Thus, I spent many hours at the dining room table one summer peeling off backing and setting bases squarely onto adhesive strips packed five by five across and four deep in little folded cardboard boxes of a hundred, neat as you like.

Now that I understood a bit more about the concept of wages, I worked hard to supplement my meagre pocket money. For the first time in my life, I felt the satisfaction of earning a financial reward for a job well done. Rather than fritter away my seven pounds immediately on comics and sweets, I pushed the unimaginable wealth through the slot of my Mr. Bump money box, content to squirrel it away for future use.

Except that I wasn't neat enough. One day, not too long afterwards, Dad arrived home with a stern face and delivered the news that my work had not been up to standard. In my haste I'd stuck the bases awry, and my entire output was unacceptable to the client. Hardly surprising from a ten-year-old, I suppose. When he told me, without emotion, that I must return all my earnings, I was absolutely devastated. I refused. I cried. I couldn't believe it was happening, but he stood firm. I guess he was teaching me a valuable life lesson.

He waited patiently while, tears streaming down my face, I retrieved the coins from my money box with the aid of a butter knife inserted into the slot. I must have hated him at the moment I handed over the money, and I can only hope that inside he was at least a little bit upset, although outwardly he offered nothing save an explanation that shoddy work was undeserving of payment. I learned many lessons that summer—about remuneration, quality control, and investment versus expenditure—but most of all, I learned about work ethics, about doing a job to the best of my ability, a lesson that has stayed with me throughout my life.

My parents were both quite strict, but Dad was, in fact, amazingly patient and preferred to deal with us reasonably before meting out actual punishment. This was usually via a tedious lecture; sometimes it seemed as though the sentence for our misbehaviour was to be deliberately bored to tears. If we broke something, we had to pay for it with our pocket money. When I was a little older and broke a window with a carelessly thrown tennis ball, I had to fix it myself, puttying in a new pane from a rickety scaffold. Hands-on smacking was reserved for the most heinous of crimes and then done in a measured, sympathetic manner. This was before physical parental discipline was widely considered to be a bad idea.

I was only four years old when I set fire to the curtains in my parents' bedroom. I didn't do it on purpose. I was merely experimenting with the box of matches I discovered in the corner of the lounge, dropped accidentally by my aunt or uncle on one of their Sunday visits. Prior to the admonitions of Welephant, the UK cartoon fire brigade mascot, who chanted, "Matches, matches, never touch, they can hurt you very much," I didn't judge them dangerous. I started small, lighting the corner of a stack of LP records, but that burnt out too quickly to satisfy me. In stark contrast, the curtains went up a treat, so fast that my little brain recognised the danger, and I ran to the bathroom to fill a soap dish with water to douse it. By the time I returned, the blaze had far outgrown that pathetic measure and was verging on engulfing the entire wall. I realised I had to do something more, but rather than tell my parents, who were blissfully unaware downstairs, I returned to the bathroom and started filling a bucket. This operation took long enough to have condemned the whole house had not the fire been discovered and dealt with in my absence. When I finally struggled up with the sloshing container, the flames had thankfully been extinguished.

My troubles, however, were only just beginning. Dad guilt-tripped me into confessing by telling me they'd have to tear the walls apart looking for an electrical fault, a highly expensive operation. Then came the smacking: scheduled in advance and to a pre-agreed number of strokes. His large hands, rough with twenty-five years of manual labour and plastic burns, were sharp on my legs and buttocks and I blubbered uncontrollably. I could feel his reluctance, though—see it writ large upon his face. It really did pain him to hurt me in this way, but I had to be taught the danger of playing with fire.

The sun is long gone by the time we arrive in San José. Not wishing to subject Dad to an extended and probably fruitless search for public transport, we jump in a taxi to the hostel. Money has been flowing away the last few days: the dive trip, the flight, the Belizean taxi driver who tried to double his quoted fare on dropping us at the airport, the forty-dollar departure tax, and now this cab. I'm trying desperately to keep track of which of us has paid for what in an attempt to maintain a fair division of costs. He doesn't appear to care, though, and it's tempting to let things slide, except I can't, because if they slid in my favour, I wouldn't be able to forget it. I still feel guilty for never repaying a sum of £12.95 he loaned me when I was fourteen, so I balance the accounts in my head as we go along.

"Not much going on here," I remark as we look around the building, getting our bearings after checking in. From the décor of the bar, tucked away in the corner of the pool patio, this hostel looks like it has its crazy moments. A list of bizarrely named cocktails is scrawled on a blackboard above the shelves of spirits, and the obligatory photos of drunken young things are pinned up on the wall by the pool table. I'm still eager to join any sort of carousing on offer, but tonight, there are just a handful of chilled-out backpackers conversing in low murmurs, probably about how wild their weekend was. It is a Monday, after all.

"I'm sorry, I didn't catch that," states Dad, bending forward and turning his head to present me with a hairy ear canal.

"I said, there's not much going on here." I enunciate into it, taking a seat.

"I'm sorry," he apologises again. "I'm going deaf. It must be irritating having to repeat yourself all the time."

"Well, maybe a bit," I admit with a sheepish shrug.

"Maybe you could alert me before speaking?" he suggests. "Tap me on the shoulder or say 'Peter' to get my attention." As if I would ever call him Peter! "I do have a hearing aid in one of these vest pockets, but I dislike it and never use it." My eyes roll of their own accord. I mustn't be too harsh, though; I confess to being a bit of a mumbler, and I sometimes think things out loud that aren't worth repeating. That must be annoying too, especially for the hard of hearing.

"I used to party, you know," he says, apparently wishing me to know he wasn't always a boring old grouch. "I used to be the life and soul." I find this hard to imagine but nod encouragingly. His eyes get that far-off look, and I'm not disappointed. "I was still a beer drinker in those days. Everyone danced the twist. I had a reel-to-reel tape recorder!" he announces with pride, as if it were the sixties equivalent of the latest Xbox. "I was the instigator behind all the parties. My friends' mothers used to shout my name in rage." I blink in astonishment, and then chuckle as he raises his voice to yell his own name in imitation of an angry parent. "I was the one who led astray their precious children. John's mother particularly held me responsible for any misdemeanour he committed."

This is news to me, and pleasant news at that. In fact, this sounds like an entirely different person. "I've never heard of a John," I remark, eyebrows raised.

"Yes, John down the road seemed to take a liking to me for some reason, so we'd spend time together, and I made friends with Alan at work because I saw him every day." After being sacked from the television repair shop for consistent lateness and absence ("I've always had trouble getting out of bed in the mornings," is his only explanation), and still fifteen, he started at an electrical wholesale company for two pounds ten shillings a week. This is where he met Peter Jackson. A few years older, tall, self-assured, and extroverted, Peter was a peripheral figure in my early childhood. He would loom above me in his uniform dark-brown suit, teasing me with his gruff, pipe-tobacco-laden voice. Despite their diametrically opposite personalities, Peter somehow became the best friend Dad had his entire life.

It's a misconception that Aspergians are unfriendly or loners by choice. They desire friends and companionship just like the rest of us; they just don't know how to get people to like them. Although as a young man Dad found it difficult to interact with people, he and Peter formed a solid friendship and, like many Aspergians, he used this as a gateway into society. He didn't interact with other people except through Peter for some time, but that was good practice, and eventually, he befriended the rest of Peter's circle.

There was table tennis in the company store, which the two Peters played each day during lunch break. They became very good, able to stand well back from the table and conduct endless rallies, smashing and defending relentlessly. They got so proficient that the boss organised a tournament with another company based purely on the skills of his two best players. Despite his obvious ability, Dad was mortified at the thought of performing in front of strangers and didn't show up. The company team was thrashed.

The Peters remained friends even after Dad moved onto other jobs, including rubbish bailer, warehouse assistant, motorcycle mechanic, and vacuum cleaner salesman (at which he must have, quite literally, sucked). They used to meet in the evening and talk into the night while roaming the streets. Dad had a secondhand BSA A10 Golden Flash and Peter a Dayton Albatross De Luxe Twin, and they'd spend the weekends riding their motorbikes from town to town throughout the West Midlands, just cruising for the fun of it.

One dark night, they rolled up to a T-junction, preparing to turn left. Neither of them saw the third motorbike coming from the right, and couldn't hear it over the sound of their own engines. They always suspected it hadn't turned its headlight on. Dad pulled away first, followed a second later by Peter, which is when the two-stroke Francis-Barnett ploughed straight into the latter's right flank. "All I remember is hearing the crash and jumping off my motorcycle, dropping it, and running back," says Dad. Peter had been thrown up in the air and landed on his head. Fortunately, he was wearing a helmet, the peak of which buckled down and broke his nose, but nevertheless, he sustained serious head injuries from which he never quite recovered.

Dad tends to play down the accident, which my Mum describes as 'horrendous.' "It was a pretty close call for me, I suppose," he says, shifting in his seat. It's getting late, but I'm really enjoying this insight into his past. I'm curious, though, if he felt any guilt for pulling out first, as guilt is an indicator of empathy.

"Why would I?" he replies. "I didn't do anything wrong. It was just bad luck on his part. I don't think he was relying on me having seen that the road was clear because we were side by side." This lack of guilt is a result of having carefully analysed the sequence and found himself blameless. I'm certain many neurotypical people would feel guilt for not noticing the oncoming bike, whether or not they had a realistic possibility of doing so. In a way, though, that is lying to oneself, whereas his analysis of culpability and subsequent lack of remorse is pure.

"You're very susceptible on two wheels," he continues. "Nothing much has to happen for you to fall off." He used to bang his ankles up quite often as they'd be trapped under the bike during a fall, and he probably visited hospital half a dozen times with minor lacerations. "I had a skin graft on one occasion," he remembers. "My ankle was damaged, but I can't remember much about it. It must have been quite bad. It's just a hazard of motorcycling." Like many Aspergians, he has a studiously exact vocabulary, always using full words, e.g. motorcycle and telephone. He calls my siblings only by their full names, Matthew and Victoria, whereas I railed against the name Daniel so forcefully as soon as I could talk that I became Dan by default. I later had it officially changed.

The two Peters had a birthday card they used to send back and forth every year. It simply said: "To Peter, Happy Birthday, From Peter." I remember it sitting on a shelf in the corner of the kitchen until it was time for Dad to send it back. Fortunately, this was only a matter of weeks, whereas Peter J. had to keep track of the same card for eleven months. It must have gone around for twenty years before drifting out of circulation. A few years after we moved to Cornwall, Peter suffered a minor heart attack. It became difficult to stay in touch, although Dad admits never to have been much good at correspondence anyway. Now in his late seventies, Peter apparently has a mobile phone, but doesn't use it for text messaging. He doesn't use computers either. He writes letters longhand and uses a postage stamp.

Nowadays, Dad is once again short of friends. "I think I was fifty before I started to feel I could deal normally with people, but even now, I try to make friends and can't. When I first moved to Spain, I went to a snooker night in one of the bars," he says more softly, the chirrups of insects his only competition. The young travellers have retired, leaving us alone by the pool. "I was probably the worst player there. There were four of us, and one said to another, 'How about if you and I have a practice one night?' 'Yeah, okay,' came the reply. So, I said, 'Good idea. Who'll practice with me one night?' Silence. Absolute silence. I tried again: 'Anybody like to practice with me one night?' Nothing. It was embarrassing." I feel the heat of shame on his behalf, and my eyes drop automatically to the floor. How could someone be so rude?

"Men don't want to know me. They don't get the feedback they expect from another man. I try to say the things I know I'm supposed to say, but it rarely fools them." He's quiet for a second before the light returns to his eyes. "Although sometimes when I meet somebody, I come away thinking, 'I pulled it off! They thought I was normal. They didn't see this thing in me!'" This success is echoed in a passage by John Robison: "As I've gotten older, I have taught myself to act 'normal.' I can do it well enough to fool the average person for a whole evening, maybe longer. But it falls apart if I hear something that elicits a strong emotional reaction from me that is different from what people expect."[14]

"I have difficulty gauging who is a friend and who isn't," continues Dad, half to me and half to himself. "Sometimes people come along who are very nice to me and so I think they're my friend, but in actual fact, they're not because they're nice to everybody." He sighs heavily. "I don't have different degrees of friendship, either. If someone's a friend, I feel obliged to do anything for them. That's what you do for friends. That's a little rule."

He's always had a problem in trusting the wrong people too quickly and been let down time and again by those he thought were friends. He once lent a retired English couple in Spain his GPS, and they lost it but didn't apologise or offer to replace it. He was shocked and felt utterly betrayed. These were people he identified with, and it turned out they had no respect for his property. He thought they were closer than they thought they were.

"I remember one time I decided to have a party at home," Dad recalls fondly, unconsciously straightening his back as he zips back fifty years. There's a gleam in his eyes that could derive from pleasure, although it could just be from the outdoor lighting reflecting off the surface of the pool. "I think it may have been my twenty-first birthday. We made the usual invitation calls, but then I remembered that Stan, one of the gang, was in London." He didn't know where in London, but he had Stan's sister's phone number, so the day before

14 Robison, *Look Me in the Eye*, 31.

the party, he and John set off to find him. They called her when they arrived in London, in the middle of the night. She didn't know Stan's address but remembered the street name and that he was three doors away from a synagogue. They found the house, and fortunately there was still a light on downstairs, so Dad knocked on the window and was told there were some guys lodging upstairs. He knocked on that door, but there was no answer.

"The door was not locked, so we entered, found Stan in bed, and drove him back to Birmingham for the party." He smiles. He's always been proud of his ability to locate people. His thoroughly systematic thought processes would have made him a fine detective. "Those were my happy years," he concludes, the warm glow of reminiscence spreading across the table and enveloping me in its embrace. "I enjoyed myself."

Chapter 5

Aflunters

"Would you like anything to drink?" he asks as we sit down for his morning brew. San José is no oil painting, just another Central American capital of buildings, roads, and people, and it's hard to see past the next street corner. The day is a roaster, but no matter the temperature, Dad never removes his multi-pocketed vest. I'm nervous of him carrying all his valuables about his person. He looks like an easy target; a group of child thieves would make mincemeat of him. I'd be more comfortable, and it would require less mental arithmetic, if I controlled all the money, but I can't possibly emasculate him by suggesting such a thing. After all, he's just starting to relax his wallet, allowing himself a nice meal and a daily cup of coffee.

"No, thanks." I shrug after perusing the menu. The most tempting item is passion fruit juice, but three dollars is more than I would personally spend on a glass of juice, so it would feel wrong to accept it from him. "I'm alright."

"Hmm, maybe you're right," he replies, replacing the menu on the table. "I won't have anything either."

"What? No!" I splutter, suddenly aware that I'm inadvertently sabotaging his efforts to spend. He must be encouraged to use his hard-earned wealth to enjoy himself; otherwise, what was it all for? "You should enjoy your coffee. You deserve it."

"Possibly, but I don't actually need it," he decides. "If you don't, I don't."

"Okay, okay!" I scowl, throwing my hands up in a gesture of submission. "I'll have a passion fruit juice, thank you." Apparently, I must act like a decadent wastrel so he can become one. Mealtimes are when the disparate nature of our budgets is most apparent, because if there's one thing I am most certainly not, it's a gastro-tourist. Whether at home or abroad, I eat mainly to fuel my body. Sure, I have some flavours I prefer over others, but in the end, it all goes down the same way. I can't see the point in spending twenty bucks on the same quantity of food as I can get for two; I'd rather spend my money on other things. That said, wherever I am, in the spirit of cultural immersion, I try to eat almost exclusively the local cuisine. On my budget this usually takes the form of street food or the staple dishes at basic eateries. Hence, in most of Central America, rice and beans will be my daily fare, usually with chicken or grilled beef.

"So, what do you want to do?" I ask Dad after reading him the list of San José's attractions, mostly museums, parks, and markets. We only have the morning before heading to Monteverde, which is probably more than enough. What I want to do is get a yellow fever vaccination. I'd held off in Sydney due to the cost, knowing a jab would be cheaper here. In fact, it turns out to be literally a sixth of the price.

No reply is forthcoming, but I'm pretty sure he'll agree to whatever I suggest. I learned the hard way to be picky when it comes to choosing travel companions. For my European Interrail odyssey, I talked one of my best friends from school, Simon, into accompanying me during the summer break after our first year of university. We arranged the trip months in advance, but by the time summer rolled around, he had fallen for a Californian student, Stephanie, and invited her to join us. Fair enough, I thought. The more the merrier. Then she wanted her younger sister to come along, and her sister invited one of her friends. Suddenly, Simon and I were outnumbered.

Still, I was not unhappy with this arrangement. I pictured lying on golden sand beaches next to a pair of gorgeous young things in skimpy bikinis, charming them with my sparkling wit and English accent until they could resist me no longer. At that time, I imagined American girls the way many in the Muslim world now imagine all Western women—as harlots of loose morals who'd more than likely jump me by the end of the first week. "How do we know the USA is tilted?" went the joke. "Because everything loose ends up in California." Surely this was an amazing opportunity to lose the burden of my innocence? How wrong I was.

I was woefully unprepared for international travel. I didn't have a guidebook; I didn't even know such things existed. My main goal was to tour the famous archaeological sites of Italy and Greece, but beyond that, I didn't much care where I went. I was travelling through Europe! With one of my best mates! Even a bad day travelling was going to be amazing, I reasoned. Stephanie and the girls had bought a *Let's Go Europe*—the classic American young travellers' handbook—and used it to plan their (and by default our) route. Again, I wasn't fazed. I wanted to see all of Europe, so wherever we went, I would be happy. Wrong again.

In short, we didn't get on. We didn't share the same sense of humour. They were too serious, too easily offended. They thought me rude. I thought them uptight and stopped imagining them as possible conquests after a couple of days. Also, their trip was being underwritten by their parents, whereas I ran out of money halfway through. By the end, I couldn't participate in any activities and could barely afford to eat. I just mooched from city to city, walking around the free sights and staying in at night. I chewed dry baguettes while Stephanie, an anti-consumerist vegetarian Wiccan, would happily buy a McDonalds burger for a chained-up dog because it 'looked hungry.'

Worse, their planned route was far from interesting to me. Three days in a medieval Italian walled town with no money is more like a punishment than a holiday. If I was in the same situation now, I'd quickly wave farewell and strike out on my own, but at eighteen, I didn't have the confidence. That wretched month almost put me off travelling for life, and I never again committed to sharing a trip with a total stranger. A friend, or relative in this case, who goes along with everything I say is a dream companion.

"I'll do what you do," says Dad, matter-of-factly. "You're the Captain."

And so to Monteverde, a pocket of lush cloud forest protected by a biological reserve nestled atop a mountain range in the country's northeast. Costa Rica isn't like the other countries of Central America. Rather than being a plaything of foreign governments and private corporations, pillaged, cheated, and invaded by one means or another, Costa Rica has evolved as a holiday destination for US tourists. Thus, instead of the poverty of ex-banana republic Honduras, the canal intercourse of Panama, or the political turmoil of Nicaragua, Costa Rica is relatively well developed, and much of its pristine jungle remains intact. One of the drawbacks of this prosperity is that it sometimes feels like part of the US, with its boutique coffee shops, bicycle helmets, and prices to match.

Santa Elena, the closest settlement to Monteverde, is really just a village with a few shops and pensions. Up here the sky is white, the air damp, and mould thrives on the concrete walls. The words 'cloud forest' conjure images of huge trees dripping with moss and vines, like the backdrop of some elaborate fantasy film set on a faraway planet. The 'nature trail' outlined in my guidebook more accurately resembles a steep and muddy road up which I trudge for an hour to a lookout above the town. It's really just a car park for the communications tower housed there, and all I can see is a wall of cloud and drizzle that the wind drives into my eyes.

For the afternoon's entertainment, I've booked myself on a canopy tour, an opportunity to zip through the treetops suspended by a harness attached to a steel cable, and fortunately, the clouds begin to dissipate as the sun reaches its zenith. I'm driven from Santa Elena in a minibus with a fancy paint job to the company HQ, where I discover zip-lining is a popular activity among people half my age. Canopy tours are *huge* in Costa Rica. Every tourist town that can lay claim to a straggly copse of guanacaste[15] has one. With the rate of deforestation in Central America, these flying foxes may one day be the only reason any trees are left standing.

In the harness fitting area, I judge myself alone in the over-thirties age group while the under-twenties are heavily represented by

15 Costa Rica's national tree.

American school groups. Between us lies a category sparsely populated by sensible German couples in Mammut-branded outdoor clothing. Standing in the back corner, waiting patiently for the fun part to begin, I wish I had someone to toss around jokes with and build a frisson of excitement. I can't start a conversation with one of the excitable people around me until I'm offered some sort of invitation, but that doesn't happen today. I may not be socially retarded like my old man, but a spontaneous introduction is still a bit of a stretch.

After a safety briefing, we begin the course from a wooden platform built around a sturdy tree trunk. Cables above my head lead gently down between the trees to a similar platform, and it only takes a matter of seconds for the guide to clip my harness onto the cable and wave me away. I push off and slide down, blurred foliage whizzing past my ears, to the next station. The initial rides are quite tame, giving nervous punters the opportunity to bail out before it gets serious, but this company (along with most others) claims to have the single longest zip-line in Costa Rica—around one kilometre. That's quite a distance to fly, especially when hung spectacularly high across a valley between two forested ridges. When we reach it, the persevering mist obscures the far end of the line, so the riders before me shrink to small dots before vanishing into the cloud. I can't say for certain we aren't all being shot into some giant tunnel that leads straight down to hell.

I choose to do the big one 'Superman style,' which means that instead of sitting up in the harness, I hang face down like a corpse being airlifted off a mountain. You wouldn't want to be scared of heights, that's for sure. Once clipped in, I launch into the sky, quickly clearing any foliage and zooming along a hundred metres above the ground. It's a unique experience, as close to flying as I'll ever get, but the highlight comes courtesy of the hitherto troublesome weather. As I glance down, the low-lying mist refracts some stubborn rays of sunlight that have struggled through the cloud layer and creates a rainbow directly below me. So far, so what, but instead of descending from the sky to a pot of gold and a betrayed leprechaun, the coloured ribbon describes a perfect circle around and slightly below me. I gasp as my gaze follows the ring of shimmering light, which surrounds me like a magic force field. The illusion lasts only a few seconds before I look up to see the landing platform approaching at sixty kilometres an hour, a guide stationed and ready to brake me. Monteverde truly is the land of rainbows.

I return to find Dad in a state of agitation, huddled nervously on the edge of the bed in our room. "You left me defenceless!" he blurts, his tone edged with hurt.

I blink in surprise as I set down my pack, wondering what strife he's got himself into now.

"I was kidnapped!" he exclaims improbably, but before I can think of a response, he continues. "All I wanted to do was sit quietly and read, but Louis found me and forced me to go to breakfast with him!"

"Who's Louis?" I ask, brows knitted, but I can't help the beginnings of a smile forming when I realise that kidnapping may be a slight exaggeration.

"The pension owner! He took me to his favourite café, told me what to order, which was far too much by the way, and over the next hour proceeded to tell me his life story while drinking beer on my tab." Oh, the horror! By this time, I'm starting to chuckle, sensing his outrage is only half serious. "Now we're best friends!" he wails, as though Louis has planted cocaine in his luggage and shopped him to the *policia*. "He wants to find me on Facebook! I've been hiding in here ever since." Obviously, Louis hasn't realised that Facebook is my father's worst nightmare, a new millennium kick in the teeth for friendless losers like him.

Just then, Louis himself arrives, a jovial, middle-aged fellow with big teeth and a trim moustache. "You have one of the best fathers in the world!" he announces grandly. It's all I can do not to erupt into laughter. "I am come to visit him in *España*," he continues in muddled English. Both of us are absolutely flummoxed as to how this guy could have mistaken Dad for a people person. Then again, Louis is a talker, and Dad qualifies as a good listener purely by virtue of staying silent.

He'd probably be a valuable asset to a suicide prevention helpline, even despite his complete lack of empathy. Life can be so ironic!

I have a deep fascination with staring into live volcanoes; that eerie red glow from within the breast of the earth lulls me into a state of intense hypnosis. I always gaze fixedly into the void, imagining what would happen should I leap in, my body burning up like a satellite re-entering the earth's atmosphere, a second of white-hot pain before disintegration. Indonesia, Vanuatu, Stromboli, the DRC—I'm always chasing that closeness to the fabric of our planet, the opportunity to experience the lazy flow of molten rock, the angry bubble of escaping gas. Hence our next destination—*La Fortuna*, where nearby *Volcán Arenal* is famous for offering amazing views of lava and flying lumps of red-hot rock.

The rain is heavier here, hammering on the tin roof over our heads. The drains in the courtyard gurgle like demented baby giants. The weather has deterred any other guests, so we can take the cheaper dormitory option safe in the knowledge that nobody will join us. Worse news is that Arenal is currently enjoying a period of inactivity. Of course, I could have obtained a seismicity report ahead of time and discovered this for myself. I could have checked the local weather as well. I could have read numerous reviews on TripAdvisor, watched YouTube videos and questioned a local tour company. Come to think of it, I could have planned the entire trip in advance using online timetables and accommodation booking websites, found the best deals and vouchers, and thoroughly researched every possible activity before accepting or rejecting it, always knowing in advance exactly what was in store. But where's the fun in that? Where's the mystery, the flexibility? Admittedly, there are times when a little preparation can save a lot of money, or offer more freedom, but generally, I'd rather be disappointed every now and again than have everything calculated to three decimal places.

With practically the only reason for our visit hiding away like a depressed old man in his bedroom, we make plans to leave *La Fortuna* the next day. However, there's still one activity we could enjoy: the geothermal nature of the area has resulted in numerous local hot springs, and who doesn't like a nice soak in a hot spring? You guessed it.

"You want to do what?" he exclaims. The fancy resort in town is out of my budget, so I'm trying to sell him on a visit to a natural thermal pool in a river outside of town. This has many advantages: you are at one with the landscape, sitting in a flowing spring instead of artificially pumped water, surrounded by rocks and trees instead of tiled walls and floors, and heated by Mother Earth herself rather than cold, hard electricity. Plus, it's free. On the downside, we'd have to somehow get there and back, and it's still raining. "You mean . . ." he says, working through it in his mind. "You mean you stand by a river, in the rain, and take your clothes off?"

"Well, yes," I admit, doing that 'so what' shrug with my neck that makes me look like a bullfrog.

"Then you walk across some slippery rocks to sit in the river, in the rain?" he continues, as if struggling to understand a complex Agatha Christie plotline.

"Yes, but that's the fun part," I point out. "Being immersed in hot water while it's cold and raining outside, like those Japanese macaques with snow on their heads. It's nice. It's, y'know, fun." I don't think I'm getting my zeal across effectively.

"Then you dry off, in the rain, and change into clean underpants?" I'm foundering now. He's making too much sense, and I can feel my own enthusiasm waning. "People who are seventy-two have to worry about catching colds and falling over," he reminds me. "Our bones are brittle." He's right, of course. I can see he's trying. He wants to do what I want to do, but he's stumbling. "How about I come along but I won't get in with you?"

My shoulders slump. "No, it'd be no fun sitting on my own." This is no use.

"You're frowning, son," he accurately detects. I have a vertical crease above my nose that wrinkles when I'm pensive. It's an expression he's obviously taught himself to recognise. "Is it because of me?"

"Well, sort of," I say. I'm a bad liar.

"I'm sorry. I wouldn't want to do anything to make you frown. I'll come along quietly."

"Forget about it," I mutter, perhaps a little too tersely.

"That's what people say when they're still annoyed," he observes.

"Annoyed with you going on about it, yes," I counter. I don't want to get cross with him, and I hate myself for doing so, but travelling with an aged parent requires a surfeit of patience, a virtue of which I have only a finite supply. I close my eyes and force myself to calm down. He doesn't mean it. He's trying really hard. I forgive him.

"I'm sorry, son." His voice radiates genuine remorse. "Have I talked you out of it? How about I take you to the other place?" he suggests. "The indoor one."

"But that's, like, thirty dollars each," I argue, dismissing the suggestion out of hand.

"It's okay," he says, trying not to let the pain show. "I'll pay." My ears prick up. He must really feel bad. Can I allow him to buy my forgiveness with hot water?

Yes, I decide, I can.

And so we find ourselves, side by side on bar stools, warm water up to our waists, sipping cold drinks. The resort is actually quite impressive, with numerous pools fed by hot waterfalls cascading off boulders. Small channels lead from one open-air room to the next and loungers are lined up beside the pools, although the night air is too chilly to use them. Coloured lights cast a pleasantly subtle glow around the place, and thick foliage hides the plumbing. This is something of a treat, actually, as I usually consider these places only for the wealthy. Jeez, I really have to get into this money-spending thing.

"So, what shall we talk about?" asks Dad, opening the conversation on his customary tack, and he literally means anything at all. Hans Asperger first described the eponymous condition as being characterised by, among other things, excellent logical abstract thinking, and while no officially recognised correlation exists between AS and high IQ, many commonly accept a link. After all, the two share the traits of detailed thinking, unwavering focus, and often obsessive interest in a single subject. According to Temple Grandin, Dr. Nancy Minshew of Carnegie Mellon University theorizes the ability of people with Asperger's to process both the individual words they hear, the signifiers, and what they stand for, their denotation, may partially explain their high IQs.[16] Many recognised geniuses in history have displayed AS symptoms, particularly low empathy and antisocial behaviour, and had a diagnosis been available, would almost certainly have been labelled as such. They include Sir Isaac Newton and Nikola Tesla, among others.

In 1983 Developmental Psychologist Howard Gardener described nine different kinds of intelligence.[17] My father more than qualifies in the field of logical-mathematical intelligence, having an amazing capacity for maths and engineering and easily comprehending electronics and plumbing systems and, more recently, computing.

"My mathematics was outstanding," he says now, not boasting, just factual, "especially mental arithmetic. I never used to have to think, even. The problem would be in my mind, and the answer would be there with it. It's gone now, though." I remember him stressing the importance of mental arithmetic to us as children, a skill that has stood me in good stead, and he was very useful as a source of help during my A-level maths course, I can tell you! I'd also classify him as above average in spatial, linguistic, and bodily-kinaesthetic intelligences.

His fascination with designing systems led to him dabbling in invention. He was actually working on a self-stirring saucepan in his garage when a version was released commercially. He pondered long and hard on perpetual motion, on creating a system so efficient that the initial energy input keeps it going forever, like a wheel that never stops spinning, even though the current laws of physics determine such a machine is impossible. In his spare time, he loved jigsaws, mahjongg, and cryptic crosswords, and still does. As children, he bought us constructional systems like Lego and Meccano and joined us in

16 Grandin, *The Way I See It,* 191.

17 See Appendix II

building with them. He embraced technology far more than I do. We were the first family I knew of to buy a VCR—Betamax, of course, because he'd done the research and decided it was the superior system (which it was; VHS only won the format war by offering lower prices).

We were also the first to own a home computer, an Apple II,[18] which he used for bookkeeping. He wrote his own accounting software and once spent two days designing a moving image of a sword in response to my request for a fantasy fighting game. In modern terms, this necessitated teaching himself machine code, a language used to write instructions for computers, over the course of the weekend. I was disappointed with the result, I was hoping he'd design the equivalent of a first-person shooter purely for my amusement, but I now see the outcome was remarkable. He took my idea, determined to start at the very beginning, and briefly made an obsession of it.

In AS, such skills are related to being a pattern thinker, one of three different types of specialised thinking.[19] Pattern thinkers have superior abilities to perform mental rotation tasks and are often very good at computer programming, engineering, or music. Dad programmed and maintained all the machinery in his factory, often inventing new parts and systems to make it more efficient. If a machine broke down, he'd find the problem using a multi-meter and circuit diagrams spread across the floor. He did all the repairs and DIY at home, from hanging wallpaper to unblocking drains to installing a new kitchen. Admittedly, this was probably because he was too stingy to pay tradesmen, but the fact that he can teach himself any technique from a book and replicate it is nevertheless impressive.

When we moved to Cornwall, he converted the shell of a barn into his new factory premises, literally rebuilding the entire structure from scratch using his *Reader's Digest* DIY manual and only employing professionals for the roofing and stonework. He has incredible willpower; when he sets his mind to a task, he will complete it. My parents

18 With 4KB of RAM!

19 Grandin, *The Way I See It*, 16. The others are visual thinking and verbal thinking, according to Temple Grandin.

used to smoke until, after returning from a European ski trip, he decided they would quit immediately. It didn't matter that they'd just bought several cartons of duty-free cigarettes; they gave them away and never smoked again. He took up the habit of chewing his tongue instead. I'd like to think I've inherited his do-anything attitude, although, as I'm not very practical, mine is in a more abstract sense. I grew up thinking I could be anything I wanted: archaeologist, hiking guide, travel writer—and I have. The history of my employment has been a succession of hobbies used to derive income.

"I must apologise for not doing more activities with you," he says eventually. We've been content just soaking our loins in the hot water in companionable silence. "I'm still lethargic from the sertraline." He must be feeling bad because I had to go on the canopy tour alone, which is ridiculous, and I tell him so. "You mustn't hold back from doing what you would normally do," he urges, consternation lining his forehead. "If you want to go and make friends with people, do it!"

"I will," I promise, touched at his concern, "but speaking of friends, what happened to yours?" I ask, trying to prompt the next part of his story. "Where are John, Alan, and Stan now?"

"Well," he says after a pause to shift his memory into gear, "when I was twenty-two, I went to work in my mother's shop in Northfield and lost contact with most of them."

"A shop?" I frown. "But I thought you were some sort of electrical genius?"

He was. He proceeds to explain how his employers at the electrical wholesalers encouraged him to enrol in a three-year course at Handsworth Technical College to obtain his National Certificate of Electrical Engineering. They paid for his first year and allowed him to attend one day a week. Despite his dreadful school experience, he was happy to go. He felt that at college he'd be treated as an adult, and since he was going voluntarily, he couldn't be criticised for failure. In his first-term exams, he scored 100 percent in mathematics and 98 percent in principles of electricity. At the end of the year, he was rewarded with book tokens and free entry to the second year. Although he moved onto other jobs, he continued his studies, again winning free entry to the third and final year. By this time, he was working as an estimator for a company in West Bromwich manufacturing crane control gear, but he was again fired, and left the course to drive a taxi.

"What?" My hand jerks involuntarily, and I slosh cold beer into the water, where the foam drifts into my belly button and nestles into the hairs there. "You left the course in which you were top of the class and getting free tuition? But why?"

"I just got bored," he admits, polishing off his margarita. "It wasn't difficult enough, not challenging. When I left school, I said to myself, 'Never ever regret leaving school early because it was the most terrible experience of your life. You must never think to yourself that you should have stayed,' and I never have. I didn't say that when I left the college course, though. I was very foolish not to complete it."

Not long after that, he and his mother became business partners at her little shop, the Cottage Stores on Hanging Lane. Dad's job was to get up at the crack of dawn, go to the vegetable and meat markets in the centre of Birmingham, and bring the produce back to the shop. After preparing it for sale, he fetched dry goods from the cash and carry wholesalers, then served in the shop all day. At 7:00 p.m. they closed, he mopped the floor, cleaned the equipment, and restocked the shelves. He had no time left to maintain friendships.

"Didn't you mind missing out on the motorbike rides and the parties and all that?" I couldn't contemplate suddenly ditching all my mates.

"Not really," he admits. "Work is ideal for people who have trouble socialising. During my marriage, I used to avoid most things by work. It was somewhere to hide. Anyway, I just lost touch with them after that." Aspergians, more so than regular people, tend to have trouble maintaining friendships. In terms of Howard Gardner's nine types of intelligence, they fall short in interpersonal intelligence—the ability to understand and interact effectively with others. Also called emotional intelligence, this category encompasses all the behaviours Aspergians generally struggle with, e.g., social awkwardness, misunderstanding situations, etc.

Shortly before I turned twenty-one, I decided that, after finishing university, I would spend a year in Australia. I can't say why I decided this; the thought just popped into my head one day and immediately stuck. I mean, it was a good idea! Before I was a regular traveller, the thought of relocating to a new and vast country on the far side of the world was a little daunting, so I wondered aloud to my family whether we knew anyone there who might be able to help me out on arrival. Dad had applied back in the 1970s to be a 'Ten Pound Pom,' an Australian migration scheme which, in an attempt to populate the island-continent, offered British subjects boat passage for ten pounds with good employment and housing prospects at the other end. He was refused due to his medical history. If it wasn't for his depression, I could've been a naturalised Australian before I was even aware of it.

It turned out that Dad's old friend Stan had moved to Sydney many years before, and Dad assumed Stan's brother, Sid, still lived in Birmingham. Proving his knack for locating people, he picked up the Birmingham residential phone book and proceeded to call everyone named Perks, S. It took only three or four calls until he was speaking with Sid, who supplied us with an address for Stan. We wrote to him via Airmail, and soon, I had an open offer of accommodation in Sydney, a welcome launch to my year in the antipodes.

It wasn't until fifteen years later that I emigrated properly. Having met Gerda in Mexico and fallen for her in London, I was in danger of losing her when she decided to move back to Africa. We made a deal. If she would stay in England for one more year while I rebuilt my bank account, I promised to move to Cape Town with her for a year, from where we'd apply for Australian visas. That second year turned into three but, with her hairdressing qualifications, the plan worked. We were accepted Downunder and have never looked back.

Dad may have sought refuge in work, but he was a disaster as a shopkeeper. "I was absolutely atrocious," he admits. "Customers in those shops come in to talk, bored housewives after a chat, and, of course, having a chat was totally out of my league. I remember that for some time my mother was upstairs convalescing after an illness, so I rigged up an internal telephone system, which was most unusual in those days. I could put the customers on to her and she could chat to them while sitting in bed."

He was also far too trusting; he didn't know people shoplifted. There was a broken window around the back of the store, and it was a long time before he discovered that children would go around and reach in there to steal bottles of lemonade. "I must have lost a lot of stock because I was so naïve." He worked out later that they'd also come in and ask for something from the storeroom, then help themselves to all the sweets while he was in there. I can picture it now: a rowdy group of boys thinking it a right lark to pay a visit to the shop on Hanging Lane after school and nick a few bars of chocolate. That weird Mr. Slater didn't have a clue!

"This is a nice, long ride, isn't it?" he announces out of nowhere. We're en route to Tortuguero, a small village on the Caribbean coast, famous for its turtle nesting beaches. He's right, it is, but it's strange to hear him say so. I turn and examine his face as the foliage passes smoothly behind him. He's smiling. I take a photograph.

"Am I dreaming, or are you actually expressing a positive opinion?" I ask, mock-serious.

"Maybe it's the effect of the magic tablets?" he suggests, a twinkle in his eye. "Soon, I'll be giving you input and asserting myself and everything. Then you'd better watch out!" I settle back in my seat to enjoy the scenery, optimistic this could be the start of a newfound positivity.

Surrounded by an extensive national park of thick jungle cut by muddy brown rivers, Tortuguero is a haven for the three species of sea turtle that use its sands to incubate their eggs. Our vessel—a large, open-sided skiff—is a transfer from the inland town of Cariari, but progress is slow enough to enjoy the sights and sounds. We glide across the smooth water, occasionally disturbing nervous herons that take flight gracefully downriver, or sunbathing reptiles that dart quickly into the sluggish depths. On both sides is foliage too dense to contemplate movement: a massed tangle of vines, branches, and leaves, a thousand shades of green dappled by sunlight. The canopy is alive with twittering birds, and the understory a constant hum of insect activity. Cruising along a river through a national park is a lovely way to get from A to B.

Tortuguero is situated on a narrow spit of land pressed between the ocean and a finger of water that creeps parallel to the coast, like the tusk of a narwhal poking into the sea. The channel joins with others, plus the rivers flowing down from the highlands, to form a neat network perfect for navigation. The village itself is chopped straight out of the jungle, a flat triangle of land located on the bend of the lagoon, where the sandbar thins to less than a hundred metres wide. The town's jetty leads to a small clearing with a lawn and benches, from which a single long street leads in both directions. This is another town free of motorised vehicles, save the decaying remains of what looks like a bulldozer, more rust than metal, slowly sinking into the ground.

The town is entirely reliant on tourism, hence the dozens of flaking, wooden signs advertising restaurants and accommodation along the main drag. Everywhere I look is evidence of a populace clinging on to its toehold in the wilderness. The 'street' is a concrete walkway raised above the flood-prone, muddy land, and every telegraph pole or fence post serves as an improvised trellis for the ever-creeping vines that seek to reclaim the area for the forest. The rain is holding off, but the iron sky is daunting, and the tang of salt from waves crashing onto the other side of the isthmus is pungent in our nostrils.

I find us a lovely guesthouse away from the main strip, large and clean with a high, breezy deck perfect for reading, writing, and generally chilling out. The season for turtle hatching is still a few weeks away, and so we're the only guests. Leatherback hatchlings begin to emerge first, and green sea turtles three months hence. The occasional hawksbill might be around laying, but it looks like the closest we'll get to viewing these charming creatures is the morbid collection of skulls dotted around the place. Hiring a guide to take us to the beach at night will likely reveal nothing more than driftwood and litter. Visiting fascinating seasonal destinations at the wrong time of year is always a little frustrating, but we couldn't plan our entire trip around the turtles of Tortuguero.

That evening we sit on the deck and drink Cuba libres. After the initial mutual apprehension at spending so long in each other's company, we seem to have settled into a more comfortable space. Dad no longer feels the need to force conversation, and we can coexist in relaxed quietude. He's still in a good mood tonight—he seems to like Tortuguero—and he even makes a planning decision: we'll stay an extra day here and get the boat transfer to Limon, about seventy kilometres down the coast. That's what I call progress!

Despite the companionable silence, it's not long before my impatience to hear the next chapter of his life story gets the better of me, and I coax from his lips what turns out to be a defining event. Only a couple of years after moving to Northfield, on the dark night of October 31, 1965, Dad's mother died suddenly.

A heavy smoker, every winter she'd be racked by a terrible cough. "It's my only bit of pleasure," she'd say of the habit. That particular autumn she'd been ill for weeks with a pain in her back, which her GP diagnosed as strain from the coughing. When Mike came to visit one day, he was aghast at her condition and immediately took her to see his own doctor for a second opinion. She was diagnosed with pleurisy, an inflammation of the tissues lining the lung cavity, and ordered straight to bed with daily penicillin injections. They never got to determine the underlying condition causing the pleurisy because two days later she had an enormous haemorrhage and died instantly.

"I had always thought I wouldn't be dismayed at anybody's death." His voice has lost none of its usual confidence, but for the first time, I sense a reluctance to discuss a topic. He's not looking directly at me as he usually does during our chats. "I used to wonder how I would feel if my mother died suddenly and be unable to imagine any grief. When it actually happened, though, I was absolutely distraught." He shut the shop for only a day or two but was devastated for months afterwards and withdrew from that Christmas altogether. He couldn't have anything to do with it then and has not enjoyed a single Christmas since 1965.

"I suppose it was the shock rather than the emotion," he says, quickly regaining his composure. "It was out of my control. I didn't think I'd be sad, but it certainly affected me. I don't expect anybody to die now that would cause me to suffer great grief, but maybe it will. Grief hits you without you thinking about it sometimes."

"So, if I died, you wouldn't be sad?" I ask, a half smirk collaborating with raised eyebrows in a virtual billboard of mischievousness—which he completely misses, of course.

"I really don't know," he states, candid as always. I manage to hide my dismay behind a sip of rum and Coke, the clinking ice painfully loud in the ensuing quiet. It's almost like the very birds in the trees have paused their singing in disbelief at his words. 'Did he really just say that?' they twitter softly to each other.

"These things happen," he continues, blissfully unaware. "People die and getting upset about it doesn't seem to be a logical thing. I never go to funerals. I don't understand the reason for going. If my brother were to die, I wouldn't go to England to his funeral, and people would think badly of me. If you were to die, I don't know what my reaction would be because grief is not a pre-thought-out thing. Since my mother, I have heard of several other relatives dying which didn't affect me in the least. I don't like to see others upset, mind you, because they are living people and maybe I could help. I can't do anything for dead people." It seems his thought process isn't able to conclude that by attending a funeral he *is* helping the bereaved through their grief, but I don't tell him that.

Thinking about it, I'm not that upset. He's being totally honest, and that's who he is. At least he's finally admitted to feeling an emotion, albeit unwillingly, as if genuinely surprised by his vulnerability. After all, a lack of empathy doesn't necessarily preclude feeling emotions, only displaying them and recognising them in others. Whenever previously I've accused him of displaying emotion, he's managed to wriggle out of it, attributing his actions to logic, or acting, or something else.

"I'm an emotional mirror," he once said, "If you're kind to me, I'll be kind back. I don't really generate emotions of my own." It's almost as if he feels the need to act the part of the Aspergian by not admitting to feeling anything, yet this seems out of character. He's not deceitful by nature. "I feel anger sometimes," he concedes when I press him. "That's an emotion." In fact, anger is called a secondary emotion because it is usually used to protect the mind from a primary emotion, such as shame, and he says he feels no shame.

"What about hate?" I ask, genuinely curious. "Do you feel that?"

"I don't hate anyone," he states, decisive. If that's true, he's a better man than I. "I cry when I watch my favourite film, though."

He seems oddly pleased with himself. The film in question is *Random Harvest*, from 1942, about a young WWI veteran who loses his memory. He proceeds to fall in love and marry, but a subsequent automobile accident restores his pre-war memories while erasing the post-war ones. He returns to his old life, ignoring his shattered wife, who must struggle to find a way back into his heart. It's a real tear-jerker, which it would have to be to break through to his circuit board of a heart. "I'm more affected by emotion in film than in real life," he concludes. Again, there's that note of pride I can't quite reconcile with his character. I'll have to keep prodding away at him on this point.

We've never really spoken about his own mortality, save for a brief lecture on how to handle his many diverse financial portfolios in the event of his death, which I immediately forgot. I'm unsure whether it's better to ignore the possibility altogether and save myself the pain of forethought or to inure myself to the expectation. That way, when it happens, I'll be able to shrug it off as cold and unemotional as he would. I don't imagine he's too worried about his own passing. Maybe Aspergians take it all in their stride due to a logical disbelief in the afterlife. I recall him saying once he didn't mind what we did with his remains; we could throw them in a bin bag for all he cared. On another occasion, he said we should throw a New Orleans-style jazz funeral with upbeat music and dancing, although I can't imagine who he thinks would attend.

Dad had been running the shop full-time for several years when his mother died, receiving only four pounds per week in wages, and there was some concession to this in her will. It was only a matter of a few hundred pounds or so, but despite her being of sound mind and there being no evidence she'd meant otherwise, Mike disagreed. It was his opinion that the solicitor who drew up the will had misinterpreted her wishes, and that his share should be more than the will specified.

Dad didn't want to fight. "I'll let it go," he thought to himself at the time. "He's my brother, and if that's how he wants it, let him have it. I don't want to fall out over it. Family is more important than money."

Either way, business was not good, partly because of Dad's 'devastating' way with people, partly the shoplifting, but also due to the opening of a new-fangled 'super market' on Northfield's main shopping street. The supermarket model was always destined to destroy local grocery shops, and this one was the death knell for the Cottage Stores. Because he was losing so much money, he started working at his brother's injection moulding business, running the shop in the daytime and a machine through the night. Eventually, he shut the shop altogether and worked for Mike full-time.

Oddly enough, I was living just outside Northfield during my first year at university, twenty-five years later. I'd gravitated back to Birmingham to study and my digs were within walking distance of the site of the old store. He'd sometimes come up from Cornwall to visit customers and take me out to dinner, but he never mentioned the place. He shrugs when I ask him why. "Perhaps it never occurred to me."

That evening, as he sometimes does, he laughs as he's getting into bed. I love it. At first, I assumed he'd thought of something funny, but no, it's just that the sheer pleasure of taking the weight off is all it takes to laugh with pleasure.

"My mother used to laugh when she got into bed," he says.

How peculiar. I guess some people laugh with relief or nervousness. I'm pretty sure I only laugh when things are funny, and sometimes not even then.

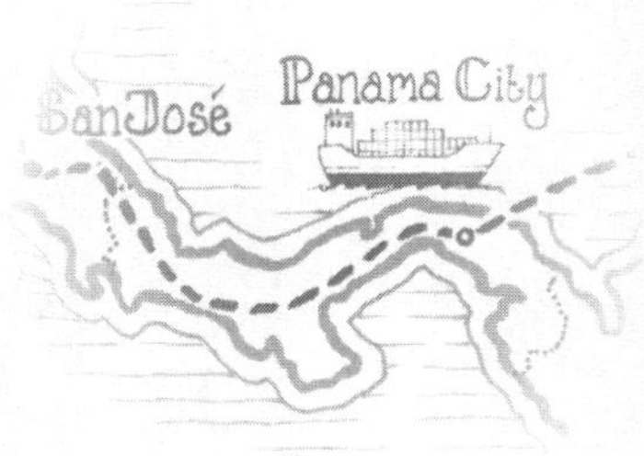

Chapter 6

Atrabilious

The Demons
By Peter Slater

The demons are coming. I can feel them draw near.
I've been chosen again and again. I must fear
the havoc they'll wreak when they come down to roost
in that part of my brain that is theirs when they choose.

They'll persist with their presence. They won't let me rest,
interfering with views that I've put to the test,
invading my thoughts, changing my plans.
Why do they plague me? I don't understand.

The cloud in the sky that was yesterday white;
today has turned black and moved to a site
directly above me and low near my head.
It presses upon me. They're here as I said.

The demons have found me. They know who I am.
They know that I'm worthless, a fraud, and a sham.
I don't deserve friends, family, justice, or love,
happiness, life, wealth, loyalty, or the Lord up above.

I belong in the dirt, back under my stone,
poor, sick, and friendless, in pain and alone.
I'm short of the mark, a total disgrace.
Down in the dark and the cold is my place.

You must keep your distance, whatever you do.
I'm afraid, if you don't, they'll get hold of you, too.
Look away and don't witness the way that I am.
I'll be back as I was if only I can.

You can't help me, I'll taint you, save yourself, do.
If you stay near me, you'll suffer too.
Run for your lives as fast as you can.
The demons have found me. They know who I am.

There's no mirth now. Yesterday's opinionated and involved trip-planner, the man who claimed to laugh himself to sleep, has gone, replaced by a silent, sullen, lump of human. It's best not to attempt conversation. Perhaps I dared hope my cheerful demeanour had permanently brightened his mood, or rather I was purposely forgetting the truth: depressives aren't cured by interacting with happy people, and I'm not even a particularly happy person. They will always have lows, and this was what he was trying to warn me that day in Tulum.

"There will be days when depression will prevent me from speaking," he'd said. "And if we get up one morning and you're talking to me and I have trouble forming answers for you, I wouldn't want you to think it is something you've done. Don't think it's your fault. It isn't. It's me."

When I realise this, my heart breaks anew. I immediately forgive him all the small annoyances that have been plaguing me for the last couple of weeks—the forgetfulness, the deafness, the social paralysis. I berate myself for my impatience; this is a man who needs all my sympathy and help, and it's unforgiveable of me to get angry with him. His depression hasn't relented; I've just been spared it thus far. I pray fervently that it's not reliving the loss of his mother that's brought this on. If the blame lay with me . . . I push it out of my mind, hoping this cloud will pass soon—for his sake, not mine.

It probably doesn't help that we've risen at 6:00 a.m. for a dawn canoe trip through the channels of the national park. In ironic contrast to my companion, the skies have cleared, and it looks like the sun may make an appearance for the first time in days. Our small canoe, paddled silently by our guide and his son, can approach astonishingly close to wildlife, and we catch some good sightings during the three-hour trip.

Nosing in among the musty-smelling mangroves, we spot tiger herons, blue herons, egrets, and parrots. Iguanas swim clumsily across the narrow canals or sit motionless on branches like knobbly green statues. Spectacled caiman perch in the high reeds, pretending to be invisible, and a blue morpho flutters by, a dash of brilliant cobalt, stark against the vibrant greenery of the rainforest. Howler monkeys are always fun—it's hard to believe such an almighty racket can emerge from the throat of such a small primate—and my heart leaps when our patience is rewarded with a fantastic sighting of a three-toed sloth, a fluffy teddy bear hanging lazily from an arm and a leg way up at the top of the tallest tree on the river. With a glazed expression, adorable smile, and mop of hair like a bad toupee, he gazes out over the tree-tops like he can't remember how he got there. And this is just a fraction of the fauna that hides within the thirty-thousand-hectare park, including jaguars, manatees, tapirs, basilisks, and poisonous frogs, most of the rainforest creatures of Central America, in fact. Unfortunately, recent logging, both legal and illegal, has opened areas of the park to poachers and endangered the protected species therein.

I'm disappointed not to see a toucan, one of my favourite birds, but all in all, I enjoy my morning. Dad seems to loosen up a bit in the afternoon, and I persuade him to join me for a stroll in a part of the park accessible by foot. Due to a signage malfunction, the two-kilometre trail south of town turns into five kilometres, but he copes well. He's slow but steady, like a lumbering tortoise but without the communication skills. One possible symptom of AS is a lack of coordination, and while this isn't readily noticeable, he often sports bruises and cuts on his limbs he doesn't remember acquiring. He seems to be losing feeling in his extremities.

"He isn't that clumsy, but, my goodness, have you ever seen him run?" my mother once said. "When he starts to run, everybody looks—arms and legs out in every direction; a remarkable sight. He doesn't do it very often."

"Rubbish," was his one-word rebuttal. I don't recall ever seeing that spectacle, but up until my teenage years, he still played tennis and squash. Apart from walking, it's the only exercise I've ever seen him do.

An unusual movement draws my attention to a peculiar vein of glittering green shards cutting straight across the jumble of roots and undergrowth. The floor of the forest is rife with leafcutter ants, their scuttling bodies wearing a rut through the leaf litter of the walking path. I'm fascinated by the dual carriageway of tiny red bodies marching along, half carrying their carefully cut bounty, waving it above their heads like placards at a political rally. The columns go on and on, a trail within a trail, seemingly without beginning or end, just an infinite convoy of life making all of humanity seem inconsequential by comparison.

We cut through to the beach, all but deserted under the once-again pregnant sky. A few locals mooch about, playing with children or just sitting and staring, and the sea looks more like the Pacific than the Caribbean, big rollers crashing in and foaming on the brown sand. Tree trunks, seaweed, and plastic jetsam decorate the shoreline, long enough in both directions to disappear into a distant haze of sea spray. Another curious trail confronts us, this time carved into the sand. From the high-tide line, a shallow furrow leads to the top of the beach, flanked by diagonal divots, and at its end, an area of disturbed sand. It can only be the spoor of a turtle, come in the night to lay her eggs and, by the look of it, very recently. She would be one of the first of the season. What a treat!

Tortuguero has been the highlight of Costa Rica, but to be honest, I haven't been impressed enough with the country to loiter longer. It feels like an American overseas territory plonked down neatly in the middle of the troubled region, like a jungle theme park run for US holidaymakers, undoubtedly beautiful but bearing little relation to the rest of Central America. I like my developing countries to be just that—developing. The more a land is culturally removed from home, the more interesting it is to visit.

Panama curves like a loop of intestine running east to west between two continents, joining them together while simultaneously separating two giant bodies of water. The kinked isthmus, gateway to Colombia and the vastness of South America, is probably not somewhere you'd normally think of as a holiday destination (unless, of course, you are Panamanian). Another victim of corruption, coups, and political bullying, Panama is currently enjoying a period of calm and prosperity and has one of the fastest growing economies in Latin America. It uses the US dollar as its currency and seems to be reinventing itself as a regional service and logistics hub, a sort of Central American version of Dubai.

From *Puerto Viejo de Talamanca*, a pleasant beach town near the border, we make our way to a disused rail bridge over the Sixaola River, which we cross by foot. Now *this* is the way to enter a country! From the frontier town of Guabito, it's a simple matter of catching a public bus to Almirante then a ferry across the bay to *Bocas del Toro*, an archipelago of small islands a few kilometres offshore. The main island's town, known as Bocas, has a reputation as a party hot spot, a reputation I fully intend to investigate. The journey takes a good few hours, but Dad has thankfully emerged from his latest nadir and shows no sign of flagging.

"I'm not tired right now!" he announces at one point, pathetically pleased with himself. His body must be getting used to the effects of the sertraline.

Although Bocas, confusingly, has more than one street, the town is only about six blocks by eight at its widest. We run out of buildings only five hundred metres from the jetty, where we find a likely looking hostel—a big, old, creaky wooden building. Stepping inside confirms its external appearance as a true backpacker's destination, the interior a labyrinth of narrow stairways, open dorm rooms, balconies, and furniture. The bathrooms and kitchen are poky, and the reception area, which seems to be in the centre of the common room, is an avalanche of receipts and flyers. An adjoining bar, really just the front room of the house, looks like it's hosted many a raucous evening in its time. Polaroids on the wall celebrate the perseverant folk who have completed the '100 Beer Challenge.' Every vertical surface is gaily painted with myriad designs, from dolphins to sunsets and mermaids, obviously the work of artistic guests decorating in exchange for free accommodation. Indeed, all the staff seem to be travellers who were passing through and decided to linger. I love it immediately, but I can see the old man is apprehensive. It's a lot of people in a small space.

We get some interested looks as we check in. I imagine he's probably the oldest guest they've ever had, and even I'm twice the age of these gap-year kids. We must look a right pair. It suddenly strikes me they might suspect we're some sort of *May to December* gay couple. "Is that his dad or . . . y'know?" I can practically hear people whispering, and I have to stifle a giggle at the thought.

There's no such phrase as *en suite* in this place, but we secure a twin room on the first floor that's close enough to a bathroom to mollify my cohort. The corrugated tin roof beneath our window is littered with discarded Balboa beer bottles, and the less said about the garden the better. I'm itching to get downstairs and make some friends, or at least quash those gay rumours.

Fortunately, that's not necessary—everyone we speak to loves our story and openly admires Dad for undertaking this trip the way he has. I feel self-conscious calling him Dad in front of strangers, as though it reduces me to a six-year-old again, but pride blooms within me at the room's mood of approval. He *is* doing well. It's a brave thing to suddenly up and go backpacking in a developing region at the age of seventy-two.

I'm also pleasantly surprised by their willingness to engage him. There's one particularly loud Australian surfer who treats him just like a regular person, as if he didn't look like a cross between Santa Claus and a cowboy from the old West. I cringe at the surfer's colourful language, which he shows no intention of moderating in the presence of an elderly gentleman, but Dad is unphased. "Look at me, having a conversation!" he boasts after the guy leaves and celebrates with a little dance.

When I was that age, I wouldn't have bothered talking to an old man. *Pah*! Old folk are boring, I would have thought to myself. With some sadness, I realise that, to these teenagers, I *am* the old folk! At least Dad is so advanced in years as to be a genuine curiosity; I'm just slightly too mature to be acceptable. I should be down the road in a middle-of-the-range hotel with my suitcases and airport transfers and day trips in air-conditioned tour buses, chatting to a really lovely retired couple from Portland, Maine about the trip they took last year to the Galapagos Islands and how they got a magnificent picture of the blue-footed boobies and wasn't the buffet delicious, etc. I shudder. Screw that!

Not everyone is so forthcoming. I see several pairs of eyes turn away after flicking over us. It serves me right, really. Fortunately, enough non-ageist backpackers accept me as one of their own, and I leave Dad for the evening to catch up on my partying. It's a Tuesday night, but that means nothing in a place like *Bocas del Toro*. After drinking games at the hostel, I follow a bunch of twenty-somethings to *La Iguana*, a nightclub built out on stilts over the bay. A large opening in the plank floor is illuminated by bright underwater lamps, fish nibbling the weeds of the sunken posts. It's positively encouraging patrons to drink n' dive. I'm too self-conscious of my forty-year-old body to strip off in a crowded nightclub, but others aren't so shy.

Sitting in a dark corner, watching the youngsters flirting with each other, I decide I should call Gerda at the next opportunity. Neither my wife nor I are needy partners; we don't get anxious spending time apart. Although, of course, we do miss each other, it isn't the disabling kicked-in-the-stomach feeling of unutterable loss that some couples experience (or claim to experience). When Gerda visits her family in Namibia for a few weeks, as she does every couple of years, I don't dread being alone. I look forward to being able to write uninterrupted, or to catch up on the films and TV series she doesn't like. I love not making the bed and consuming all the food in the house before going shopping again. I know for a fact she also relishes her 'G Time,' as she calls it, when I'm away.

So instead of needing to speak every day or wish each other goodnight (now that such an indulgence is possible in this era of telecommunication), I'll phone once a week if it's convenient. It's not unusual to make one of these sporadic calls only to be informed she's eating, watching TV, or has had a hard day and isn't in the mood to talk. I confess I'm disappointed when this happens, but I'd rather have that occasional reaction than a clingy wife who needs reassurance on a daily basis. Does that make us a bad couple? Are we doomed to one day fall out of love, our marriage fizzling out in divorce? Absolutely not. Time apart strengthens our bond, and our lack of need for communication bears this out.

Mingled with the fun of the evening is a soft sadness. Nights out will never be as enjoyably carefree as they were when I was young, dumb, and single. Age makes one cautious; twenty years ago, I wouldn't have hesitated to leap into that square of pale-blue water. In fact, I remember doing just that in a waterside bar on the island of Utila off the coast of Honduras. Did I, or did I just watch others doing it? I honestly can't remember. Nineteen-nineties Dan may also have ended up with one of the seemingly inexhaustible supply of pretty Dutch backpackers, and maybe that's the deeper truth of why present-day revelry can never live up to the halcyon nights of my youth. Gerda is everything to me, and I would never cheat on her, but there's always that small part of me that misses those uninhibited possibilities.

While he has problems speaking the language of men, Dad is much more comfortable talking to women. "Give me a woman any day of the week," is one of his maxims. "Men, you can keep. They seem to have this secret code involving a grunt and a nod or a wink, to which I smile and nod back dutifully while not having a clue what may have passed between us. Women, on the other hand, mature women at least, appear to have a greater knowledge of life itself and of the trials and tribulations of existing in the world, and so are much more interesting to chat with."

This conversational ease with women doesn't extend to initiating romantic involvement, however. "I never in my life had a girlfriend that didn't approach me," he admits. "I was never able to chat girls up. It was partially a lack of confidence, as I didn't think anybody would be interested in me." He met my mother at a party when he was eighteen, although it was more like she met him. I know the story well. He was by himself in a corner when she detected him, just sitting there quietly. Presumably, Peter Jackson had dragged him along, and he was pretending to be a regular person but not altogether succeeding. The first thing she noticed was that he wasn't dressed like the other guys; he was wearing a collared shirt. This would have been common enough at work but not at a party, and he had the sleeves rolled up to the elbows, which wasn't the fashion at all. Brenda was intrigued. She was fourteen, and the average boys she met didn't dress or behave like that.

"So, do you fancy him then?" said her mischievous friend Debby.

"Oh, yes," she replied. He was handsome, despite his bad dress sense. So, Debby dragged her over and introduced them. Mum was mortified, but my parents ended up spending their first evening together. He was much better chatting in a one-on-one situation than in a crowd, especially to a female, and when her father came to collect her, she knew she wanted to see him again. Initially, Mum was attracted to Dad because he looked unusual and wasn't talking to anyone, two undoubted facets of his AS. He was alone because of his lack of social and conversational skills, but to her he was a 'dark, handsome stranger.' It's not unusual for women to be intrigued by men who keep to themselves, the 'strong, silent type,' and they can unwittingly fall for Aspergians for this very reason.

Somewhat brazenly, Mum called the party to speak to Dad as soon as she arrived home, and they made a date to see each other that Sunday. They walked around town and sat in the park, and by the end of the day, she knew she was attracted to his mind as well as his striking features. She could see the intelligence there, which is another frequent explanation of attraction by women to AS men.

They started stepping out regularly, going for rides on his motorbike, her in the sidecar, but he soon put an end to it. "My big brother says I mustn't go out with a girl for more than three weeks or she'll get too attached," he told her. "At your age you don't need to get attached, so I'm not going out with you anymore. But we can stay friends." Mum was devastated, as would any teenage girl be at such a blow to her self-esteem. Not having any idea how these things worked, Dad was simply following Mike's instructions, but he lacked the ability to see the effect of his strategy and improvise based upon her reaction.

They both moved on to other relationships. Encouraged by his success, and maybe wanting to try his hand at 'playing the field,' Dad used to count on his fingers how many girls he could call upon at any given time. He was aiming for seven, one for every night of the week, but he only ever got to six on a regular basis. In the early 1960s, the notion of 'taking a girl out' was not accompanied by the depth of relations that are assumed today, but even so, this isn't the image of a shy Aspergian. "I was cheating, really," he admits. "Two were neighbours whom I'd known since childhood. Another two were sisters of my friend John. Sue was another who I never actually approached. She just fell into my lap, like Brenda. So, it wasn't difficult."

They still saw each other occasionally when their orbits crossed. When Mum began studying chiropody at Handsworth Technical College, he was still attending once a week for his National Certificate of Engineering. They used to meet in the canteen for lunch, but it was only two or three years later that they recommenced their relationship properly. Gradually, the other girls all fell away until the only one left was my mum.

They were engaged to be married when his mother died, although disappointingly, neither of them now remembers the original proposal. It seems to have been a mutual decision—the logical next step in the relationship. Dad only recalls his mother knowing a jeweller from whom he could get a discount on a ring, a square emerald set with diamonds on a gold band. Then Mum's father took ill and passed away. She'd lost her mother when she was thirteen and now, the death of the last solid foundation in her life freaked her out so much she broke off the engagement. A practising Catholic, she felt that God was trying to force her into this marriage, and she was not about to be forced into anything.

They were still a couple, though. She rented a one-bedroom flat in Bartley Green and would stay at the shop in Northfield once or twice a week. This went on for a couple of years before she realised she might lose him if her stubbornness continued, so she relented. She was unconcerned about his oddness. On the contrary, she adored him all the more for being a little different. She thought him intelligent, studious, and determined to be the best at whatever he did, including relationships, plus he was still clinging on to a veneer of sociability at this point.

The re-engagement was less than romantic. According to her, she said, "Can we get married now? I'm ready." He remembers it differently: "One day she said to me, 'Well, are you going to marry me or not, because if not, I'll go and marry someone else.' 'Well, alright then,' I said. I just went along with it. It was probably not a good basis for getting married."

She suspected he started to feel overly threatened when they began to make actual wedding plans. It was then that his fear of intimacy began to assert itself. Not physical intimacy, which seemed to be normal, but emotional intimacy. Because of this, as the time neared, she began to have serious doubts as to whether he could commit to the marriage. "If there's any risk you're not going to go through with it, you've got to tell me," she said, "and we'll cancel everything. Don't leave me at the altar, I really couldn't face that."

He reassured her he wouldn't but wasn't altogether convinced himself. "As the date approached, I may have liked to change my mind," he admits, stirring the pattern atop his coffee into a frothy whirlpool during my history lesson the next morning, "but you don't do that to someone when you've made a commitment." We've escaped the cramped and messy DIY pancake explosion that is the hostel kitchen and found a café on the main street for breakfast. Dad has ordered a club sandwich, careful to stipulate no ketchup. He absolutely detests vinegar and anything associated with it. It was banned from our dinner table, and Sunday evening runs to the chip shop were characterised by NO VINEGAR instructions drilled into our heads. 'If I went to Room 101,'[20] he said once, 'they'd drown me in a vat of vinegar.' Predictably, this café makes the dreaded mistake, and he has to send it back.

With his general discomfort around people, I imagine aloud that he must've been nervous of being attached to one of them forever. "Yes," he says, dead serious. "It was a bad idea, and I should never have done it. I didn't want to, but it was sort of a default situation. I actually said to her, 'Why are we going to get married? Why don't we just live together?' but under pressure from society and her Catholic upbringing, she wouldn't consider it."

"It sounds like you were never happy being married," I probe, glumly, avoiding his eyes. Could it be true that the entire basis for my life was rooted in melancholy? I refuse to believe it. There were plenty of good times, happy times. He's seeing the past now through this black lens of depression. I wish I could somehow lighten it for him, but how?

"My feeling back then was that it didn't matter very much whom you married," he continues, plunging the conversation into the surreal. "Emotions didn't come into it. It was just something that people did—you married someone, and you lived with them. It didn't seem important to me at the time."

My brow furrows, a forkful of omelette interrupted in its fateful journey to my stomach. "But surely there are some people you'd prefer to marry over other people? People you like, for instance?"

"Aspergians don't have this like for some people and not other people," he says, the first time I've heard him name his condition. He speaks almost impatiently, as if I'm just not getting it. And I don't think I am. He told me earlier there were clearly defined 'friends' and 'non-friends'; he seems to be changing his story. "The relationship thing is very strange. People are just people."

Do Aspergians even feel what neurotypicals refer to as love? This is not a straightforward question, as 'love' is probably the most

20 The torture chamber of the Eastasian government in George Orwell's *1984*.

ill-defined word in the English language, an ambiguous concept suggested by endless symptoms and individual perspectives. Remembering that the label AS refers to a wide range of behaviours on the Autism Spectrum, the short answer is yes, usually. They are not cold-hearted psychopaths, after all. They do feel their own kind of love; they just have difficulty in both expressing it and recognising expressions of love directed at them. This makes forming relationships difficult, as misunderstandings often arise from both directions.

Interestingly, psychopaths are born with Antisocial Personality Disorder (APD), a label seemingly perfect to describe Aspergians. However, while psychopaths (and sociopaths, although neither are recognised professional labels) can accurately judge the emotions of others, they don't trigger an appropriate response in them. They have little or no empathy towards anyone else. They ignore the suffering of others and manipulate people around them, usually in superficial relationships, for their own ends.

Contrast this with Aspergian behaviour: "When they discover they have inadvertently hurt another person," Baron-Cohen says, "perhaps by saying something that has caused offence, they are usually shocked. They typically find it equally puzzling to know how to repair such a hurt. Certainly, they do not set out to upset others."[21]

The ceremony was at a church in Northfield, a very small affair. I've only ever seen a few photos of the event because they never had a wedding album, only a bundle of photographic proofs. They were even stamped with the words 'rough proof'. There was always the intention to get some proper prints, but that would've cost several hundred pounds, a lot of money in those days. So they never got around to it, hence no pictures were ever on display in our home, only tucked away in an album we might fish out every few years.

In the photos, Dad is smiling. His white, even teeth positively radiate through the neatly trimmed, jet-black beard. He's slimmer than I ever remember him in real life, although his nose is still very impressive. The wedding haircut, new suit and inexpertly trimmed

21 Baron-Cohen, *The Essential Difference*, 137.

monobrow create an impression of reluctant smartification, and on closer examination, his face throws a shadow of doubt. It would have fooled the casual observer, but the longer one looks, the more one notices the black eyes set slightly too firm, the grin fixed for the camera, so unlike the soft eyes and authentic smile of the woman beside him, as radiant and happy as any young bride. I wouldn't go as far as to say his smile is fake, but I've seen him genuinely happy and it doesn't look like that.

Mum had £80 squirreled away over many years by her parents to one day pay for her wedding, but Dad had nothing to contribute. His mother had been saving loose change from the shop takings every day for years, keeping it in an old sock specifically to pay for his wedding reception, but she'd cashed it all in to lend to Mike when he started his business. After she died, Mike claimed the money had been a gift, but my parents knew well enough that it was supposed to be a loan. Again, Dad decided not to pursue it. "It's only money," he said. "Family is more important."

"Did you enjoy the wedding?" I ask, hopeful.

"I don't know whether I expressed any emotion either way," he says, not answering the question. "It wasn't a great romantic occasion, just a process one goes through." Mum is more forthcoming when I later ask her the same question: "I think he was alright. He didn't really seem happy, as such, but then I didn't know what a bridegroom was supposed to be like."

They spent a week in Mallorca for their honeymoon, but Dad didn't like being on holiday. He wasn't comfortable with the extreme changes to his environment it entailed.

"I don't like being amongst strangers," he says, "and on holiday, there's a whole load of strangers wanting to talk to you." He must have been a right barrel of laughs. Nevertheless, he perks up after a few moments' consideration, or maybe it's the effect of his second coffee. "Afterwards, I think I had a happy period. We were quite close sometimes."

Chapter 7

Myötähäpeä

Bocas is great fun, but we have a deadline looming: I've promised to be in Cartagena in eleven days to meet my mate Dave, with whom I've arranged to hike *La Ciudad Perdida*, The Lost City. Before then, we still have the remainder of Panama to traverse, and one thing on my list is the *Sendero de los Quetzales*. It's apparently possible to see the beautiful quetzal, a rare and colourful bird of the Central American highlands, on this day hike from the mountain town of Boquete. Despite his insistence ("I'll do what you do. You're the Captain."), I opt to leave Dad in the city of David and journey to Boquete on my own. He wouldn't manage the hike, so there's no need to subject him to two unnecessary bus journeys.

"Don't talk to any strange men!" I warn after depositing him in a decent hotel. I say the words in jest, but the concern behind them is real.

He waves me away. "I'm old enough to look after myself," he scoffs. True, but still . . .

On my return, two days later (having completely failed to find a quetzal), Dad is, of course, perfectly fine, if a bit bored and quite ready for the seven-hour journey to Panama City. The fine weather from Bocas continues as the bus drifts down the looping spine of the country, like a leaf washed along a winding mountain creek. The ridge of the central mountains looms large to our left, while the glittering Gulfs of Chiriqui and Panama tease us from below. It looks like we may finally have escaped the rain.

I never really considered my father to have a drinking problem, yet he's spilling water everywhere. Whenever he raises his bottle, the bus brakes or swerves, and liquid sloshes down the front of his t-shirt. The only way to quench his growing thirst is to wait until the driver pulls over to allow a passenger to disembark, then whisper, "Quick—drink!" At my urging, he jumps with realisation and struggles to unscrew the lid and gulp down some water before the jerk of the bus pulling away renders him damp once more.

"He's so cruel to me!" he complains to the lady beside him, and I cringe in embarrassment. His sense of humour has survived, at least.

Panama City is certainly the most exotic-sounding place we've visited thus far, although the tight business district of skyscrapers is far from how I imagined it. I've chosen a hostel in the old part of Panama City, *Casco Antiguo*. This network of narrow streets and plazas is the second location of the city, after the original settlement was looted in 1671 by British pirate Henry Morgan and subsequently abandoned. Surrounded on three sides by the sea, the small peninsula was easier to defend. Built in 1905, the huge, airy mansion that's to become our home for the next few nights incorporates a section of the original city wall. Luna's Castle has the decor and inhabitants of a classic backpacker hostel but with the enormous, high-ceilinged rooms and wide, wooden staircases of a colonial villa. It's the rank opposite of our cramped and maze-like accommodation in *Bocas del Toro*.

The reception opens out in a huge dining-cum-entertainment area with a vigorous game of table tennis in progress and a kitchen that looks like it could easily produce a meal for several hundred. The colourful rucksacks of departing guests are stacked against the wall beneath lurid posters advertising country-wide tours and city juice bars, items for sale, and companions wanted. This would be many folks' first stop in Central America, and for many others, their exit.

Our *Odd Couple* appearance occasions the usual double takes as we check in. We're given a map of the neighbourhood, complete with a Red Zone into which we're advised not to stray at any cost. It's three blocks away. A hollow bouncing noise announces the arrival of the table tennis ball, and the two players look expectantly in our direction. Dad, an old master of the game, bends forward to collect the ball but, over balanced by the weight of his pack, tips too far forward and falls onto his head.

I've never before been simultaneously subject to two so completely opposing emotions. The sharp flare of concern for his wellbeing is muffled by the wet blanket of embarrassment. Acutely aware of fifty pairs of eyes abruptly swivelled in our direction, I help him to his feet with the assistance of a couple of nearby youngsters. As I dust him off, I can hear the whole room thinking, *That old man just fell over. I wonder if he's okay.* He is, luckily, but if I'm uncomfortable with the attention, he is downright mortified, muttering apologies and keeping his eyes on the ground.

As soon as I know he's alright, my thoughts turn selfishly inward. How am I going to befriend any of these people now? I'll always be 'that guy whose dad fell over in reception.' I'm already well aware how little I have in common with other backpackers. I'm ten to twenty years older than most of them, I have grey in my beard, and I seem to be the only one without a cell phone. Never has it been so difficult to break into a group dynamic. Despite my efforts, I haven't so far 'clicked' with anyone on this trip as so often used to happen.

"This is a death trap!" proclaims Dad, two seconds after entering our room. "There's no way out in case of a fire," he explains to my look of puzzlement. "We'd be incinerated."

The location of fire exits in these backpacker warrens is not something I've ever taken much notice of, but it seems he's been looking out for our safety all along. This must be the first place we've slept that hasn't been up to scratch.

"One way I'm sure I don't wish to die is by fire," he urges, showing more passion than in all our discussions about love and marriage. "The prospect of having to choose between burning to death or leaping from the twelfth floor is one of my personal nightmares, and, of course, having you with me would be even worse." He pauses to shoot me a meaningful look. "Please, I want you to be more careful in future. Always express a preference for a low floor, and try to remember where the escape routes are."

It's tempting to label this Aspergian behaviour, similar to when Rain Man, having already declined to fly due to safety concerns, refuses to drive on the freeway after witnessing an accident. In Dad's case, he once read about a hostel fire in Queensland, Australia, in 2000, where fifteen backpackers burnt to death. There were no working fire alarms or smoke detectors in the old timber pub, plus the fire was started intentionally by a local man who'd expressed a hatred of seasonal fruit pickers and had actually threatened to burn down the hostel beforehand. Even so, basic fire safety is plain old common sense, AS or no. We move rooms.

"And how is Arsenal doing in the league now?" Dad asks.

Even if we both lived for a thousand years, I can't think of a sentence less likely to escape my father's lips, yet there it is. I'd have put more money on "The languid catamite spliced seventeen loquacious homunculi with eldritch velleity" than any sentence containing Arsenal. I think he's as shocked as I am, and I can feel the discomfort radiating from him and bouncing off the glass walls of the law office. Any minute now, he's going to slip and drown altogether in small talk, small bubbles of *nice* and *how* escaping from his nose as he goes down. It's as excruciating as it is hilarious.

When we embarked on a self-guided walking tour of *Casco Antiguo*, I couldn't have predicted the morning would turn out so comically. Currently uglified by copious restoration works, the peninsular suburb is a mélange of decaying colonial buildings sitting cheek-by-jowl with refurbished ones. The latter edifices house chic tourist cafés and boutiques selling Panama hats which, as everyone knows, originated in Ecuador.[22] It's the absolute model of a district in mid-gentrification. Apparently, there are still some unsightly residents inconveniently living here, but the plan is to move them into other, presumably poorer,

22 They were named Panama hats after the port from which they were shipped, having been transported overland from Ecuador

parts of the city where they'll be away from the eyes of tourists. I did spot a few loitering women dressed in colourful smocks and beaded greaves, their darker skin and slanted features characteristic of an indigenous tribe, possibly the Kuna. Far from being offended by their presence, I considered them the most genuine aspect of the place.

Our walking tour encompassed numerous plazas, churches, museums, markets, parks, and municipality buildings. The façades of once-grand colonial mansions stood peculiarly alone, held vertical by rusting steel trusses until new office blocks could be constructed behind them. The sense of history from these structures has been muted by the starkness of the restoration process, and I felt little as I explored the alleys and corners save a desire to finish the tour and move on. Dad bumbled along beside me, uncomplaining, although I felt the need to continually point out broken pavements, kerbs, and holes in the ground. He also had an eye on safety, expressing ongoing concern about accidentally wandering into the Red Zone, but was placated on discovering a wonderful cup of coffee right on its boundary.

From the corner of *Casco Antiguo,* we could see the Panama City business district, an impressive skyline of high-rise architecture reminiscent of Singapore or Doha. My eye was particularly drawn to a building of spiralling glass blocks called the F&F Tower. By happenstance, Dad actually retains a lawyer in Panama City to deal with one of his investments. It would've seemed impolite to pass through the country and not drop in to say hello, so we caught a bus around the bay, disembarking among the glittering towers. We had the address of the financial institution but no appointment, so when Dad walked into the twelfth-storey office and asked for his lawyer, the man was visibly taken aback. He'd probably never expected to meet this European client in his life, and it took him a few moments to regain his composure. With hindsight, Dad realised it was probably quite improper to show up unannounced to a business meeting dressed like a backpacker and that his associate was thinking us somewhat rude.

Now here, Dad is taking the opportunity to sign some papers in person rather than have them certified and mailed, but because of our surprise visit, it takes a good ten minutes for the paperwork to be prepared. During this time, he's forced to make unbearable small talk, his idea of hell. He and the lawyer talk about the weather, the financial climate, the new project to widen the canal, and yes, even football. My dad has never spoken about football in his entire life as far as I can tell, although, as usual, he's taught himself the right thing to say should such a situation ever occur, hence the sentence about Arsenal. Good prep, Dad!

I follow the exchange like a spectator at a tennis match, flicking my eyes back and forth between the combatants as the torture proceeds. Before each answer, his eyes momentarily cloud over and his mouth hovers open while he selects the response he thinks best. I keep a straight face, but inside, I'm howling with laughter at his increasingly nervous attempts to keep up the pretence. Thankfully, before he's forced to comment on his taste in women or beer, the papers are ready, he signs them, and we make our escape.

One of the wonders of the engineering world, the Panama Canal runs seventy-seven kilometres across the isthmus between the Atlantic and Pacific Oceans. A major waterway for international maritime trade, it removes the necessity for cargo ships to take the lengthy and dangerous route around Cape Horn at the bottom of South America. The first serious plan for a shortcut to the East Indies and China was not until 1843, when Barings of London entered into a contract, but the project never began. Despite construction of a trans-isthmus railway in the mid-19th century, a waterway was still deemed necessary, but it took until 1881 before construction began under Frenchman Ferdinand de Lesseps.

De Lesseps had recently enjoyed great success with the much longer Suez Canal, but the French were totally unprepared for the more severe tropical climate of Panama. Work quickly fell behind as floods, venomous animals, and diseases claimed many lives, but the project progressed for the best part of ten years before de Lesseps' company went bankrupt. The ensuing loss of investor money, never mind the twenty-two thousand dead workers, was a major scandal in France, and it wasn't until thirteen years later that the concession was purchased by an American company. At that time, Panama was still a province of Colombia, just about, and in a typical feat of bullying, the Americans negotiated a deal with Panama allowing them remarkable access to the canal zone in return for their support in the country's secession efforts. Panama became independent less than a year later, and the US held the rights to build and 'indefinitely administer' the canal and a strip of land five miles either side of it.

US construction followed a different plan from de Lesseps' sea-level design. Rather than dig a channel all the way from coast to coast, the new proposal saw most of the canal twenty-six metres above sea level, with ships raised and lowered by a series of massive locks. In between would be a man-made inland reservoir, the largest in the world, across which the ships would sail. The strategy worked, and after ten more years' work, the canal successfully opened in 1914. It wasn't until 1999 that ownership of the canal and all its associated land was transferred back to Panama, and only after twenty years of co-control with America.

The set of locks nearest to Panama City is called Miraflores, where that afternoon we watch the thirty-minute process of a ship's passage. I have to admit—it is pretty cool. The maximum passable width of a ship is thirty-three metres, and its height must be below sixty-one metres to fit beneath the Bridge of the Americas, a cantilever bridge across the mouth of the canal. We're talking here about vessels carrying fifty thousand tonnes of cargo and paying an average toll of fifty-four thousand dollars. There are two lanes so multiple ships can pass through the locks at once, and we can see them lined up into the distance waiting for their turn.

It's fascinating to watch the progress of the *Zim Barcelona* from the second storey of the visitor centre. As she passes through the system, the giant double-lock gates slowly open to allow water to leak through, lowering the vessel by 16.5 metres. When level with the Pacific Ocean she's pulled through by the *mules*, stout locomotives that run on tracks alongside the canal. With the drop in water level, the mule tracks dip steeply over a short distance and resemble the plunge of a rollercoaster.

To my amazement, and for the first time on this trip, Dad pulls out his phone to take a few photos of the operation. He must be really excited. As I watch him trying to figure out the complex capabilities of the device, squinting at the screen and accidentally taking videos instead of stills, I allow myself a small smile. Four weeks ago, I would have become impatient with his fiddling and stepped in, unasked, to do it for him. Now, I find it endearing.

With both business and pleasure concluded, Colombia beckons. The problem is it's currently impossible to cross from Panama to Colombia overland. Well, not impossible; more like suicidal. The only route lies through the Darién Gap, a morass of mountains and jungle deep within the green hell of the Darién Rainforest. With the remote border unguarded by government officials of either country, the route is used solely by drug and people smugglers. This length of about one hundred miles is the solitary break in the otherwise trans-continental Pan-American Highway joining North and South America. Even without dragging an elderly curmudgeon along, I would not attempt to traverse those badlands of trackless swamp, tropical disease, angry guerrillas, and doped-up desperados. Successful tourist crossings are few and far between, especially with the renewed presence in the area of the FARC (Revolutionary Armed Forces of Colombia). Occasionally, an intrepid traveller attempts it and is kidnapped or disappears.[23] I'm not taking my father there. FARC that!

Fortunately, there are a couple of overland workarounds for the Darién. The first is a lengthy and uncomfortable trek along the coast involving a combination of buses, hiking, and a motorboat across the Gulf of Urabá to Turbo in Colombia. This is undoubtedly the way I would've gone on my own, and I seriously consider attempting it with Dad, but I can't conscionably subject him to that discomfort just for my own selfish reasons. I flirt with the idea of sending him by aeroplane and making this crossing alone, until I hear about a third option—private yacht.

23 Around this time, a Swedish backpacker vanished in the area. His skeletal remains were discovered two years later with a bullet hole in the skull.

The Gulf of Darién offers a straightforward sea route from Colón in Panama to Cartagena in Colombia via the remote San Blas Islands. This has become something of a backpacker favourite, although at a cost of $550, 30 percent more expensive than the corresponding flight, it isn't what I'd consider backpacking. However, the cost is spread over five days and includes all food and accommodation, plus boasts the travel 'purity' of not leaving the face of the planet. There are cheaper operators, but when spending that long in close quarters with a bunch of strangers, crossing a large expanse of water, I decide it's worth paying more for a sturdier-looking craft.

Dad originally nixes the idea based on his lack of sea legs but offers to fly over should I wish to sail. Just as I'm making final arrangements for my passage, he suddenly decides he doesn't want to stay in Panama City on his own; he now wants to come.

"I thought you got seasick?" I ask, hand poised over the telephone in Luna's Castle. "I've heard tell that the Gulf of Darién contains some small amount of sea."

"Well, I expect I'll have to lie down for the crossing, but I hope it'll be okay," he says, faking confidence.

"Hmm, okay. You are going to be social, aren't you?" I ask, concerned I might be condemning the other passengers to five days of hell.

"I don't know," he replies, eyeing the room as if our shipmates were lined up before him. "You can dislike someone on sight, can't you?"

Of course, you can, yes, but that's unlikely to happen. It's just his way of considering every possibility to ensure he's not being dishonest. If Dad was a movie character, he'd respond to the line, "Promise you'll never leave me!" with something like, "Well, I'll try not to, but I don't have control over all the possible circumstances. I might get hit by a car or something, then I'd be breaking my promise."

I call the captain of the *Black Dragonfly* and secure the last two berths on his yacht. By this time, our margin for error has shrunk considerably—I'm due to meet Dave on the same evening we arrive in Colombia, but in Santa Marta, four hours from Cartagena. The very next morning we'll start our pre-booked, four-day hike. I disapprove of such a densely packed schedule, but this meeting was arranged many moons ago. My timing is now exceedingly tight (or impeccable, depending on how you look at it).

The good mood from Dad's viewing of the canal mechanics lasts well into the evening. If only there were ground-breaking civil engineering projects dotted all along our route, I might be able to keep him on a constant systemising high.

"I cannot allow you to not eat a proper meal," he insists, as I remove a couple of crusts of leftover pizza from the fridge. The travelling lifestyle shrinks my stomach, and I find I rarely need more than two decent meals per day. It's nice of him to be concerned, but it's my night to pay for dinner and there are no cheap options in *Casco Antiguo*. It's all candlelit restaurants for elderly tourist couples whose evening entertainment seems to consist solely of strolling around, looking at menus, and chatting about the food, both past and future. I'm sure he's not doing it on purpose, but this is amusingly reminiscent of when the family used to go out to dinner. He'd always offer to pay, but when the bill arrived, he'd discover he'd accidentally left his wallet at home. It happened so often it was a running joke, although Mum didn't seem to find it so funny.

The *Black Dragonfly* is a forty-seven-foot ketch-rigged sailing yacht hand built in Taiwan in 1981. Her previous owner fully refurbished her six years ago, refitting the interior in teak and installing modern plumbing, electrics, and toilets. She really is a beauty. Jan, her captain, is a young, blond Norwegian fellow, jovial but serious about his responsibilities. He owned his first craft at six years old, took his boating licence at sixteen, and next year will attain his International Yachtmaster qualification. He sold everything he had to buy this business and has made the crossing seventeen times in the last year. We seem to be in safe hands.

Colón is Panama's second city, situated at the north end of the canal. It has a yacht club with a convenient mooring for the *Black*

Dragonfly in between crossings, and waiting there for Jan, we meet our fellow passengers: two German girls, a Chilean/Peruvian couple, an Australian girl, and a Norwegian girl. The two of us makes eight. Most boats hole up for the windy season, but the stoutness of Jan's vessel allows him to continue running the 250-nautical-mile crossing. In fact, higher winds are better for the *Black Dragonfly* because of her weight (twenty-eight tonnes loaded). In addition to the blustery weather, Jan reckons Panama to Columbia is the rougher direction. Hang on to that stomach, Dad!

The first leg of the crossing is to the San Blas Islands, an archipelago off the cost of Kuna Yala province and, by all accounts, a paradise of classic desert islands. Of the 378 sandy humps carelessly scattered away from the mainland like thrown pebbles, just over fifty are inhabited by the Kuna. We'll spend a couple of days touring the islands before the main push to Cartagena, some forty hours further away.

Dad and I are shown to the forward cabin, a tiny, wedge-shaped room squashing together a bunk bed and small toilet. The front of the yacht isn't the best place for a seasick-prone passenger, but he doesn't want to make a fuss, so we settle in for the overnight sailing. According to Jan, the sea is mild, but from the top bunk it feels more like a herd of unbroken horses rearing and snorting beneath the hull. I find it quite relaxing actually, like being rocked to sleep, and Dad seems to be okay as long as he stays lying down. It's warm, though; my berth is like the top tray of an oven, but we aren't allowed the fore hatch open during the crossing, so I have to suffer. He takes a seasickness tablet he bought in Panama City, but he doesn't like it. "It is disagreeing with my toilet," he claims, using a phrase that hasn't been heard since Queen Victoria died.

I emerge yawning into the cockpit the next morning, the clean, salty air sharp in my sinuses. I turn slowly through 360 degrees; we're surrounded by the beautiful turquoise Caribbean Sea reflected in a pristine, cloudless sky. Not far away is a small island, *El Porvenir*, the capital of Kuna Yala province. Jan takes our passports for immigration formalities while we breakfast on fruit salad and contemplate our surroundings. The gang all seem fine, which is more than can be said for one sad-looking excuse for a yacht that limps into the harbour.

Puny next to the majestic *Black Dragonfly*, it looks battered and sore like it's just gone ten rounds with Neptune himself. The passengers stare out from the hatches like prisoners-of-war. After a brief chat with the captain, Jan dismisses him as a cowboy, an inexperienced sailor with a craft unfit for the job. They've just survived a particularly rough crossing from Cartagena during which they ran out of fuel and were forced to use their sails, being tossed about on the waves like a discarded beer can.

"These young guys just buy any old boat and think they can make a few bucks ferrying backpackers to and fro." He sighs, taking his position behind the wheel. "It's not that easy."

I don't know about the others, but I'm immediately glad I coughed up for a more expensive trip, especially when Jan describes the interior as "awash with vomit." Their desperate captain is trying to buy enough diesel to see them back to the mainland, and Jan quotes him a ridiculous price for some of our abundant spare fuel, happily gouging his business rival like a frisky bullock tossing an untried matador in the ring.

Most of the fifty thousand Kuna live on the San Blas archipelago, but rather than spread themselves out, they congregate on a few urbanised islands that end up as crowded as inner-city slums. This fact is often relayed in tourist literature with wonder, but to me, it seems no different to the rest of the world, huddling in big cities while the most beautiful countryside lies uninhabited. The group of islands nearest to *El Porvenir* has one such city-isle named Wichub Wala, and we dinghy on over for a look while we await our exit stamps.

Like any undeveloped city, Wichub Wala is crowded and dirty. Rubbish is strewn about the landing pontoon, and the island's only toilets are built on stilts out over the shallows, not nearly far enough from the shore. The sand streets that crisscross the interior are swept clean, though, and run between rows of bamboo-walled huts with tin or thatched roofs, the crowns of only about three trees left on the entire island poking out above them. Among the huts are a few concrete buildings, including a school and a single shop selling such classic township fayre as Coca-Cola, corned beef, tinned tuna, Balboa beer, Lay's chips, and bizarrely, a large baseball trophy.

A few of the huts are dedicated to the sale of textiles woven by bent old Kuna women in traditional dress—wrapped skirts with intricately embroidered blouses called *mola*, headscarves, and arm and leg beads. The skilfully patterned *mola* are the main souvenir draw, and dozens of designs hang on the walls of each store. Weatherworn old folk sit around on corners chewing the cud like they've been doing it their entire lives, which they may well have, while a bunch of schoolchildren run around, smartly dressed in spotless white shirts and navy trousers or skirts, carrying plastic rulers. I initiate a game of chase with three boys and quickly gather a good-sized crowd of curious kids who I entertain with my tongue piercing. When I produce my camera though, they scatter like a handful of dropped ball bearings. Wichub Wala is an interesting diversion, but we're all pleased when Jan returns with our passports.

Chugging between the other links in the chain, we pass numerous fantastically beautiful, postcard-worthy islands as blinding golden bumps thickly crowned with tall, waving palm trees. Some have a house or two or three; some are completely wild. Rising sea levels will almost certainly obliterate most of these atolls by the end of the century. A few other yachts rest at anchor here and there, their owners demonstrating exactly what we should be doing—kicking back on the deck with cocktails. This truly is a slice of the good life.

The next couple of days follow a pattern: I wake early, drag myself up on deck, and fall off the side of the boat. I drip dry over a healthy breakfast of fruit and yoghurt before tackling the main business of the day. It might be paddling the kayak to a deserted island, going snorkelling with Jan, or just chatting and reading in the hammock. We might visit one of the tourist islands—*Isla Perro* or *Isla Tortuga*—just a couple of thatched huts, a toilet, and a 360-degree beach. Each has a shallow saltwater well made drinkable via the filtering action of sand and palm tree roots. Sundowners are generally taken in the cockpit, followed by dinner, which is tasty but usually quite basic unless we've encountered some locals selling seafood from their canoe. I was worried about how much alcohol to bring, thinking one bottle of *Flor de Caña* (my favourite Nicaraguan rum) might not be enough, but the youngsters are all in bed by 9:00 p.m. "This is not a party boat," said Jan early on, establishing a self-fulfilling prophecy.

We snorkel around a hundred-year-old wreck festooned with coral and vividly-mottled sea life, followed by its modern counterpart—a catamaran driven onto the reef by its drunken captain three weeks ago. We take the dinghy out to One Palm Island, the archetypal desert island of single-panel comic book jokes worldwide. Just seven metres in diameter, with its lonely yet resilient palm tree dead centre, this desolate circle of sand epitomises our San Blas experience; we frolic around like loons, splashing in the shallows of the infinite beach. I'm continually amazed by the amount of time some of these girls can lie motionless in the sun, especially the Norwegian, who seems content to remain prostrate for twelve hours at a time. My mind couldn't possibly cope with the inactivity, although, who knows, maybe she's solving complex mathematical problems in her head.

The days are perfect—sunny with scattered clouds—but the nights are sweltering in our bijou quarters. Dad seems . . . content. I won't go as far as happy, but he isn't unhappy either, which is a win as far as I'm concerned. He even has the occasional dip, just a climb down the ladder and a few minutes treading water before returning, but given his tirade against beaches in the opening days of the trip, I'd say that's a remarkable improvement. He stays out of the sun altogether.

"I hate the feeling of sunscreen on my skin," he claims from the shade of the cockpit canopy. "In fact, I try to avoid creams on my skin at all costs." Many people on the autism spectrum suffer from such negative sensory experiences. The more extreme cases feel actual physical pain when, for instance, they are forced to wear rough fabric against their skin. This explains why some autistic children tear off their clothing in distress. Overly bright lights and jarring noises can cause similar anguish. Like nails down a blackboard, they're an unpleasant sensory overload. I hand him the bottle anyway and proffer my back for slathering.

He grimaces. "I'm not a touchy person, you know," he says, overcoming his loathing to slap some cream roughly over my torso. "Although I have taught myself to tolerate contact enough that I can put my arms around someone and hug them." Gratitude wells up from the pit of my stomach. "I found it was very encouraging for other people to have a contact relationship with me," he continues, "but I had to learn that." At this, my heart goes out to my mother. How hard must it be to love a person who resists affectionate contact?

Dad doesn't involve himself much in group conversation, but I can see he's trying now and again to be sociable. His improvement has been a very gradual process, from deepest black in Mexico through incremental relaxation in Belize and the inklings of pleasure in Costa Rica, culminating in actual enjoyment of the workings of the Panama Canal. I'm sure the sertraline is mostly responsible for this regeneration, but I'd like to think my company and our shared journey have also helped exorcise the black dog.

When the yacht's Italian cook, Martina, asks if he's ever been to her home country, I sense a halo of warmth appear around his head and spread down his body. "Oh, yes," he replies, his eyes lighting up like dawn breaking over Venice. "In 1973, I applied for a job as an electrician at a company which dealt with production line machinery in automobile factories. They didn't ask for my qualifications but just assumed I had some." He adds with a cheeky smile, "Which I didn't." The mere mention of Europe is bringing back memories of better times, although, to reach them, he had to go through hell.

With his mother's shop finally out of business thanks to both supermarket and thieving kids, Dad started working full time in Mike's injection moulding business. He'd work very long hours, rising at 6:00 a.m. to get the machines running before the other employee arrived at 8:00 a.m. In winter, this meant boiling a kettle, climbing a scaffold tower, and thawing out the coolant pipes so the cooling system would run. If the machine operator didn't have to waste time prepping the machines, he could concentrate on running them, thus saving Mike money. Then one week he returned from a short holiday to discover that Mike hadn't attempted to maintain his morning preparations for the other operator. Obviously, that meant they weren't that important, so he stopped doing them.

Later on, when there was a nightshift, he'd be on call in case a machine broke down, which they frequently did. He'd mend it by telephone if possible, but if not, he'd get up, get in the car, drive half an hour, mend the machine, and come home again, then get up the next morning and go to work as usual. In other words, he ran the whole factory 24/7 while Mike and his business partner Norman worked nine to five in their office across town.

He did all this out of a sense of duty to his brother, but he was also aware it was important for him as an employee that the business was successful. The truth is that long hours at work are part and parcel of being a productive Aspergian. Tasks that entail good systemising can be complex and require intense concentration to complete, often over a long period of time with no distractions. Low empathising is an aid in this regard. Having little interest in how others are feeling—e.g. a wife trapped at home coping with young children—makes it easier to focus.[24]

Linked to this is a deeper truth: instead of emotional attachment, Aspergians find more fulfilment in overcoming intellectual challenges.[25] They immerse themselves in their work to the exclusion of other humans, and for many, it doubles as a hiding place from real life. It certainly was for Dad: "When I worked for my brother, I used to work seven days a week. On reflection, I find it was really a way of avoiding interaction with other people. It's an excuse you can use to avoid society. 'I'm sorry, I have to go to work.' "

Another reason Dad continued working all hours was because Mike and Norman had been promising to make him a partner. "Don't worry, Peter," they'd say. "Soon we're going to give you a piece of the business." This mollified him enough to keep on running the factory, but every so often he'd ask them, "Have you sorted this piece out yet? How much are you going to give me?" and they'd um and ah and procrastinate. This went on for a couple of years until, finally, just

24 Baron-Cohen, *The Essential Difference*, 123.
25 See Appendix III

after I was born, they called him into a meeting and made him an offer: for every year he worked from then on, he'd receive a two percent stake, up to a maximum of ten.

"That was a great shock and a disappointment," he'd explained to me. "It was nothing like what I'd been anticipating. Ten percent on the spot might have been a minimum for the sort of work I'd been doing."

Mum was less reticent: "If they'd slapped him in the face with a wet fish and stabbed him in the back and cut his balls off, they couldn't have upset him more. Having started with zero experience, he'd taught himself to programme those machines until he was better at it than anyone else. He'd worked so hard, tackling all the problems, and doing an amazing job. That really knocked him off course."

Even that was an understatement. He had a nervous breakdown. He stopped working. He stopped doing anything. He sat at home and stared at the walls. Mike paid him six months' sick leave before cutting him off. Diagnosed with clinical depression, he was prescribed an antidepressant. It's unlikely his cracking up was in response to that single stimulus, however it was more like a culmination of stress factors, the ludicrous partnership offer being the final straw. There was the pressure of working for and with other people, never easy for an Aspergian, plus thirty years of pretending to be a person he wasn't, forcing himself to fit into a critical society in which he knew he didn't belong. He felt alone, isolated, excluded. Asperger's Syndrome in adults is often linked to depression for that very reason. According to Professor Baron-Cohen: "In most cases, these patients also suffer from clinical depression, as they have not found an environment, in terms of a job or a partner, that accepts them as different. They long to be themselves but instead feel forced to act a role, desperately trying not to cause offence by saying or doing the wrong thing, and yet never knowing when someone is going to react negatively or judge them as odd."[26]

My parents were also dealing with money problems at the time. With my brother a toddling one-year-old and me growing ever

26 Baron-Cohen, *The Essential Difference*, 141.

larger in my mother's womb, they'd sold my Mum's house in Bartley Green and bought a new four-bedroom detached house in Streetly for £17,000. They'd taken out a large mortgage and the balance of the money was to come from the sale of the Cottage Stores land. After the closure of his mother's shop, the building had been declared unfit for human habitation and placed under a demolition order. Dad did the job himself with a sledgehammer. In any case, that sale had fallen through due to a slowdown in property prices, and they'd needed to take out a bridging loan to complete the purchase of the house. Thus, they moved in with very little money and couldn't afford much decoration or furnishing. The house was a bare shell until Mum got a loan on her private account to carpet the bedroom and living room.

They were managing to keep up with repayments, but property prices stopped growing altogether then began to fall, prompting the bank to threaten foreclosure on the bridging loan. This may have been another significant factor in the breakdown and is certainly what Mike would attribute it to. "I don't know if Mike ever knew what he'd done or thought it a tiny bit unreasonable," Mum says. "But then Mike never does think that Mike has been unreasonable."

It's hard for me to reconcile these negative examples of my uncle's behaviour with my memories of him. He was a jolly figure, always joking with us children, and we loved to visit that half of the family. The adults all seemed very friendly in those days, and I'd like to believe Mum was a forgiving soul and only became indignant when I dragged the subject up from the depths much later, after her life had fallen apart.

That period remains the worst trough Dad has ever experienced, but he never contemplated suicide: "The brain shuts down, protects itself. I can't remember thinking about anything. Suicide has never been an option." This perspective contrasts starkly with recorded figures for suicidal thoughts among Aspergians, according to the Autism Research Centre at Cambridge University. They report late-diagnosed AS adults are ten times more likely to have suicidal thoughts than the general population, and AS adults with depression are four times more likely again.[27] It has been postulated that Aspergians' rigid thinking style makes it harder for depressed adults to see any other way out.

Eventually, the bank did foreclose, and my parents' only option was to put their new house up for sale. They got a few hundred pounds less than they paid for it and moved into a rented home. Thankfully, Dad was recovering by then and took himself off the anti-depressants, but he couldn't have gone back to work for Mike. It was too painful.

This is when he got the job as an electrician. He worked initially at the British Leyland factory in Birmingham before being sent to an assembly line near Valencia in Spain, wiring up machinery, debugging it, and modifying it as necessary. "I was responsible for the interlocking wiring between machines for the whole assembly line," he tells Martina, the sea breeze blowing his white ponytail softly about his head. "I loved that job. I was good at it." He gestured to me. "You all came out to live in Spain. It was great."

It's not often I hear him express such enthusiasm. Undoubtedly the reason he chose Spain for retirement was his memories of this period, some of the happiest of his life. For the systemising brain, the predictability of working with machines is comforting. They do as they're told, and they don't talk back or sulk or have mood swings. It's much easier for an Aspergian to have a good relationship with a mechanical appliance than with a human. As long as one understands the machine, one is in control.

"I understood electricity very well when I was studying it, but I found a lot of other electricians didn't. They did all the courses and passed the exams, but they didn't really understand what was going on in detail. Much like now, people who repair computers probably don't know how a diode or a semi-conductor actually works, whereas I did." He could look at a wiring diagram and see instantly what was wrong and how to improve it. He used to modify machines while they were running. "I could see that a particular bit of wire wasn't going to be in

27 Sarah Cassidy, "Suicidal Ideation," 142–147.

use for another twenty-seven seconds, and I would rewire it in that time without interrupting production. I don't think many other people have that same ability."

Indeed, it sounds like he had an almost savant-like aptitude with wiring systems. Unfortunately, his employer went bust less than a year later, but because he'd made some friends from that job, he decided to follow them to another company. He was sent to Bolzano in Northern Italy, where the family joined him again. I have vague memories of the farm where we stayed, the Röllhof. This was in South Tyrol, a part of Italy that identifies as German and uses that language. Most particularly, I remember Herr Röll pinching my cheeks good-naturedly with his strong farmer hands and making me cry.

Apart from over-enthusiastic Germans with cruel fingers, it sounded like we were having the time of our lives. I'm loving reliving my childhood through my father's eyes, being reminded of long-forgotten details, and learning new ones. Unfortunately, things were about to take a turn for the worse. We were stationed in Foggia in Southern Italy when Mum became pregnant with my sister, Vicky. She took the family to stay with her sister, Jean, in Birmingham, but it was a difficult pregnancy, and she was very sick. Dad frequently had Jean on the phone, telling him he should be there, and in the end, he felt pressured to quit his dream job and come home.

Needing employment at short notice, his only option was to return to his brother's factory, the source of his greatest distress. On the day he was to leave Italy, his manager belatedly offered him a temporary exchange with a UK electrician. He'd be able to stay with us during the pregnancy and birth and return to Italy afterwards. The man even had a stack of business cards freshly printed and ready to hand over, 'Peter Slater' bold against the cream background. Regrettably, having already agreed to work for Mike, and being a man of his word, Dad had to refuse.

"It was the biggest mistake of my life," he says, turning his eyes heavenwards. "I was back into plastic moulding."

Everyone is visibly downhearted when, at 5:00 p.m. on the third day, we batten down the hatches and haul up the anchor for the last time, ready to set sail for Cartagena. We lounge around the cockpit in the late afternoon sun, enjoying the breeze of motion and discussing the dreaded crossing. According to the clever-clogs computer, which takes into account prevailing currents and wind speed and direction, if we average a speed of six knots, we'll arrive in thirty-four hours. Unlike the dismal yacht from day one, we have GPS, radar, satellite phone, VHF radio, and a life raft—pretty much every conceivable safety precaution. Jan will stay at the wheel the entire way, but for now, he sets a line behind the boat and soon catches a sizeable barracuda. I sit on the bowsprit and watch the sky go dark. Dad is already horizontal in his bunk. He tries to read but feels immediately nauseous.

I spend half the night dozing in the cockpit, subliminally enjoying the cleanest air of my life. I take watch for an hour while Jan gets his head down, then retreat to my bunk. The cabin is sweltering with the hatches closed, but I manage to sleep, often waking in mid-air when we crest a particularly large wave, before crashing down onto my mattress and back into slumber land. When Jan unfurls some sail to stabilise the yacht, we tilt about thirty degrees, making it much more difficult to use the toilet, or even walk to it. My body is forced into the bulkhead, inches from the sea, which swirls on the other side of the porthole like a tiny washing machine on a violent spin cycle. That night, I dream I'm a homeless person bedded down for the night in a twenty-four-hour laundromat.

At breakfast, Dad stays in his berth, only able to manage a few slices of mango from his prone position. His bladder is full, but his prostate has swollen from the stress, and he can only squeeze out a couple of drops of urine at a time. He must be in pain, but only his furrowed brow indicates his discomfort. I fret uselessly, wishing I could open the hatch and relieve the temperature a little, but Jan won't allow it. When I check on him an hour later, he's bathed in sweat, naked, and trying to urinate into his water bottle while lying down. He can't even lift his head to drink without feeling his gorge rise. I fetch a straw for him to sip from a cup as I empty his pee bottle, but he starts retching behind me. I grab a carrier bag into which he vomits messily.

"I'm getting myself into a bit of a state here," he says, wiping his mouth. My heart breaks at this ridiculous understatement. "Please look in on me a bit more often." The words are forlorn but the tone even, the poor wretch. I sit beside him all afternoon, or nervously in the gangway outside, trying to read. I don't know what else to do. He knew he was a bad sailor, damn him! What was I supposed to do? Tell him he couldn't come? Reject his wishes like a child who isn't tall enough to ride the rollercoaster? He's old enough to make his own choices, and then some!

The next time I enter, the cabin stinks of sweat, old puke, and urine. I damn Jan and unfasten the for'ard hatch, tying it open with my elastic washing line. The claustrophobic atmosphere lessens somewhat, and he forces down a few potato wedges Martina has prepared, afterwards stabilising a little and dozing off, thank goodness.

Up in the cockpit, Jan is cheery as ever. "This is a very, very smooth ride," he smiles while the coats hang away from the kitchen wall at a sickening angle. As we settle down for another night, I can't think of anything but the pain of my own flesh and blood, and my inability to do anything to ease it.

We arrive in Cartagena at 4:00 a.m. after a thirty-five-hour crossing, dropping anchor quietly and lying still until 7:30 when we can disembark. I leave Dad to dress, frightened of how he'll look in daylight. The other passengers are aware he's had a rough crossing, but I haven't revealed the extent of it. I imagine them looking at him with pity or, worse, distaste, and feel morbidly embarrassed on his behalf. When he does shuffle out, he hides his distress well. He's a little more bowed than before, is certainly moving slower, and his face looks a couple of years older, but his walk is steady as he makes his way stoically down the gangplank and into Colombia. What have I done to him?

Part II

A Solitary Man

Chapter 8

Begrutten

"I need to get this man to a toilet!" is not something I ever imagined myself saying, but that's exactly what I'm thinking as I step off the gangplank. I draw C$300,000[28] from an ATM at the port, and we jump in a taxi to central Cartagena, only a short walk away. I check Dad into the first mid-range hotel we come across and order him to empty his bladder while I pay for the room.

I'm counting out ninety thousand Columbian pesos onto the reception desk—not cheap, but hopefully he'll be able to move hotels tomorrow—when I pause, mid-riffle. The financial cogs in my brain are squeaking into movement for the first time today, and I rewind thirty minutes. It takes a few seconds to remember, calculate, and check the facts before the pain hits, then I'm tempted to scream out loud, right here in the lobby. I gave the taxi driver sixty thousand pesos instead of six thousand! That's an extra twenty US dollars, and the dishonourable swine didn't say a thing! I clench my teeth, eyes, and fists in frustration. I can't blame him, though, only myself. What an idiot! I haven't made such a costly currency mistake since Italy, 1992. On that occasion, I tracked down the hapless bread-seller in Naples' *Piazza Garibaldi* and rescued 90 percent of my lire, but that's not going to happen here. The pesos are gone forever.

I feel awful when I tell Dad and insist on paying him the difference. "No, that's not necessary," he replies, waving his hand dismissively.

28 Colombian pesos

"You were acting on my behalf." He's probably got bigger things to worry about than twenty bucks, the same things that distracted me when I should have been getting to grips with the currency. Despite his stable new surroundings, he still can't coax his urethra into action, although he tries frequently. In the meantime, he sits in the hotel lobby, checking emails and updating me on the latest global financial crises and moves by governments to steal people's money. "Cyprus plans to introduce a tax on personal savings," he informs me, "and the US is making it illegal to unlock phones!"[29]

Alas, I cannot stay to nurse him—I must rush to Santa Marta to meet Dave, who has come all the way from the UK for our trek the following morning. I feel like a terrible son, but what could I do if I stayed, anyway? I'm not a doctor. The prostate will fix itself given a chance to relax, I rationalise. By the time I return in six days, he'll have fully recovered. He's not the sort of person who needs comforting, anyway; I suppose that's one benefit of the AS. On the contrary, he's urging me to go, so I do.

It's late afternoon by the time I reach the intercity bus station and transfer to the long-distance coach to Santa Marta. It's a protracted and cheerless journey, my mind turning over and over the abandonment, and it's almost midnight by the time I arrive. Reasoning that Dave's probably doing his nut by now, I catch another taxi to the Drop Bear hostel (managing not to overpay the driver by a factor of ten this time), rush to dump my things in the dormitory, and seek him out.

A couple of lifetimes ago, when I was a chemical engineering undergraduate, Dave was one of my fellow students and thus one of the first northerners I ever befriended. University was a time of discovery for everyone, brought up as we were in our own parts of the country and ignorant of "foreign" cultures save what we'd seen on television. Certainly, Cornwall was a far cry from the wilds of Guisborough, Dave's hometown in North Yorkshire. He may have spoken funny, but he liked the right sort of music and had a marvellous dry sarcasm

29 This law lasted just two years before being reversed.

which matched my own. He was also an enthusiastic user of the common room pool table, where we gradually bonded over green baize battles. Short of stature with shoulder-length hair and an impressively thick goatee beard, his was a face among many during my university years. Come graduation, we both stayed on in Birmingham, thus managing to keep in touch as other friends fell by the wayside. Now, twenty years later, we've reached the stage in our friendship where we're comfortable holidaying together in a formerly violent cauldron of super-rich cocaine barons, unhinged government forces, and paramilitary guerrillas.

Colombia has, to put it mildly, a troubled past. Last time I was in South America, the country was one huge no-go area. I managed to sneak into the extreme southeast corner, the tri-border with Peru and Brazil, to spend a few days exploring the tributaries of the mighty Amazon before continuing upriver to Iquitos, but that was the extent of my incursion. The *Sierra Nevada de Santa Marta,* where we're heading tomorrow, was completely out of bounds. Even this hostel building, a lovely 1970s private mansion, has a dark history. The Australian owner proudly explains it used to be the headquarters of a notorious drug cartel. It was designed with hiding places for the huge volumes of cash the drug trade generated, a satellite dish to communicate with associates in Jamaica and the US, and two escape tunnels. Deceased Colombian kingpin Pablo Escobar used its secret basement as one of his numerous safe houses when the government forces were closing in on him.

Founded in 1525, Santa Marta is one of the oldest New World settlements on the continent. Conquistadors forged inland from the Caribbean coast, claiming land for Spain, and killing the indigenous tribes. Their numbers decimated by murder and smallpox, the natives were deemed subjects of the Spanish crown and enslaved. New Grenada, as the region was christened, went through several incarnations before independence came in 1819, led by Venezuelan-born Simón Bolívar. The extensive new country, Gran Colombia, actually comprised present-day Colombia, Venezuela, Ecuador, Panama, and parts of Guyana and Brazil. This mega-state, with Bolivar as president, didn't last long, and after forty years, the present borders (including Panama until 1903) were established. Relative peace lasted all of about eighty years before the eruption of a new political conflict elegantly dubbed *La Violencia* (The Violence). Although the two main parties involved eventually formed a coalition to end the troubles, over 220,000 civilians are thought to have died.

"Apart from fever, vomiting, jaundice, kidney failure, and bleeding from every orifice," ponders Dave, the next morning, "what's the worst that can happen?" When I finally found him last night, he'd been resigned to the fact that I wasn't going to arrive in time and he'd have to holiday alone. Having recovered his composure, he's light-heartedly listing the symptoms of yellow fever, just one of the insect-borne diseases rampant in the jungles of the Sierra Nevada. These unpleasant bodily reactions are a point of particular interest to Dave, nowadays clean shaven and presentable for his career as a corporate IT consultant, because his body wouldn't accept the yellow fever vaccination due to a previous long-term medication. While it's good he's remaining philosophical, the answer to his question is long and frightening.

In September 2003, eight foreigners hiking in this area were kidnapped by guerrillas from the National Liberation Army (ELN). Ten years after Pablo Escobar's death, Colombia was just beginning to register on the radar of the most adventurous backpackers. However, the country was still riven by warring factions. Several left- and right-wing paramilitary groups were carrying out a punishing multi-front guerrilla conflict against government forces from makeshift bases deep within the mountains and jungles.

The hikers were woken in the night and told two tourists had been killed further along the track and that the army would be escorting them to safety. In fact, ELN guerrillas marched them hundreds of kilometres in the opposite direction, forcing them to walk for fifteen hours at a time on a diet of rice, yucca, and cane sugar—a somewhat more extreme trek than the one they'd signed up for. The abductees were taken further into the jungle and held at a base deep in the mountains while the guerrillas demanded an investigation into human rights abuses. Days grew into weeks and months as an international team investigated the reports, and it was only after 102 days that the ELN released the hikers unharmed.

This incident is far from the back of my mind as we're collected from our hostel after a few hours' sleep and taken to the offices of Expotur, one of only four companies registered to run tours into the mountains. Their most popular trip is the hike to *Ciudad Perdida*, The Lost City, with three options following the same 46.6-kilometre route and costing the same—about $250. Although unconstrained by time, Dave and I have chosen the four-day walk over the five- and six-day choices. We figure the longer options mean a slower pace with more breaks, and we like walking, not waiting.

Ciudad Perdida is known as the Machu Picchu of Colombia—a spectacular archaeological site, remnants of a lost civilisation, deep in a forbidding mountain range. The *Sierra Nevada de Santa Marta* is the highest coastal mountain range in the world, topping out at the summit of *Pico Simón Bolívar* (5775 metres). Established in 1964, the National Natural Park is a sanctuary for flora and fauna, as well as home to thirty thousand indigenous peoples of the Kogi, Arhuaco, Kankuamo, and Wiwa cultures.

From Expotur, we're loaded into Jeeps and driven a couple of hours to the small trailhead town of Machete, an eerie name for a remote, peaceful village. Eating a brief lunch while our guide organises the mules and muleteers to transport our food along the track, we observe with interest some groups just finishing their trek; do they look relieved, scared, or bored? On the contrary: loud, sweaty, and muddy, they down their cold *cervezas* in the sun, laughing and singing. It's a good sign.

For the first day, Dave and I are lumped in with a larger group doing the five-day tour, and we're soon tramping across a shallow river and out of town behind our guide, Miguel. The track is wide and thick in places with churned-up mud, testament to its use by livestock. Farmhouses nestle in the misty valleys, surrounded by cultivated land. At one point we actually have to step carefully over a couple of pigs wallowing in our path, but we progress steadily uphill and eventually enter the jungle proper.

We stop repeatedly for rest breaks; snacks of pineapple, passion fruit, or *lulo* (a kind of tree tomato); or to swim in cool river pools. Miguel gives us an idea of what birds and animals we might see if we keep our eyes open. Due to its isolation from the Andes, the Sierra Nevada has developed distinct flora and fauna: orchids carpet the forest floor; blue morpho and mariposa butterflies add colour to the air; there are jaguar, tapir, brocket deer, and red-tailed squirrels; and the trees are alive with toucan, hummingbirds, and parrots.

That night, lying in my hammock, I realise I'm actually missing my father. It's only been a couple of days and I'm loving being with Dave, but here and now it finally hits me: I've come to treasure every moment of Dad's company, from chatting over his morning coffee, strolling around town, deep and meaningful discussions over dinner, to the quietude of our bus and boat journeys. I love hearing his little nuggets of wisdom, even if they sometimes go against my natural instincts. I wish I could predict every question I will ever need an answer for, gather them all together, and grill him thoroughly while I still have the chance. He's my go-to, my fall-back, my oracle. I believe he can calculate the best way to do anything. Through the story of his life, unfolding piece by fascinating piece, I'm slowly discovering the individual components of his being, diodes and resistors on a vast and complex motherboard which controls his behaviour.

Surely, today, he'll have managed to empty his bladder. I try to imagine the discomfort, the feeling of an overfull water balloon and the pressure against his dysfunctional sphincter. After three days it would be agony. If I was religious, I'd be praying for him with all my might, but instead I cross my fingers and project a stream of hope up into the night sky, where it dissipates among the stars.

We're woken at 5:00 a.m. by a gangly youth named Jerry, a kitchen boy. "Why do we start so early?" I ask him, rubbing my eyes. I may love hiking, but that doesn't make me a morning person.

"*Es muy lejo*," he answers (It's very far). We're scheduled to walk sixteen kilometres to catch up with the group that left the day before us, a decent hike which we're delighted not to have to drag out over two days. After more steep and heavily used tracks, which must turn into mud chutes after a few minutes of rain, we're strolling through sun-dappled glades with mossy trees and chirping birdlife. "Is that a scarlet-fronted parakeet, or a crimson-backed tanager?" I ask Dave, pointing out one specimen.

"I dunno," he replies. "Which way is it facing?" We'd certainly have benefitted from Miguel's toucan-spotting abilities here. Jerry is good value ("I drink ten beers while wait in Machete," he boasts to us, "and now I sweating alcohol"), but most of the day, he rushes off ahead or lingers behind to chat to mates.

Our path passes a Kogi village of circular, stone huts inhabited by chickens, pigs, and ducks. A group of children, dressed in white cotton smocks, jet-black hair roughly trimmed, peer out at us. They stare silently, not shy but curious. The Kogi are direct descendants of the native Tairona people who originally inhabited *Ciudad Perdida*. When the conquistadors arrived in the early sixteenth century, they chased the Tairona from their coastal settlements, forcing them to take refuge high in the Sierra Nevada. This isolation protected them throughout the next century, but eventually Spanish settlers encroached further inland, and clashes were inevitable. The tale is a familiar one: eventually the Tairona chiefs were sentenced to death, their villages burned, and populations scattered. The Kogi now live in the same, simple way as they have for centuries, growing crops (cocoa beans, bananas, yucca) and raising cattle up in the clouds.

Our trek has coincided with *Semana Santa,* or Holy Week—the week before Easter and the largest holiday in Catholic Latin America. This is the park's busiest time of year and Camp 3, with an official capacity of about thirty, has to accommodate over a hundred hikers tonight from a fistful of countries. Hammocks swing bum-to-bum, and drying laundry fills every available line. Juan, our new guide, informs us the group we were supposed to join has already gone up to see the ruins, having (unsurprisingly) arrived with a whole afternoon to spare. All the better for us—it means we'll have him to ourselves tomorrow.

The kitchen seems to be dishing out chicken and mashed potato on a rotating basis and random bodies are sleeping, chatting, or bathing down in the Buritaca River. Kogi women and children hang around the camp waiting to consume any leftover food. I wish we could interact better with these people, but we share no common tongue, and even the international language of pulling faces at the babies evokes no reaction. All the guides are *mestizo*—of mixed blood descent—a completely different culture.

After an uncomfortable night of bumping hips with neighbouring swingers, and the loud *wheep-wheep* of tree frogs, we rise with the sun. Juan takes us the last kilometre along the river to the start of the steep ascent necessary to reach *Ciudad Perdida*, a punishing slog of something like fifteen thousand steps. The Lost City, actually called Teyuna, is believed to have been inhabited from about 800 CE until its abandonment nearly four hundred years ago. It remained overgrown and lost to all but the local indigenous population from the seventeenth century onwards, until discovered by looters in 1972. Archaeological interest was triggered when artefacts from the culture began appearing for sale in Santa Marta's markets, and the site was fully excavated and partially reconstructed by 1982.

The city is characterised by circular structures spread around the 80,000 m^2 site. These homes, plazas, storage areas, and ceremonial buildings, some which have been cleared and their retaining walls rebuilt, were situated on terraces and connected via a series of contour paths and steep stairways. With a population of approximately two thousand people, Teyuna was the main town of the Tairona, but numerous other small settlements still lie undisturbed in the surrounding jungle.

As we explore the various dwellings, Juan explains aspects of the Tairona culture, in Spanish. We had specified an English-speaking guide because my Spanish is still rudimentary at best, and Dave's even ruder, so we miss a lot of detail. Well, all the detail.

"I like a bit of mystery with my Lost Cities, generally," comments Dave, "but this is ridiculous."

While not quite matching the stature of the Incan city of Macchu Picchu, Teyuna culminates in a magnificent central terrace, a series of circular lawns that stand proudly clear of the surrounding jungle. The last section to be built features the most elaborate and complex stonework, certainly a place of ceremonial or religious significance.

I puff up the final slope. It's humid, and sweat is running off me like the early-morning dew dripping from the leaves of the rainforest giants. Reaching the top of the steps, I look out over the heart of Ciudad Perdida. The view of the ruins, guarded by soaring peaks and wreathed in swirling mist, is just magnificent. I turn to congratulate Dave, but he's been replaced by a stern-looking man in combat fatigues, holding an automatic rifle. He gestures toward me with the barrel, and smiles. Thoughts of ELN and FARC guerrillas flash through my brain. *This is supposed to be safe* is my first thought, closely followed by *Gerda is going to kill me*! I needn't have worried, though; the soldier's smile is genuine, and he just wants to shake my hand. The Colombian military now have a permanent settlement at the ruins to prevent a repeat of the kidnapping, and although I'd have loved to spend more time hiking here, fifteen hours a day for three months might be pushing it.

Five days have now passed since I left Dad and I'm desperate to discover how he's progressing. I call his hotel in Cartagena from Drop Bear reception, but they can't locate him at that moment. Instead I call Gerda over the hostel's Wi-Fi. The signal is better if I'm near the router, so I wedge myself into a bay window near the computer terminals where the noise from the bar isn't too loud. The connection is stable, but her voice has that faraway resonance that fails to convey any warmth; she sounds distant and sad. While the awkwardness of communicating by phone is mutual—she much prefers face-to-face contact—tonight her unease is amplified. I soon discover the reason; after a few stilted pleasantries, she reveals she's spoken to Dad.

"Oh, great," I say. "How is he doing?"

"You need to talk to him," she replies, with an air of something left unsaid.

Little do I suspect the web of communication that's been spun in my absence. Gerda, concerned after I told her about his prostate problem, sent Dad several emails but received no reply. I'd given her the hotel's name, so she called there but couldn't communicate with the Spanish speaker who answered. She then told my sister who, using Google Translate, wrote them an email, again with no reply. By this time, Gerda was very worried. Her second call was luckier and she managed to get through to him.

"I know. I've been trying." I assure her, the edge of the window frame digging into my spine. "We're going back to Cartagena tomorrow. I'll see him then."

"You need to talk to him now," she repeats. "He's not well."

Her words ignite a tiny spark of panic in my brain. It's so small at first as to be non-existent, so I ignore it. "What do you mean 'not well'? What did he tell you?"

"You need to talk to him yourself," she says a third time, reluctant to elaborate. She obviously thinks that whatever has happened is best heard directly from him, whereas I disagree. I think she should tell me immediately, and I make increasingly stern enquiries until she gives in. "He's going to have to go home," she admits.

"What? No!" I declare, my voice rising two octaves. "He was fine. He'll *be* fine." In my worst musings, I never considered that this silly incident would be so serious. I wouldn't allow the possibility space in my head. I still won't, but the faint spark has found a fuel source, and the resultant flame is growing quickly. Even now, I know its light will reveal the truth, but I try to block it out, to pile thoughts on top of it, to smother it with denial. "He just needs a few days' rest, that's all," I try to convince her, my fingers unconsciously tightening around the phone. "He doesn't need to go home!"

"I'm sorry," she replies, softly, "but he does."

"N-No, not yet!" I stammer, but even though my tongue is still in defiance, my brain has finally caught up with her words, and my stomach lurches. The blaze in my mind has eclipsed all, providing searing clarity. My vision blurs as tears spring to my eyes at the thought of losing him. The more I consider this disaster, the more of a mess I become. Snot bubbles out of my nose, and I cringe into the window, acutely aware of the hostel environment and occasional passing youth; although, at this moment, I don't much care what anyone thinks.

I can't remember the last time I cried; it must have been years. When Gerda and I first moved in together—a shared house in Shepherd's Bush, London—she'd asked me about my parents and why they got divorced. I avoided the question, brushed it off. I'd dealt with the situation badly when the end had finally been announced, retreated into the denial in which I'd sought comfort for years. I didn't know the actual reason for the break-up, and I didn't want to know because it would almost certainly reveal that at least one of them had done something bad. Whenever the question was asked, I'd clam up, or mumble some generalised offence, like 'they just didn't try hard enough to stay married.' Like a typical man, I was avoiding a conversation about my feelings. Gerda pushed me though, she kept prodding and poking until I cracked, a few drops of saltwater dripping through the fingers that covered my downcast face. Having proven my sensitivity to the topic, she backed off, changing the subject to crack a silly joke. It was the only time I'd come close to acknowledging the truth.

I remember how Dad used to comfort me when I hurt myself, reverting to humour to distract me from my weeping. "Naughty table," he'd scold, slapping at whatever offending furniture I'd fallen into. When I vaulted over the handlebars of my BMX bike, smashing up my elbow and face, he barely offered any sympathy before launching into a terrible Dad Joke routine. "Who 'nose' how you managed to do that." He chortled as, through my tears, I examined my damaged snout in the living room mirror. "There's 'nose' saying how bad the damage is!" Angry at his mocking, I refused to react, but the barrage of puns was relentless and eventually, despite my best efforts, I had to smile. He'd won; the pain was forgotten.

Nowadays, the only tears I shed are likely to be while watching a film, an embarrassment which happens more and more often as middle age encroaches. I'm beginning to see how Dad can be so affected by *Random Harvest* and yet so apparently emotionless towards real people. It's pure empathy, but empathy for fictional characters. How does one rationalise that?

"Strangely enough, it's at the happy parts I get upset," he'd explained. "Not the sad parts. Expressions of great love do it for me because I know the sadness in their future. They don't know what's going to happen to them, but I do, and that's what gets me."

My mind flicks back over the best memories from the past month—the boat ride to Tortuguero, the hot springs resort, even his conversation with the Australian backpacker in Bocas—and forward again to the present. The parallels to *Random Harvest*—the innocence of that happiness and our ignorance of this future sadness—hit me even harder. He can't go now! We're really connecting; we're having fun. But it's much more than that: every minute of every day I've felt a warmth being around him, a safety, a ghost of the protective aura I felt as a child, when I knew nothing could hurt me because he was around. It's absurd, of course. I'm the one protecting him, or I'm supposed to be. I've completely failed as a minder. What am I supposed to do now? The selfish bastard was supposed to spend three months with me—that was the plan!

Gerda is silent on the other end of the line. I can almost hear her thinking, *This is awkward. What do I say now*? I get a grip and wipe my eyes. Maybe she's misunderstood the situation. It was probably a bad line, and English is her second language, after all. I'll see him tomorrow afternoon; we'll soon sort this out.

I bid farewell and fire off a quick email: 'I just spoke to Gerda. She said something is wrong but won't tell me what. What is wrong? We're coming tomorrow.' I simultaneously receive one from Gerda: 'Thanks, my love, for ringing me. I don't want you to be sad. Good luck with your dad and be strong, okay? Things will work out for the best. He does not want you to worry. Miss you very, very much, and wish I could hold you in my arms and legs.' She has a way with words, so she does.

I find Dad at the computer in the hotel where I'd left him. He looks the same as ever—not dishevelled, not hunched under the weight of stress, not even particularly unhappy. You wouldn't know there was anything wrong.

"I have to go, Sunshine," he apologises lightly. "I am sorry. There was always one thing that could necessitate me having to cut short our trip, and it has happened."

I've left Dave at our hostel, and I'm glad I did. I foresaw a re-emergence of emotions and indeed struggle once more against the unlocking of my tear ducts. My eyes glaze over and I stare at the ground, just managing to keep them from brimming over. I am gutted. If only I'd been a bit more miserly and opted to fly, he'd still be okay, and our long-planned and semi-executed bonding session wouldn't be over.

"I don't think it was the sea-sickness that did it, but lying down for thirty-six hours," he explains, his crooked pelvic posture in the chair testament to his discomfort. "Anyway, my prostate finally closed up, and after you left on Sunday, I couldn't pass urine at all. By Monday morning, my bladder was overfull, and I was in pain. I was in and out of hospitals all day, and now I have a piece of pipe attaching me to a plastic bag which I have to carry around. I can't pretend to be a backpacker with that. I'm more like a *bag*packer. In any case, the doctor says I have to go home and have the operation." It's probably the only silver lining to this miserable raincloud.

Apart from the apology, Dad seems pretty upbeat considering the circumstances, even philosophical. "Maybe we can finish the trip later?" he suggests, but he knows as well as I do we'll never have another chance. Quite apart from the difficulty of finding time and money for such a jaunt, he's only getting older. Before we know it, he'll be pushing eighty and some other problem will have arisen. In my heart, I know this was our chance. I grasped it with both hands and juggled it like a tricky catch in the outfield, but ultimately, it popped out and fell away.

At least Dad is mobile now, so after collecting Dave, we head to his favourite coffee shop. They've met a couple of times before, most recently at my wedding, but I can't detect any trace of recognition in the old man's greeting. There's no lack of friendliness there, though. He seems to flick an internal switch the moment he's required to interact with my friends, as though erecting his façade of sociability. When, as teenagers, we'd bring mates home for dinner, he'd always make an effort to speak to them, but his attempts at affability would come out as a barrage of questions. 'Where do you live? What do you do? Why do you like this-or-that?' He'd take the same questions regular people would ask, the ones he'd learned from observing others' conversations, and make them sound like a job interview. It was part amusing and part cringeworthy.

It doesn't take long for Dad to elaborate on the details of his ordeal. "That day I stood over the lavatory and nothing happened. What to do? I went to a clinic early the next morning where I asked if they could fit me a catheter. The procedure is simply to grasp the penis in one hand and force a tube down its 'throat.'" If there is one thing I never want to experience in my life, it is catheterisation. The very thought of it makes me shiver so violently that I have to get up and walk around. "The nurse attempted to do this," he continues. "She failed. She called the lady doctor on duty. She also tried, with the same result. They commandeered a passing nurse and invited her to have a try. No success. Pretty soon there was a queue of enthusiastic ladies all wishing to be the one to succeed. I think I was handled by more girls that morning than in the whole of the rest of my life. But they all failed."

Throughout this description Dad is as animated as I've ever seen him. He's using his hands and his body to convey the operation and his reaction to it. His eyes are wide, his monobrow kinking and unkinking in the centre like a galloping centipede. Dave leans forward, his face a massive grin, as eager for details as a ghoulish medical student.

"They told me the problem was caused by a blood clot," Dad continues. "More likely they had caused the bleeding by repeatedly attacking my prostate with their tubes. They tried thinner ones and more rigid ones, still without success, so eventually they decided I should see a specialist.

"His waiting room was full. I drew their attention to a notice on the wall promising priority to the aged, but it made no difference. I waited and waited. The waiting room eventually emptied, except for me. Finally, a nurse arrived who spoke English, and I explained my problem. Of course, she and her companion felt obliged to try to fit the catheter themselves before consulting the specialist. They failed. I was left in a cubicle in a hospital gown. While I waited, I strolled around the cubicle only to discover I was leaving a trail of blood wherever I walked. Someone had to mop it up. By now it was late afternoon. I hadn't drunk anything or eaten the whole day. I asked permission to go out to a shop. It was refused. Eventually, the specialist arrived."

Dad is reaching a crescendo, but by this point, I'm crouched over with my legs crossed, my face scrunched up like a discarded newspaper.

"I didn't think you were squeamish, son," he interjects with a devilish grin. I'm only grateful our fellow coffee shop denizens don't speak English. Even had we been in the drawing room at Buckingham Palace, I'm sure it wouldn't have stopped him telling the story.

"He tried the usual method first to fit the catheter and failed, of course. He sent for his toolkit, which had the appearance of a set of spanners in a roll, or, more appropriately, a set of torture instruments for the inquisition. His hand went in and came out with what I can only describe as a hook of the type that dockworkers use to carry sacks. It had a T handle at one end and a large curve. He inserted it at one angle then rotated it to another. He fed it inside until he came to the obstruction and gave a sudden push. 'I think that's in,' he said. I decided that wasn't too bad a price to pay. He withdrew and turned to his assistant. 'That was number fourteen,' he said. 'Pass me number sixteen.' So, I had to accept sixteen, eighteen, and twenty, maybe even twenty-two, each with a bigger diameter. Finally, he selected a thinner one, onto which he threaded the catheter. Having finally successfully inserted it and withdrawn the metal, he put the end of the tube into a receptacle and drained off a litre and a half of fluid. What a relief! Then he fitted me with a bag and left."

At this denouement, I abruptly rise to leave, overwhelmingly desirous of the fresh air and traffic noise of the outside world. When I hear them burst into laughter at my retreating back, I'm grateful for the comic relief our situation so gravely required.

It takes a few days to organise Dad's flight home, time during which I'm by turns tortured and pathetically grateful. Dave is to leave the same day and I, too, to Venezuela, to continue the trip alone. The able-bodied pass the hours touring the main sights of the beautiful old city—the gold museum, the Palace of the Inquisition, the *Castillo de San Felipe de Barajas*—while Dad rests, and we all pretend what is about to happen isn't about to happen. The architecture is outstanding, many of the stone buildings dating from the middle of the sixteenth century, when a fire razed the original wooden settlement, but I can't seem to summon up much appreciation for them in my current mood. Cartagena isn't short of visitors, though, and seeing one of those ridiculous Segway tours rolling slowly through the UNESCO World Heritage Site almost cheers me up.

In the evenings, Dave and I go out drinking. This is a popular traveller's hub, so there are plenty of people about. I favour *Aguardiente*, a robust drop (literally translated as "fiery water") made from distilled sugar cane with anise. I probably drink too much of it, desperate to lighten the heaviness of my heart. When sufficiently lubricated, I ask Dave what he thinks of my father, trying to get a handle on how he might come across to a casual acquaintance. Sometimes I feel I'm too close to the subject to assess him accurately.

"He reminds me of you actually," says Dave. "He's got a wry sense of humour. He seems like a cool guy."

A 'cool guy' is not how I would've described him, but then Dave's unlikely to tell me to my face that my Dad is a pitiful killjoy.

"He hasn't been overly friendly, but then he is quite ill so I can't really blame him for that. He's taking it very well, I must say." I tell him about the Asperger's to see if he's observed any of the symptoms, but he shrugs. "No, I didn't notice anything untoward about him."

This doesn't really surprise me as Dad can be a superlative actor at times. The way he turned on the chattiness the moment Dave arrived was in marked contrast to that painful performance with his lawyer in Panama City. While I'm also hopeless at small talk, I'm worse at feigning interest in other people's stories when I couldn't give a flying toss about them.

Our last evening together is a melancholy one. Dave actually seems more affected by the unfortunate circumstances than I would have expected. "Well, this is all a bit shit, isn't it?" he announces morosely. He even emailed his boss to ask for a holiday extension but was denied. It would've been great to have him join me through Venezuela, even as a sort of substitute father, and I really appreciate the gesture. I don`t mind being alone *per se*—I travelled solo around much of the globe before I met my wife—but I'm not looking forward to it now.

"So, what's been the highlight of your trip?" I ask Dad while Dave is off packing his bags.

"Hmm, well . . . I don't really do favourite parts. You're asking me stuff I don't understand."

"Oh, come on!" I plead, raising my palms to the sky. "You must have some parts that you remember more fondly than other parts?"

"Overall impression—I enjoyed it," he admits. "I'm glad we did it. I was remembering the other day the locks in Panama." The contented faraway look in his eye is interrupted when he catches me scribbling in my notebook, tiny shorthand legible only to its author. "What are you writing about me in your little book?" he asks, pointing with his nose at the journal that is never far from my hands.

I've been taking notes the entire trip—it's what travel writers do—but I confess that most of them have been about him. I have an unformed notion that he might make a good subject for a future book. Being no fool, he must have suspected as much. In 1907, the *Times Literary Supplement*, reviewing Edmund Gosse's book, *Father and Son*, famously raised the question of "how far in the interests of popular edification or amusement it is legitimate to expose the weaknesses and inconsistencies of a good man who is also one's father."[30] Worth bearing in mind, to be sure, but my father is neither weak nor inconsistent, and though I might expose some facts he might rather keep hidden, such a project would surely reveal him to be a troubled, yet kind and peaceful man who deserves much respect.

30 Ann Thwaite, "Daddy Dearest."

Chapter 9

Sillage

Alone at last, but not in a good way. The night bus to Maracaibo in Venezuela is surprisingly comfortable, with plush, roomy seats and overly enthusiastic air conditioning. Dave left mid-morning for Bogota, and I put Dad into an airport taxi a few hours later without ceremony. He doesn't like goodbyes. He did donate his remaining pesos and US dollars to my travel fund, so his disappearance wasn't a total loss! Despite him downplaying his feelings, I'm convinced he had an enjoyable trip. I must believe this in order to feel I haven't failed him.

Unwilling to hang around in Cartagena, now a cache of unpleasant memories, I transferred to the bus station early and killed time among the trinket stalls and cafeterias, blasted on all sides by noisy Latino families yelling and laughing over their greasy, home-cooked meals. I had time to email Gerda a final Colombian dispatch: "I'll get on that bus tonight a sad person but get off in Venezuela completely clear and ready for a new and different trip. Bring on Part Two."

"Oh, my dear, you will be fine, and so will he," she replied. "It is sad, very sad. Even I am sad. I was glad you were together. I do not like it when you are on your own. It is not what I like."

Her unorthodox syntax cheered me up a little, and she also forwarded an email Dad had sent her while I was away hiking: "Dan has been brilliant on the trip. He has done all the organising, translating, worrying, leading, and even carried both backpacks on one occasion to save me a walk. He has managed to find a private room for us every night. I'm treated like backpacking royalty. I'm so sorry I have to let him down. I'm fine now, just disgusted and embarrassed at being an old guy with a bag and anxious to get the operation organised so I can be 'normal' again."

His words are like salt in my wounds. Him let me down? He's so wrong.

"You just get better," she'd ordered him. "Go get your operation. Dan is used to travelling on his own, and he will want you to do that as well. It was bound to happen sooner or later. I was very worried, but I'm glad you are okay now. You can tell Dan the news. I will not tell him yet."

I keep to myself, earphones a permanent fixture on the sides of my head. I stare out the window, reprogramming my in-brain trip computer to take account of the new circumstances, trying to stay positive. At least I won't have to fret about long bus journeys now, plus I'll be able to hike up Roraima in southeast Venezuela, a bucket-list fixture for the last ten years, without leaving Dad alone for another six days. On the other hand, accommodation is going to cost twice as much. The hotels around the Caribbean are going to bankrupt me!

During the night, the bus passes through Santa Marta and on towards the border, a zone infested by black-market fuel vendors. Venezuela's huge crude oil reserves, the largest in the world, have long meant the population benefitting from ridiculous subsidies on domestic fuel. For seventeen years the price of petrol has been fixed at the equivalent of 1 US cent per litre (compared to about $0.85 in the States and over $2.50 in Norway[31]), a luxury that is causing serious economic strife for the country. Naturally, entrepreneurial Colombians have devised devious methods of smuggling untold quantities of gasoline over the border to sell to their neighbours. Cheap, illegal gas is advertised on the roadside via a gangly youth waving a siphoning tube and funnel at passing cars.

At 5:00 a.m. we reach the border at Paraguachón, still three hours short of Maracaibo. Bleary-eyed passengers troop off the bus to obtain

31 Trade Economics, "Norway Gasoline Prices."

exit stamps for Colombia, before walking a short way to the booths on the Venezuelan side. A group of young Germans embarked at Santa Marta, artistic types with torn clothes and dreadlocks, and I eagerly earmark them as possible future companions if they continue on to Merida.

When I reach the Venezuelan immigration window, the unshaven official takes one look at my passport and shouts at me in rough, heavily accented Spanish. I look at him blankly. Frowning, he shouts the same thing a couple more times before getting bored of my increasingly desperate shrugs and waving me away without issuing my *tarjeta de ingreso* (tourist card), without which I can't enter the country. Now what? I can't do anything other than re-join the back of the queue.

Now the last bus passenger requiring a stamp, my nerves are taut as I reach the window a second time. What could be the problem? With my UK passport, I don't require a visa, and I don't have an onward ticket as I'll be leaving by land again. The immigration officer rolls his eyes when he sees me gracing his presence once more. Maybe he's unhappy at having to work the night shift. The air is sticky with humidity, and his uniform stained with sweat patches. This time he shouts louder, presumably prefacing his rant with, "You again? I already told you . . .," but I still can't understand his words. My Spanish just isn't good enough under duress.

With the bus driver no doubt tapping his watch, a couple of the Germans come back to see what's taking me so long. With their superior language skills, they translate the grumpy man's demands—I must show him a booking for my first night's accommodation in the country. My brow furrows; this shouldn't be necessary. They asked the Germans for no such proof. My new friends, though I'd have preferred to meet them under better circumstances, argue robustly in my favour, but to no avail. I'm not to be admitted without this irrelevant paperwork.

I watch haplessly as my backpack is unloaded and the coach accelerates away into the night, dust thrown up by its wheels obscuring the faces of the Germans sadly waving goodbye. They look worried, and no wonder–while my guide book has no entry for Paraguachón, it describes Maicao, ten kilometres back in Colombia, thus: "Widely and justifiably known as a lawless town and far from safe—stay there as briefly as possible." Alone in the darkness of no-man's-land, my first feeling is relief that Dad isn't here with me, my second, a strong sensation that I should hide. Miraculously, one of the shacks in this short strip of wooden buildings houses an internet café, outside which I camp until dawn.

The connection is painfully slow, but I eventually secure a booking at a hostel in Merida, print out the confirmation, and make my way back to Venezuelan immigration. Instead of promptly processing my tourist card with a gay smile as he welcomes me to his country, my nemesis, now at the wrong end of a very long shift, directs me inside the building.

I groan. What *now*?

I'm led into a bright, bare office where I'm joined by a well-dressed female customs agent who proceeds to conduct a lengthy interview. Thankfully she speaks softly, using vocabulary I can understand, and for the next hour she interrogates me about my recent history, future plans, and life motivation. While my luggage is thoroughly searched in another room, she goes through my wallet and money belt, unhurriedly counting all my cash, maybe judging how much she can squeeze me for. She asks if I'm travelling alone, where I'm going, and my business there. She takes my camera and scrolls through the photos of the last five weeks. I watch them as she clicks, her gaze stopping to linger on the frames showing my father. I catch the one of him snoozing gently in a deckchair under the palm tree on Caye Caulker, resplendent in his many-pocketed vest. There he is gazing out the window on one of our many bus journeys, water bottle held tight in his veined fist, and next, he's posing in front of an ancient fire truck down one of the side streets of *Bocas del Toro*.

"Who is this man?" she asks, pointing at him. He's swimming in the pristine ocean off the *Black Dragonfly*, white hair floating around his head like a ruff, his alabaster shoulders receiving a rare glimpse of sun as he aims a discomforted glance at the lens. His omnipresence has aroused her suspicion. Maybe she's also jumped to the Toy Boy conclusion? Under the circumstances, the idea is no longer as amusing as it was.

"He's my father." My voice trails off into a whisper.

"Where is he?" she presses, her crisp delivery slicing through my feeble one, and I'm forced to relive my loss, explaining in broken Spanish the barest details of his sickness and subsequent evacuation. She glares at me suspiciously while I speak but evidently decides to trust my word. She photocopies my passport and hostel booking, explaining that she's charging me twenty dollars for the use of the copy machine. She emphatically staples the greenback to the rest of the paperwork, both of us knowing it'll be in her purse as soon as I'm out of the door. I'm not in the mood to argue, though, not today. I just want out, a wish soon granted. Passport stamped and only six hours behind schedule, I shuffle into Venezuela and thumb a lift the rest of the way to Maracaibo.

The city of Maracaibo dominates the west of the country and the Gulf of Venezuela. Below it, Lake Maracaibo, the site of the country's crude oil reserves, bulges out below Tablazo Strait like a water balloon. My corrugated seat in the back of a pickup truck gives me a great view of the ever-thickening traffic converging on the city centre. The roads are dominated by old US sedan cars, classic 1970s models like the Plymouth Valiant and Chevy Nova. Due in part to President Hugo Chavez's dubious economic policies, these old monsters hold their value better than new models and are cheaper to maintain. The road behind me resembles a grey canal crowded with metal barges. They're so big I could probably leap from bonnet to bonnet all the way to Caracas.

I only stay in Maracaibo long enough to eat and change buses, the prospect of the twelve-hour leg south to Mérida making me wish I was still in detention at the border. Dad will finish his journey to Spain before I finish mine, and probably be in considerably better shape at the end of it. Mind you, it can't be fun flying with a colostomy bag.

The passenger in the seat beside me attempts to start a conversation, just being friendly, I suppose, but my grunted replies soon put him off. I can put up with a little idle chitchat in order to get to the true purpose of a conversation, but I can't see any benefit in discussing the weather with a person I'm never going to see again. I guess that makes me unfriendly. Come to think of it, I'm much like my father in that respect. I plead guilty of sometimes using conversation only as a means to transfer information. When I write business emails, I address the issues at hand then force myself to return to the beginning and preface them with futile questions like "How are things with you?" so I don't come across as rude.

The more I think about it, this last month together has served to highlight similarities between us I'd never previously noticed. Research suggests that although its causes remain mostly unknown, it's widely accepted that genetics play a key part in the development of AS. Kenneth Roberson, an Asperger's psychologist from San Francisco, states, "It is likely that a complex combination of factors unfold gradually to cause Asperger's . . . [but that] people with Asperger's tend to have parents and/or relatives who have similar behavioural symptoms." He goes on to say, "This does not mean that Asperger's is caused by one gene passed down from parents to children. It's more likely that a common group of genes combine to render an individual vulnerable to developing Asperger's, and it is the combination of genes that determines the severity and symptoms for each individual."[32] In other words, Dad was destined to be this way, condemned by his DNA to a life adrift.

This leads me to question who in his family displayed similar behavioural symptoms. From everything Dad told me about my paternal grandfather, Walter, he showed little emotion. Also, he was a successful toolmaker, a skill which required good systemising. Could he have been on the spectrum? There's no way to know now. On the other hand, there's my uncle, Mike. My memories of him don't suggest a typical AS profile. He's easy with people and a good salesman. On balance, I doubt Mike is anything but normal.

32 Roberson, "What Causes Asperger's Syndrome?"

The next thought is more worrying: if the condition is hereditary then which of my father's offspring may be affected? My sister? My brother? Me? My younger sister, Vicky, is well-ensconced in as normal a life as it's possible to have. She has a husband, a mortgage, and three children. She's gregarious, loves having a social life, and is hopeless with computers. I don't for one second think she's at risk, but one of her sons is overly sullen and uncommunicative. Has the AS skipped a generation, which it certainly can, or is he just a typical teenager? The thing about acquiring a wide knowledge of AS is that you suddenly see the symptoms all around you, whereas the people displaying them may be doing so for completely different reasons, such as depression, introversion, or downright rudeness.

My brother is a different matter entirely. When asked what he does, Matthew describes himself as "achieving flow[33] through software engineering." When pressed, he'll state his occupation as a community currency engineer, a self-styled career rooted in altruism. Five years ago, having amassed a considerable knowledge of computer programming, he thought to himself: 'What can I do that is worthwhile for the world?' He decided to hack the financial system and help small community groups find alternatives to traditional money systems. He built accounting software so they could easily devise and run their own economies, and designed time banks with which they could exchange services instead of money. His work is parallel to his lifestyle, which sees him reject money, a home, and most possessions. He lives out of a small backpack and travels the world, working only for food, accommodation, and expenses. This is, of course, a trifle eccentric.

"A home and possessions don't provide happiness, so why bother with them?" he explains, when I contact him via a chat app the following day. Like me, he's much more comfortable using this method of communication. His telephone manner is about as expressive as the

33 *Authentic Happiness,* 2002. According to psychologist Martin Seligman, Flow, or Engagement, is one of the three kinds of happiness, along with Pleasantness and Meaningfulness.

voice of a GPS unit directing someone to the supermarket, except when he gets indignant or amused, then his pitch wobbles like a pubescent teenager. He's like an unrefined version of our father, which I suppose he is. As someone who seems to be permanently online, it's a relatively simple task to get hold of him at any given time, but I'm lucky he's in the mood to chat. I imagine he's probably designing a world-changing cryptocurrency in between his responses to me.

"Well, it's convenient," I reply.

"Exactly!" he announces triumphantly, totally misunderstanding.

"No, I mean it's convenient to have them," I clarify.

"No, it's just clutter. I haven't paid rent for nearly a decade. I only wear donated clothes. I don't eat for pleasure; I'm just doing what is expected of me. Generally, I would eat less food if I was presented less, and I would probably lose weight."

"But you do get pleasure out of working," I remind him.

"I don't quite see it in that way." There's a pause while he types. "I don't talk about pleasure and happiness at all. It simplifies things. There are some things I would rather do than not do, that's all."

He seems to be content with his choices, and I'm happy for him. Eccentricity in itself is not a symptom of AS but can certainly derive from its symptoms. Matt is happy in his lifestyle because he sees no need for company, or happiness *per se*, hence his preference for the word "flow."

"Everything he did was eccentric," he writes when I ask for childhood memories of Dad. "When I asked for a BMX bicycle one Christmas, he sat me down and made me discuss exactly why I wanted one, since I already had a road bike. After numerous questions, we got right down to the nub of it, which was that I wanted the feeling of going over jumps and flying through the air. When I got my BMX, he set up a big ramp at the bottom of the driveway, but the feeling always seemed to be so brief as to be elusive. To talk a child right down to the innate reason for wanting a particular toy, that was eccentric." To be fair, only a similarly minded child would have accompanied him that far. "I don't remember particular times of fatherly affection as such, but then that wasn't important to me. I didn't miss it. The affection was in being treated like an adult. Once, when I was about twelve, he tried to tell me about the troubles in Northern Ireland. That meant more than any physical affection."

I stare at the screen for minutes, awaiting his next pearl of wisdom, my eyes going numb. I imagine him suspending our conversation to make a small fortune in Bitcoin, which he'll later lose down the back of the sofa.

Finally, he says, "When I started having difficulties at school, because I was a bit weird, Dad told me I was better than everybody else. He told me I was special, that I was like him. He knew he was different somehow, and he saw the same thing in me and taught me his coping mechanism. From that day on, I was an arrogant little brat. I had to deal with a superiority complex. 'They're all morons,' he'd say. 'If they dislike you for no reason it's because they're morons,' which was very comforting at the time because I was quite distressed with some interaction I was having at school. I had difficulty joining in."

I remember seeing my brother being bullied. Our primary school playground had a shed at one end, behind which was naturally the venue for all sorts of mischief. I would've been about seven and him eight, and I walked around the corner one day to see him on the ground, a group of boys pulling him around by the hood of his duffel coat. I'll never forget the look on his face—there was no crying, no wincing in pain, just a fixed look of stoicism, boredom even, as he waited for them to get tired of their abuse and leave him to get on with his life. To this day, I'm ashamed I didn't report this bullying to a teacher. I just walked away and left them to it. I don't even know why.

"Much later," he continues, "when I eventually read about AS, I worked out that Dad had it worse than me. He had grown up in a much more socially rigid society that had less tolerance, and because I went to university, I had more freedom to experiment in social ways and more intelligent people around me, which helped. I also had the benefit from his experience early on, so I didn't spend decades asking myself what was wrong. I was working on the solutions much earlier."

In contrast to my sister, who would spend her childhood days teaching our cat to read and naming inanimate objects after her school friends, teenage Matt embarked on a complex statistical project recording the details of every song in each week's Top 40 chart countdown. Months and months of handwritten sheets listed chart positions, movement, number of weeks in the Top 40, etc. It was exactly the sort of narrow but deep interest one would expect to observe in a child on the low end of the spectrum. Come to think of it, I took over those charts when he lost interest, and turned them into a school statistics project. Anyway, now he works in computer programming—say no more!

My brother accepts his characteristics and plays to his strengths to maximise the work he's doing, and he's comfortable with that. Just before a dodgy Venezuelan internet connection ends our conversation, his musings reach their conclusion: "I'm not as bad as Dad, but slightly worse than you."

Surrounded by snow-capped mountain peaks, Mérida sits in the northern strand of the world's longest mountain range, the Andes, and is a favoured hangout of backpackers and domestic tourists escaping the pressure of big cities. Venezuela has a chaotic history of revolutions and coups, and my visit has coincided with political upheaval following the recent death of popular president Hugo Chavez. Election campaigns for his successor are well underway, and most buildings are smothered with posters and murals, mostly supporting presidential hopeful Nicolás Maduro, who was handpicked by Chavez to succeed him.

The hostel I was forced to book at the border now seems like a lucky break when I find myself among other travellers, and I'm soon invited to join them at a bar that evening. Most seem to be on holiday from teaching or NGO jobs elsewhere in Venezuela, or freelancers with a laptop and no fixed abode. So, after one of the most magnificent steaks I've ever tasted, for a paltry seven dollars, the night becomes an enjoyable pub crawl through the central district's hopping bar scene. I imbibe freely in an attempt to forget my woes, until long-overdue sleep drags me under.

The surrounding mountains provide a host of outdoor activities, but my head is too muddled the next morning to undertake any of them. I'd intended to ride the *Teleférico*, one of the world's longest and highest cable car systems, from here in town to the summit of *Pico Espejo*, some three thousand metres up in the clouds. Such a rapid ascent could certainly result in Acute Mountain Sickness (AMS), so passengers are recommended to stop at the three intermediate stations to aid acclimatisation. AMS combined with a nasty hangover would undoubtedly be quite unpleasant, so it's probably to my benefit that the system is closed today as it has been for the last five years.[34] Instead, I make a spur-of-the-moment decision to catch a Jeep to a mountain village called Los Nevados. After a brief email check, which reveals Dad has safely arrived ("Still sleeping the journey off. Proper reply later."), I'm outta there.

I have plenty of time to regret my spontaneity during the five-hour ride up and down the tortuously steep unpaved roads snaking through the Andean foothills. *Pico Bolivar*, the country's highest mountain, is only a handful of kilometres away, and at times, the ascents are so abrupt that our vehicle overheats and needs to be rested, stones behind the wheels keeping it from rolling back downhill. Head banging and stomach queasy, I want nothing more than to be teleported back to my bed in Merida, curtains shut against the harsh highland light. The views are good, admittedly, but not what my nauseous guts can appreciate right now.

In *Los Nevados*, I check into the nearest *posada* and collapse into a brief nap, waking in the late afternoon feeling much more acceptable. With most of the day gone, I settle for wandering the steep cobbled streets of the village. Perched on the low end of a ridgeline above a seemingly bottomless valley, whitewashed houses topped with terracotta roof tiles surround a small church and plaza. The aged locals hide their weather-beaten faces under wide-brimmed hats and scurry

34 It finally reopened three years later, in 2016.

up the inclines, legs strong from a lifetime of practice, while I hunch over, wheezing. Men lounge around chatting and cackling, while the women always seem to have somewhere to go. Over the *posada* wall, I watch a friendly game of *bolas criollas*, a Venezuelan version of *bocce* or *pétanque,* underway about ten metres down the mountainside. In the other direction, one could follow the ridge all the way to the top of Venezuela without ever crossing another valley.

Without doubt, *Los Nevados* is the very encapsulation of its charming reputation, but it's unfortunately marred this evening by an airbrush artist who spray-paints a pro-Madura mural on one of the walls of the plaza. The image—South America containing a vastly enlarged Venezuela, all encircled by a heart—is an ugly, red wound on the pretty breast of the town, but the locals applaud enthusiastically while a press photographer snaps pictures. I can't tell if this is a publicity stunt to impress Caracas voters or if the townsfolk are Maduro supporters who have commissioned the eyesore.

Loitering in the plaza, I somehow find myself in conversation with seemingly the only *Los Nevados* resident under the age of sixty-five. She suggests that rather than returning to Merida, I hire a mule to take me to *La Cruz del Alto*, a high pass close to the summit of *Pico Bolivar*. From there, I'll be able to hike back down the mountain underneath the disused *teleférico* line to Merida, staying overnight in the hut of a reclusive farmer named Pedro. Ever the fan of a circuit adventure, I decide this sounds like an ideal plan, and make preparations for the morning.

My muleteer is a jolly, nameless chap with a dodgy moustache and a colourful Merida t-shirt underneath his shabby bomber jacket. With a mule each and a donkey for my backpack, we wend our way slowly uphill from *Los Nevados* on a rough track of broken stone, surrounded by the low scrub of Andean alpine tundra in its many shades of green. The clouds hang low, obscuring the uppermost ridges of the range but never quite discharging their cargo of raindrops. We clip-clop quietly along, encountering no other riders, and whenever I glance back, my companion is fiddling with his cell phone. Higher and higher we climb, up vertiginous ridges and through hanging valleys, until we brush the undersides of the clouds themselves. It's a beautiful, peaceful ride which obliterates the painful memories of yesterday's torture by Jeep, and when we crest a broken pass five hours later, marked by a plain wooden cross, I'm sad to realise we've reached *La Cruz del Alto*.

The air is thin at forty-one thousand metres, but fortunately, after shouldering my pack, I only have to walk downhill. I wave farewell to my silent friend as he nudges his mounts back onto the broken rubble that constitutes the flank of *Pico Bolivar*, and turn my nose northwest to survey the thin, grey line of the track. It contours the mountainside ahead before plunging into the swirling cloud, looking like the most desolate path in the universe. I hope this Pedro chap really exists.

Despite the bleak premonition, it isn't long until I come across the dull shape of a building looming out of the mist. Close up, I recognise it as a defunct *teleférico* station, shuttered and wind-blasted, the ground around it strewn with derelict and battered cable cars in a scene resembling some bizarre, long-forgotten skyway pileup. After a brief examination, I'm kind of glad the system is closed; I wouldn't have wanted to trust my life inside one of them. This is *Loma Redonda*, the second-highest station on the route to *Pico Espejo*, and from here, my trail should follow the marching pylons all the way back to Mérida.

Two hours of walking later, in a muddy rut beyond a second station, I find a small signpost for *Casa del Pedro*, the name spelled out in twisted lengths of barbed wire nailed into the wood. Fortunately, the dwelling is more welcoming than the signage—but only just. The two huts which comprise Pedro's mansion are simple, mud-walled structures with corrugated iron roofs, perched on a rare patch of flat land with a ridiculous view of the surrounding peaks. Were it a nice day, I could sit here all afternoon, but the chilly wind and rain-threatening skies chase me inside.

The main hut's interior is scarcely more furnished than its exterior, and Pedro makes my muleteer look like a relentless chatterbox. Frowning, bearded, and taciturn, he reminds me of a certain close relative with a very similar name. When I greet him cheerily with "*Buen dia, señor*," he replies by pointing to a scrawled English sign on the wall: "Do not call me *señor*. *El Señor*[35] is in the sky. My name is Pedro." I see.

He takes some of my money and shows me to a bunkroom, the whitewashed walls cracked, grimy, and dusted with cobwebs. Each amateurishly nailed-together bunk has a thin mattress and the sort of pillow on which one would be wary of placing one's boots, never mind face. Fortunately, the linen that covers them both is clean. It's charming. Really.

Pedro gestures me to join him in the kitchen, recognisable as such only by a wood-fired stove in the corner, underneath which crouches a forlorn-looking mongrel greedy for its meagre heat. We sit at the table. He stares at the wall. I read my book. After a while he asks if I've brought anything to eat. I'd assumed food would be available, and with this being an impulsive addition to my itinerary, I didn't have any anyway.

"I'm sorry, no," I tell him with a grimace. Maybe I could have hunted down a packet of two-minute noodles in Los Nevados. "Can I buy some?"

"No," he grunts after giving me a long stare, but proceeds to boil a pot of plain spaghetti, half of which he serves to me topped with cheese powder. He won't accept my money, though. "Tell your friends they must bring food if they come here," he says, referring to all the *gringo* travellers who will stay with him from this point forward.

"Okay," I agree blankly. I don't say more. I tend to follow people's lead when it comes to conversation: if they are garrulous, I reply in kind; if they are mute, then so I will be. Sitting here with this other Pedro, it's impossible not to think of Dad. Were his current partner to leave him, or die as I gather Pedro's did, would he sit alone in his big house in Spain, a recluse, staring at the walls and eating plain pasta? I can definitely see it. Part of him would love to be a hermit, I know. On the other hand, I can also imagine him taking in paying guests. He'd show them to their rooms with forced politeness, but once settled he'd sit them down and open with his customary, "So, what

35 *El Señor* can also mean The Lord, as in God.

shall we talk about?" He'd then proceed to interrogate them with the skill, if not the menace, of a Gestapo officer. No doubt he'd sometimes be disappointed in the quality of conversation, but if the visitor were intelligent and receptive, they could have a whale of a time.

Once, after I'd left home, he decided to pretend to be a tramp. He was interested to know where the homeless passed their nights in winter. He donned work clothes and his old sheepskin coat—a ragged, lamentable garment, full of holes and tied closed with a piece of string—the one my mother was embarrassed to be seen with. He drove into Plymouth, parked, and walked around until approached by a likely looking fellow, to whom he explained that he'd just arrived on the bus from Birmingham and was wondering where to sleep. The man offered him some floor at his place and advised him not to be in Union Street at pub closing time, as he'd likely be beaten up by drunken youths. At some point, the man stopped to talk to someone else and Dad kept walking. He'd heard about a hostel somewhere around the back of Union Street, so he drove over there to find it. He was slowly cruising the streets when a scantily clad figure appeared from the shadows and asked if he was looking for business. He said no, wished her goodnight, and decided to go home.

Along with ridding themselves of the complications of people and society, hermits are subject to a loneliness more complete than any I've ever experienced. Isolation from the rest of the human race. The more I consider this, the more my heart goes out to Pedro. He doesn't exactly look happy to be here. I want to start a conversation with him, to show him friendliness, but I'm intimidated by his silence and my less-than-fluent Spanish. Before I can conquer my fears, he abruptly announces that he's going to bed. It's 5:30 p.m. and still light. Sitting alone in the gloomy, soot-stained kitchen is all too much, and I soon follow suit.

I can't wait to get away the next morning. After bidding Pedro the briefest of farewells, I ramble down through the Andean foothills for a couple of hours, diverging from the *teleférico* to reach the suburb of Mucunutan on the outskirts of the city. From there, I catch a local bus to Mérida's central station, where I plot a course straight across Venezuela to the south-eastern region of *Gran Sabana*.

Located in the tri-border area incorporating parts of Venezuela, Guyana, and Brazil, the *Gran Sabana* is a landscape of rolling grasslands decorated with *tepuis*—free-standing, flat-topped mountains that typically feature towering, vertical cliffs on all sides. It's one of these *tepuis*, Roraima, that I've long been anticipating visiting. Given both the political climate and Caracas' reputation for violent crime, I decide to avoid the north of the country entirely and go via Ciudad Bolivar, a supposedly charming, historic city on the Orinoco River. I'll also be bypassing *Los Llanos*, a vast wetland area of central Venezuela famous for its wildlife. I'd originally planned for the two of us to go there, but now I fear it would be an expensive and lonely excursion.

Expensive and lonely; these two side effects of my new solo status dwell on me for the duration of the nineteen-hundred-kilometre journey to *Ciudad Bolivar*. The added costs are purely logistical and to be expected. They shouldn't impact me too much for the present but will start to bite once I hit the Caribbean islands, not exactly backpacker-friendly territory. As for the latter condition, meeting people was sometimes awkward with the old fella in my shadow, but at least I knew I had him to fall back on should I fail. By contrast, in Mérida, drinking with the guys from the hostel, I couldn't shake the feeling of solitude. I never lacked for companionship with Dad, even if we weren't speaking. It was the most comfortable of silences; a few words would suffice to recharge the ambience. At least I don't have to worry about him anymore. He's in safe hands now.

I miss him, though, and contentedly pass many road hours reliving times of closeness between us, not just in this last, too-short month but throughout my life. Playing catch in the backyard when I was obsessed with cricket at school; learning to ride a bike, him running alongside with a steadying hand on my seat; helping him lay the foundations for the outhouses in Cornwall, hard work but so rewarding. Each of these moments was like a layer of protein strengthening the bond between us, a mutual respect formed over the course of my childhood. When the old car my brother and I shared wouldn't start, he dedicated a whole Saturday morning to removing and completely stripping down the alternator, cleaning it, and putting it together again. He'd never done it before but reasoned that must be where the problem lay, and when it was reassembled, it worked perfectly! I treasured the dinners we shared while I was at university when he'd visit from Cornwall. One night, I ordered a vindaloo curry; it took me two sweaty hours and several litres of water to finish, all while he asked me probing questions about my chemical engineering course. Happy days.

Fuelled by the memories, I start to draw parallels between father and son over the long hours of rumbling tyres and bus-station loitering. We're more alike than we might seem. As well as avoiding chit-chat, I also detest the sweaty, skin-on-skin feeling of shaking hands, only forcing myself to comply in a business environment. The rest of the time I get away with a friendly fist bump and crooked smile.

I appreciate directness. If I'm going to a dinner party or barbecue, and I'm told to bring nothing, that's exactly what I'll bring. If the host wanted me to bring a starter or a bottle of wine, then they should have said so. I was good at maths and physics in school. I make a lot of to-do lists, and I like orderliness and routine in my day-to-day life, but at the same time, I crave new situations. Any weekend that passes without a new, or at least rare, experience leaves me with a sense of disappointment.

I love collecting things. It started with Star Wars figures (I still have a large and valuable collection), but then I'd pretty much label any group of related objects as a new collection and add to it. Decks of cards, alcohol miniatures, sticker sets, Mr. Bump memorabilia, toothbrushes; I'd collect anything. My most ridiculous ideas were seventy-nine pence price labels and identical wooden chip forks from a hundred different chip shops. Dad's collecting career began and ended with Dinky Toys, a range of beautifully made diecast, zinc alloy miniature cars which he played with lovingly as a boy and still keeps in pristine condition in storage.

What was it my brother said? That he was "slightly worse" than me? Although I'd mused before about the similarities between myself and my dad, I hadn't considered that I might actually be on the spectrum too. I guess I shouldn't be that surprised. After all, if Autism Spectrum conditions are strongly genetic in origin, and therefore, AS is heritable, then it's completely possible. Now that I begin dissecting my behaviour, the character trait that most worries me is my lack of empathy.

Professor Baron-Cohen gives a far better definition of empathy than I could: "Empathy is about spontaneously tuning in to another person's thoughts and feelings, reading the emotional atmosphere, effortlessly putting yourself in another's shoes, sensitively negotiating an interaction without hurting or offending the other party in any way. A good empathiser can immediately sense when an emotional change has occurred, what the causes may be and what would make that person feel better or worse. Less skilled people might only do it when reminded, or by practicing, not spontaneously. Other people's feelings matter less to them. Empathy is the glue of social relationships and provides a framework for the development of a moral code."[36]

I believe I can put myself in another's shoes. I can sense when an emotional change has occurred. The trouble is, unless that person is personally connected to me, I don't much care. The problems, pain, and death of complete strangers is inconsequential. Why wouldn't it be? I don't know them, and the news has no effect on my life. I understand their friends and families will be sad, as I would be if something happened to mine, but a stranger in a news report? Thousands of deaths happen every day due to murder, disease, and accident. If one truly empathised with them all, one wouldn't be able to get through each day. And how can one care about some strangers and not others, just because of some vague commonality? "Seventy-Six Dead in Kabul Car Bomb" versus "Local Toddler Dies in House Fire"—I don't differentiate between the two.

My brother is more abrupt. "People are getting burnt to death in houses all the time," he said to me during our webchat. "I can't

36 Baron-Cohen, *The Essential Difference*, 23–27.

empathise with all of them just because they're on the television or in a newspaper. Some people might feel they should care, but that's just because we are wired to care more about things close to us."

A comparison to other peoples' degree of empathy can only be speculative because we can't ever know how anybody else actually feels inside. We can only guess that from what they display. My father doesn't accept he's low on empathy, arguing that since he doesn't know how other people feel, how can he classify his own quotient as 'low'? When he told me this, I sensed he was just being contrary, probably as a result of being constantly reminded, in books and articles, and also by me, that as an Aspergian, this is how he's supposed to be. There must be a correlation, though, between the way people feel and the way they act. I think it's fair to say that, unless everyone fakes their emotions all the time, I display—and therefore feel—less. When it comes to the death or illness of strangers, I rarely raise an eyebrow, never mind burst into tears. Could I have been on-spectrum my whole life and never realised it?

With these thoughts bouncing around my mind, I drift off to sleep, my head resting against the windowpane. A blanket wrapped around me fends off the vigorous air conditioning, only part of the reason for the chill gripping my body.

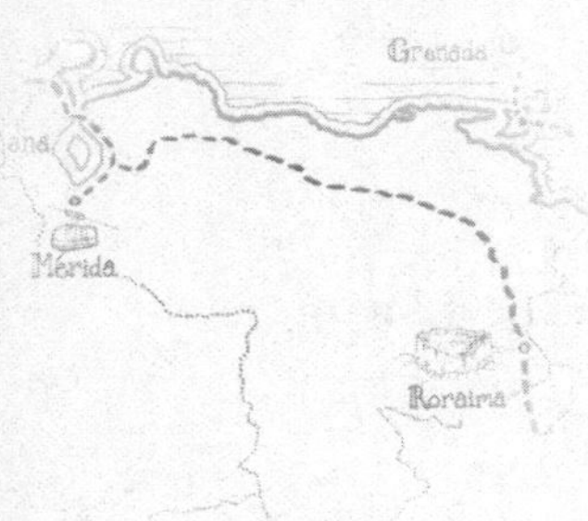

Chapter 10

Jouska

I wake in *Ciudad Bolivar*. The first leg to Barinas, although simple on paper, was unfathomably lengthy. On arrival there, I discovered my onward connection to *Ciudad Bolivar* had been cancelled, leaving the quickest option via *Puerto La Cruz* on the north coast, a huge detour. Those fifteen hours, plus the four-hour wait, *plus* the five hours to *Ciudad Bolivar*, bring the total journey to twenty-four hours. I feel like death warmed up and award myself a rest day.

Ciudad Bolivar is pleasant enough to stroll around, with a cathedral, parks, plazas, and stately administrative buildings, but the highlight is the magnificent Orinoco River gliding past the waterfront, its opposite bank nearly two kilometres distant. Just upstream is the Angostura suspension bridge, which was the only crossing of the river along its entire 2140-kilometre length until the opening of a second bridge a hundred kilometres downriver seven years ago. The structure looks stunning silhouetted before the setting sun. Above all, though, just not being on a bus is what makes the day so enjoyable.

I'm sitting in a café, enjoying the golden sheen on the water, when at last I receive a proper email from Dad. I read it slowly, savouring both the contact and his particular syntax. The cadence of the words in my head conjures an image of him next to me, slouched a little on the plastic chair, rubbing his face and fishing in his Aladdin's cave of vest pockets for his reading glasses to peruse the menu. He mentions briefly making an appointment with a prostate specialist in Plymouth, then goes on to ask several questions about our movements near the beginning of the trip, specifically the flight between Belize and Costa Rica.

"I need you to give me a summary of our travels to help with my memory," he writes. "For example, I can remember you deciding we should take a flight to Costa Rica and that there were two legs, but I cannot remember being at any of the three airports or sitting on an aeroplane with you. Did we do that?"

I frown, worried by the disintegration of his memory. This happened literally five weeks ago. Can this short period which has meant so much to me be so easily erased from his brain? I'd hoped we'd be able to share this experience for the rest of his days, but that won't be possible if he can't remember it. I remind him of the fare argument in the airport taxi and the exorbitant Belizean departure tax, two financially related incidents I calculate most likely to jog his memory.

I wander aimlessly for the remainder of the evening but can't focus on my surroundings. My thoughts are caught in an eddy that swirls around this central concept of my similarity to my father. I may be shocked by his failing memory, but mine is also deteriorating. How long before I forget the details of that unremarkable flight? A year? Five years? While the murkiness of the mind's recollection is usually age related, there are other, more concerning parallels.

"I have to concentrate on maintaining eye contact when face-to-face," he'd told me. "I learned that by copying other people." I've never felt comfortable making prolonged eye contact. If someone looks too long into my eyes, even during casual conversation, I feel naked and uncomfortable, like they can see everything I've ever done wrong. It establishes a degree of intimacy that I don't wish to share with a total stranger, or even most friends. Meeting somebody's gaze unexpectedly, I'll immediately flick my eyes away. This probably explains why I've always been bad with faces; when I meet new people, I avoid their eyes and thus, their whole face. How could I possibly recognise them later?

I definitely have touches of Obsessive-Compulsive Disorder (OCD)[37]—everything must be in its right place, and round numbers please me immeasurably. Buying something that costs exactly the amount of change I have in my pocket gives me a real feeling of elation. I'll even choose the less appetising yet more expensive snack if it costs the right amount of money. My cheese sandwiches are a source of constant mirth to Gerda, as the slices of cheese must be arranged to exactly cover the surface of the bread with no gaps or overlapping. I mean, it makes sense. I want every mouthful to have the same balance of bread and cheese, right?

As I return to my guest house, which, as usual, doubles as the family home, I'm greeted by the unmistakeable wailing/shrieking of small children. I scuttle upstairs to my hammock and escape into my iPod. I don't generally like kids; I never have. They bore me. They're bad conversationalists, they're messy and noisy, and they tend to repeat things over and over. I don't have any or intend on ever having any. Unless a baby sprang from one's own loins, I can't think of any reason one would volunteer to have contact with it, except maybe for money, i.e., a babysitter. I'm not ashamed of my stance on children, but it seems to put other people out, maybe because I don't make stupid noises to theirs or comment on their size, intellectual advancement, or bowel movements. Given the natural self-centredness of Aspergians and my own lack of interest in offspring, it's natural to wonder how Dad behaved as a new father. Would he have seen us as an imposition? Did I bore him?

"I didn't think about having children either way as being a good or bad thing," he'd said. "It was just something Brenda announced one day—'I'm pregnant!' I had no experience at all with babies or children. I didn't know how to interact with them."

My brother was born about two and a half years after my parents got married. In Dad's own words, "After [the wedding] I think I had

37 Dongbai Liu et al, *Integrative analysis of shared genetic pathogenesis by autism spectrum disorder and obsessive-compulsive disorder.* Research published in *Bioscience Reports* suggests a possible complex genetic association between OCD and ASD.

a happy period. We were quite close sometimes." Obviously close enough for me to come along sixteen months after Matt, shortly before his breakdown. My sister arrived four and a half years later, coinciding with another of his happy periods, working abroad, and Vicky was nicknamed "The Italian Job" while in utero. Even after that, I remember incidences where Dad would sneak into the bathroom while Mum was bathing, explaining with a cheeky smile as he closed the door that she needed someone to "wash her back."

"He was very good with you all," confirms my mother when I next call her, setting my mind at ease. "He may not have been a natural, and I don't remember him reading books on how to raise children, but he had this huge intelligence. He would observe and learn. He'd think about what was required and figure it out for himself."

He played baby games like normal fathers—peek-a-boo, knee-bouncing, etc. As we got older, it was hide and seek or Cowboys and Indians.[38] He'd also sit and talk with us, or teach us board games like Ludo and draughts, later chess and, our choice, Dungeons & Dragons. (Both my brother and I were obsessed with this fantasy role-playing game, the classic 1980s geek detector.) He had endless patience. "Asperger's or not, with your own child there's a bond that's unique, especially when the father is present during labour," crackles Mum's voice down the line. He took on fatherhood like a job that had to be done, and therefore, like any other job, he had to do well. And he succeeded, if I may say so myself!

"I have no complaints," finishes Mum, "not until much later."

Australian Asperger specialist Dr. Tony Attwood writes that, "Having a parent with Asperger's syndrome can sometimes cause children to feel they are 'invisible' or a nuisance and deprived of the acceptance, reassurance, encouragement, and affection that they need."[39] This was definitely not the case for me. I remember affection and encouragement, especially with scholarly pursuits. He spent a lot

38 Dad's favourite joke: Good cowboy pointing gun at bad cowboy: "Put your hands up, ya bum!" Bad Cowboy: "Put my hands up my what?"
39 Attwood, *Relationship Problems of People with Asperger's Syndrome*, 10.

of time with my brother and I leading up to our eleven-plus examinations, an assessment in the last year of primary school in the UK which determined academic selection for secondary schools. When I passed the entrance exam for a prestigious secondary school, he was clearly proud I'd proven my intellectual ability.

Nowadays, though, he's more of a crotchety old git. "I'm waiting for my grandchildren to grow up so I can talk to them," he admitted, referring to Vicky's three boys. "I really have no interest in interacting with them as children." Without the direct bond of fatherhood, and having spent little time with them as babies, the impetus to be a good grandfather just isn't there. I'm reminded of another wry John Elder Robison observation, when friends and family reacted to the birth of his son: " 'Oooh, he looks just like you!' [they said], standard baby drivel, I figured. How could a six-pound baby with misshapen features and a head the size of an apple look 'just like me'?"[40] I couldn't have put it better myself.

Remembering that Aspergians do feel their own kind of love, I don't need to question whether fatherly love was present. That has been shown us too many times to be obliterated by the impassive words he would no doubt use should I ask him. When I'd questioned my brother about love, he'd been evasive.

"That's another word like happiness," he'd written. "You have to define it. When you define it, I'll answer you. Women might like the words, but the demonstration is more important. Is the demonstration sincere? I don't know. It's just socially appropriate behaviour." Yeah . . . I don't think that counts as love. "The trouble is that sometimes my feelings don't lead to the same behaviour as everyone else, so I have to control my behaviour; therefore, all behaviour is conscious behaviour, and I'm manipulating myself all the time.

"I've got a problem with saying things like 'I love you,' " he'd continued. "It's a contract; it can be misunderstood. Dad would agree. It happens to regular people all the time because they think they have to say it, but I don't fall into that trap. They think they have to utter this stream of syllables with no defined meaning, so they're bound to

40 Robison, *Look Me in the Eye*, 221.

be misunderstood. And that doesn't even take into account all the cultural accretions. The first time you say 'I love you' is a seminal moment in a relationship and probably means 'I want to be with you,' but I can love someone (by my definition) and not want to be with them very much." Great boyfriend material, my brother. He's forty-one and still single, by the way.

As for me, in my youth I had two long-term girlfriends in close succession who confessed to being in love with me. Although I liked them a lot, I never felt an emotion strong enough to be this 'love' that society shoves in our faces every day, so I never reciprocated, which is why the relationships ended. After the second, I seriously asked myself whether or not I was capable of love. I wasn't worried, merely curious. After almost two years with Gerda, and during a long period of apartness, it finally hit me. This must be it, I thought. It was the constant and urgent desire to be with her, the impossibility of getting her out of my mind, and when we were reunited, the utter relief that our physical separation was over. That, to me, is love.

It turns out I may be stuck in *Ciudad Bolivar* for some time. Seats heading south to *Santa Elena de Uairén*, the small town which serves as a springboard for the *Gran Sabana*, are booked solid for the next week due to a severe bus shortage. Many of the vehicles that regularly service the route have been commandeered by political parties to shuttle their supporters to rallies around the country. With all voters required to return to their place of birth to vote, this is a combination guaranteed to bring forth nationwide transport chaos. In some dismay, I walk to the city's small airport to enquire about flying, but air services have been suspended for some time.

Mounted in a flowerbed in front of the airport is an old six-seater, single-propeller light aircraft. This Flamingo G-2-W is the very one that American pilot James "Jimmie" Angel landed atop *Auyán-Tepui* in 1937 while attempting to get a closer look at the impressive waterfall that flowed from its escarpment. First spotted by him in 1933 and later named *Salto Angel* (Angel Falls) in his honour, the cascade is well-known as the highest in the world, its waters tumbling an uninterrupted 979 metres down to the rocks below. Although *Salto Angel* is deservedly one of the biggest tourist draws in the country, it gives, by far, its most impressive performance in the wet season, whereas my arrival coincides with the very end of the dry.

While trips still run, and are expensive since the only way to reach the base at Canaima is by aeroplane, I see little point in going. The flow of water over the falls is so slight right now that it blows away in a breeze, and the accompanying river trip is impossible due to low water levels. It's sad, but the decision is an easy one. Having landed successfully atop *Auyán-Tepui*, Jimmie Angel's aircraft became bogged down and impossible to use. His party of four had to make an eleven-day trek off the mountain to the nearest settlement, and his valiant Flamingo was retrieved thirty-three years later and laid to rest in this spot.

Beginning to despair that my rest day might soon become a rest week, I return to the bus terminal. Albert Einstein, the controversially undiagnosed Aspergian,[41] is credited with defining insanity as repeating the same behaviour over and over and expecting a different outcome, but this time, I do receive more encouraging news. I can't book ahead, but I'm told if I come to the terminal at 5:00 a.m. tomorrow morning, I may be rewarded with a place. Accordingly, after an early alarm and a long walk through unlit streets past shadowy figures and barky dogs, I push nervously through to the ticket booth. Lady Luck is with me, and a couple of hours later, I'm rolling east to *Ciudad Guayana*, then south on Highway 10.

Our little group pushes up the final slope through the driving rain, scrambling over a steep jumble of fallen boulders that gurgle with rainwater run-off. We're sweaty, sore, and as wet as if we've just walked

41 Muir, "Einstein and Newton."

under a waterfall,[42] but our pumping hearts are jubilant at cresting the lip of the four-hundred-metre-high escarpment at last. The great thing about *tepuis*, we think collectively, is that they're flat on top.

Roraima was 'discovered' by Sir Walter Raleigh in 1596 and first climbed in 1884 by two British explorers—Sir Everard im Thurn and Harry Perkins. Their expedition report inspired Sir Arthur Conan Doyle, author of the Sherlock Holmes stories, to write *The Lost World* in 1912, a book about dinosaurs surviving on top of a remote South American *mesa*. In the book, one Professor Challenger found prehistoric creatures and became embroiled in a war between two semi-human tribes. He escaped back to London with a live pterodactyl. I must admit I'd once daydreamed of being in the professor's sturdy hobnailed boots. How incredible would it be to discover a living descendent of that doomed epoch? Once up there, I determined to keep my eyes open!

We'd been expecting bad weather; it rains almost every day on the mountain's thirty-one km^2 plateau due to a concentration of cloud that creeps up from the steamy rainforest. Wind pushes the moist air against the warm slopes, and as it rises, it cools and condenses violently.

Another fascinating fact about *tepuis*, we learn seconds later, is that they are anything but flat on top. What confronts us instead is a landscape of freestanding cliffs, wind-carved slabs, rock pinnacles, and precariously balanced boulders with names like The Elephant, or Monkey Eating an Ice Cream. Disregarding those ridiculous monikers, I visualise every jagged silhouette as a winged, leathery lizard perched on high, eyeing us as a potential dining option. The place is a maze—without Fernando, we'd soon be hopelessly lost. After a minute's respite in the lee of the Flying Turtle, we form up and follow his squelching disco boots into the mist.

I'd reached *Santa Elena de Uairén* after thirteen hours with only two flat tyres and two stops for armed harassment. I'd been warned by a work colleague who'd come this way the previous year to be wary of military checkpoints. He'd been politely relieved of two hundred

42 We have.

dollars by a rifle-toting officer, and there was nothing he could do about it. I'd consequently hidden all my money, save a small sacrificial wedge, in my dirty laundry bag, a living maelstrom of odour horrific enough to repel even impoverished Venezuelan soldiers. Fortunately, my stink-barrier was not tested.

Within seconds of my arrival in Santa Elena—hot, hungry, and tired—I'd been pinpointed by a tour operator who'd told me the only Roraima trip for the next week was leaving at 9:00 a.m. the next day. Due to the transport issues, and the Venezuelan government closing the country's international borders to prevent destabilisation by opposition parties, there were only enough backpackers in town to make up a single group of four. My companions were two German girls and a quiet Japanese man. Some unlucky Brazilians who'd booked their trip months ago were stuck on the wrong side of the border, only a few kilometres away.

With just enough time to shower and sleep, we were driven to the small Pemon village of Paratepui. We had a guide, young Fernando, who apparently didn't mind missing polling day in favour of some extra cash. He was dressed as though he'd walked straight out of a nightclub—jeans, basketball boots, neon jacket, and earphones permanently glued into his ears—and it turns out, that's exactly what happened. We also had one porter, José. I elected to carry ten kilograms of group food on top of my own gear, effectively acting as a second porter to keep my costs down.

After signing in at *Paratepui*'s guard post, we set off across the hilly grasslands of the *Gran Sabana* to our first camp, where we had a magnificent view of Roraima and Kukenan, its striking neighbour. From down here, the wisps of clouds seemed insignificant against the deep blue of late afternoon savannah sky. It can get crowded here in high season, but the troubles meant we had the mountain to ourselves.

On the second day, we walked across the boulder-strewn folds of the foothills towards the base of the escarpment. All the while the monolith loomed closer, silver ribbons of water cascading down its cliffs. We could now clearly make out The Ramp—a fault line in the vertical wall which is the only practical means of ascending Roraima.

The *tepui* cannot be approached from Guyana or Brazil due to militarized zones and tribal tensions. We could also see what looked like a gushing torrent of freezing water running directly into our path. That was going to be a fun obstacle to tackle.

Day three was the killer. Water dripped through the cloud forest, feeding the thick moss clinging to the branches. This close to the equator, the humidity was extreme, and we were soon sweating like stevedores, but after a couple of hours, we reached the foot of the cliffs and the start of The Ramp proper. As we emerged from the trees, we were enveloped in low cloud, the combination of wind and drizzle permeating our clothing layers, but we were driven now, propelled upwards by determination.

"Ah," sighed our Asian companion, succinctly summing up our situation. "So very up!" He'd bought a cheap plastic poncho from the sole Japanese hiker we met at Camp 1, who was on his way out. He will, in turn, sell it to the sole Japanese hiker we meet at Camp 1, on our way out. I wonder how many back-to-back Roraima trips that poncho has made; it may be more experienced than Fernando!

Another ninety minutes brought us to the waterfall we'd seen yesterday, dropping directly into our path from nearly half a kilometre up. There was no way around, yet the uneven rocks made it impossible to rush; we just had to stride stoically through, thinking of the easy hiking awaiting us on top.

And there, of course, is where we've come unstuck. As Conan-Doyle puts it: "And there we were, the four of us, upon the dreamland, the lost world. To all of us it seemed the moment of our supreme triumph. Who could have guessed that it was the prelude to our supreme disaster?"[43] Fortunately, it isn't far to our 'hotel'—a series of small overhangs along the side of a rocky outcrop where we don dry clothes while José heats up some soup.

Fernando has no rainwear at all, so his clubbing outfit is soaked through, and having changed into his only spare clothing, he's reluctant to venture out again. However, with the rain easing up and a mixture of

43 Conan Doyle, *The Lost World*, 92.

cajoling and guilt, we persuade him to lead an afternoon expedition to the Edge of the World. Far from the 'thickly wooded' interior the book describes, the plateau is treeless and ridiculously cluttered with rocky obstacles, deep pools, sand, and shrubs. Reaching the edge of the escarpment is like reaching the limit of the known universe—nothing but swirling mist and a vertiginous drop of hundreds of metres. Through breaks in the cloud, we spy rainforest stretching away to the north and catch brief glimpses of gorgeous waterfalls cascading off Kukenan. On its south side, Kukenan Falls is the second tallest free-leaping waterfall in the world after *Salto Angel* at 674 metres.

That evening, huddled around a fire in our overhang, Fernando tells us why no trips run up Kukenan anymore. The silence up here is absolute, perfect for ghost stories—no bird cries pierce the air and no mammals scurry in the shadows. In a low voice, Fernando relates the tale of the 'suicide *tepui*.' Groups used to explore Kukenan as they now do Roraima, until one day, an unhappy guide leapt from those magnificent cliffs to his death. What a way to go! The reason was reported to be girlfriend trouble, a common enough motivation for jumpers, and the *tepui* was subsequently closed to hikers for the next twenty-five years. Once reopened, trips were rare and expensive, but parties did go, at least until disaster struck a second time. Another guide went missing.

"He was never seen again," says Fernando, lowering his voice to a stage whisper. "But now his spirit cries for help. Many people say so. Sometimes I have heard it in the night, even from right here in this cave. No guides will go Kukenan anymore." We glance at each other, wide-eyed, ears straining for the plaintive wail of loss, but the night remains deathly quiet.

Our objective the following day is the tri-border, an eight-hour return trip over similarly ridiculous terrain. There are fast-flowing rivers we need to wade through and a gigantic sinkhole a good ten metres across and five metres deep. When the weather permits, it's possible to jump into the pool it contains and climb back out through a slot canyon. Although the rain is only intermittent and the peek-a-boo sun fierce enough to dry us after each soaking, it would be freezing in there today, so we give it a miss.

The border marker at 2810 metres is a three-sided trig point with one country's plaque on each face, or at least it's supposed to be; the one dedicated to Guyana has been removed by nationalist vandals. An enormous territory to the east of here is owned and controlled by Guyana and makes up more than half of that country, but it is also claimed by Venezuela. This long-running dispute has been simmering since colonial times, complicated by the discovery of gold and, more recently, oil. An international tribunal ruled in favour of Guyana (then called British Guiana) in 1899, but Venezuela contested the decision and no end to the quarrel is in sight. Standing on this lonely, windswept plateau with nothing but rocks and jungle in every direction, the bickering seems childish.

It's near here I spy Roraima's most charming resident—a tiny black toad, *oreophrynella quelchii*, which exists nowhere else on earth. Due to the nature of their formation, the *tepuis* are home to many endemic species. Nestled in a crevice near our camping overhang is a unique species of pitcher plant, a carnivorous tube that traps insects, but of fauna, there is little sign. This cute amphibian is far removed from the pterodactyl I was hoping to see, but I crouch down anyway. Close up, he's beautiful—bulging black eyes stare from glistening black skin, not smooth but a rough pattern of knobbly bumps, much like the surface of his knurled *tepui* home. He perches for a second on the end of my thumbnail, swallows, then crawls down my wrist and onto a nearby rock. He's oddly reminiscent of my absentee travelling companion. A humourless laugh erupts from my sinuses. I just hope he's not as black on the inside.

Two days later, for the first time in weeks, I'm able to relax for a few hours, do some laundry, and take stock. Roraima was a terrific adventure in good company, but I'm preparing to venture further east, where fellow travellers are likely to be rare. The results of the presidential election haven't yet been announced, so there's still time to flee the country before the violence starts. An email check brings news from Dad, although bizarrely, he's still more concerned with the forgettable flight than his ailing health.

"I've remembered arriving at San José airport and taking a taxi," he writes. "And I remember looking for a yellow fever jab but can't pull an image of the hostel."

I sigh. Surely, it's more important to focus on our interpersonal experiences? Belatedly, he adds some prostate information: "Everything going according to plan. Biopsy today, but two weeks to wait for results. Be careful out there!" I will, Dad. I will.

Chapter 11

Dromomania

I love entering a country through the back door. Often one's first impression of a new land is from flying into the capital city and being greeted by stern-faced immigration officials, inflated prices, English-speaking touts, and the same fast-food chains you're trying to escape. While that may be an invigorating introduction, strolling through a barely used land border gets my vote every time. You can breeze into an apparently abandoned shed, read the wanted posters as the guard languidly stamps your passport, make small talk with customs officers, then search (sometimes in vain) for transport away from no man's land.

This pretty much describes the border between Bonfim in Brazil and Lethem in Guyana, albeit with quite a big shed. To reach Bonfim, I took a shared taxi a couple of hundred kilometres from Santa Elena to *Boa Vista* in Brazil, and another roughly the same distance from there. Boa Vista is only 660 kilometres from Manaus, the largest city in the Amazon and the northernmost point I'd reached when I was last in the area, ten years previously. Thinking of Manaus and that South American jaunt reminds me that, strangely enough, my father is not the first Aspergian I've travelled with, although, at the time, I didn't know it.

I'd been in South America almost a year by the time I reached Manaus, although Paul had joined me only a couple of months previously. I'd never thought of Paul as weird or even antisocial, only a bit shy with girls. When I was sixteen, I moved schools, naturally apprehensive of being the new kid in a well-established classroom society. One of my classes, advanced mathematics, had only six students, yet I couldn't bring myself to sit directly beside any of them; I always left an empty chair between myself and my neighbour. After three lessons, a glaring redheaded boy beckoned to the seat beside him.

"Why don't you sit here?" he suggested in a somewhat accusatory tone. I did, and we became lifelong best friends. I'll be forever grateful to him for that stark yet amiable invitation.

Paul is a functioning member of any social circle with his quick wit and wicked sense of humour combined with remarkable breadth of knowledge and the intelligence to discuss it. He's adept at event planning and will research all alternatives before logically calculating the best course of action. Those skills translate well to travel, and indeed, he requires a plan in order to proceed; he cannot contemplate going forth without one. Other clues to his condition were present: his need for routine, his obsession with cool little travel gadgets, his habit of maintaining eye contact a little too long than is comfortable, which earned him the nickname PaulEyes. With retrospect, I now recognise this as overcompensation for his natural desire to look away.

A few days in Manaus broke up our pursuit of the Amazon, all the way from its delta on the east coast to Brazil's tri-border with Peru and Colombia. One might think twelve days with no entertainment save the turbulent brown body of the mighty river would become tedious, but I never tired of watching the emerald jungle glide past with all its associated vessels, settlements, people, wildlife, and insects. Lots of insects. We slept in hammocks on the main deck of the boat, swinging hip-to-hip with mysterious, solitary men in combat fatigues and raucous, undisciplined families. We'd brought a huge sack of boiled sweets to tame the children but stopped handing them out after witnessing the wrappers thrown overboard. We couldn't really blame the young ones, though—all rubbish from the boat was swept into the endless flow that transported it away forever, at least in the minds of Amazonians. To them, the river was some sort of magic vortex which consumed and vanished all waste; it was heart-breaking.

Meals were served thrice daily, a routine which broke our lives into segments of reading, watching the river, or listening to music, activities undertaken from either the comfort of the hammock, the small area in front of the wheelhouse, or the top deck. The food was invariably meat stew, so Paul, a longstanding herbivore, simply decided to fast. He's never been that interested in food other than to fuel his body, so it was easy for him. The upper deck was otherwise reserved for socialising, and every evening, the passengers would sit around to drink, play dominoes or cards, or watch the small television above the bar. I got hooked on *Kubanacan*, a hilarious Brazilian *telenovela* (soap opera) which seemed to consist entirely of three members of a romantic triangle taking turns kissing and fighting each other. It was so bad; I loved it. Paul and I got used to playing dominoes with some of the other passengers, absolute grandmasters of the game. They'd lose patience with our slow-witted play, often calculating from the remaining tiles what we should be laying down before we did. Given time, Paul would have been a natural!

Only half an hour prior to re-boarding in Manaus, we'd realised we might require some vodka to see us through the next leg of the journey. An initial search proved fruitless, so with the clock ticking, we split up, each agreeing to buy a bottle of vodka if we located one. In actual fact, we both found a shop, and both independently decided to buy two bottles just in case the other came up empty. Thus, our starting inventory numbered four bottles of the cheapest vodka *reais* could buy.

It was in this environment that the most frustrating of Paul's symptoms manifested itself. Hugely intelligent, he's always been a fan of debate or, to put it another way, arguing. He'll argue all day long; he'll argue black is white and put up a very convincing case. He has the sort of file-indexed memory that can instantaneously locate any fact necessary to back up his position, leaving less mentally agile people groping for factual support. One's carefully memorised contention vanishes in the face of his data onslaught. It's never bothered me before, but in this setting, maybe due to a lack of mental stimulation and heightened by alcohol, his belligerence went into overdrive, and I found my patience wearing thin.

Truth be told, I enjoy a bit of debate myself, especially when I hold my own against his superior skills, but the culmination of three months of daily interaction began to wear me down. I didn't want an argument every time I opened my mouth, especially with someone who sometimes forgot the discourtesy of interrupting and talking over another person. I began to get distressed, angry, and downright annoyed by his ceaseless remonstration, and this is the thing: he couldn't tell how irritated I was getting until I virtually exploded. In between hands of dominoes we'd bicker so fiercely over trivialities that our opponents would be confused by this apparent enmity and begin to openly question our friendship. They couldn't believe two lifelong mates would shout at each other in such a way, yet Paul would press on relentlessly in the face of my obvious despair.

"Enough!" I finally snapped, after one too many nights of raised voices and hot blood. "I do not want to argue with you *anymore*!"

"Oh. Why?" he asked, genuinely confused. "What's wrong?"

I explained that his constant quarrelling was driving me insane, and like a true Aspergian, he immediately apologised and dropped the issue like it was beneath his notice. All I had to do was say exactly what I felt and not rely on my tone of voice or deepening frown to get the message across. We came to an agreement—whenever any discussion began to get a little too heated, I'd just say, "Paul, end of discussion." He'd realise what was happening and change the subject. After establishing this rule, the problem disappeared, and we finished our journey as friends.

I didn't know what his behaviour portended then, and I still rarely think of Paul as an Aspergian, but looking back, it was a clue to his eventual diagnosis ten years later. Once that happened, other pieces fell into place. That his father had AS was suddenly obvious—he also has no clue when he's angering someone, and he hates the sensory overload of foreign or spicy food. Paul's brother is also on the spectrum, and one of his sons is further along than any of them. Sound familiar? Yes, it's a family business, alright.

One thing I've learned from years of travelling off the beaten track is there's *always* a Chinese restaurant, and Lethem is no exception. Having arrived in the southwest corner of Guyana in the early afternoon, I have six hours to kill until the evening minibus for Georgetown, the coastal capital, so I take a leisurely self-guided walking tour of the town, absorbing everything of interest. Then I do it again. With still five and a half hours to go, I give in to the temptation of very poor chow mein.

From my seat, I have a great view of the inflammatory text daubed in rude letters on the opposite wall of the street. For the first time since Belize, English is the national language, although I may have been better off not being able to read this nugget of wisdom:

> **Incest mean sex between members of the family, like daughter rape father, sister rape brother, niece rape uncle, and so on. That is why the wrath of God is upon them permanently, all of them. If this world want to see piece it is bette for all of them die jost today. Romans 1:31**[44]

Despite the author's rudimentary grasp of spelling and language structure, the message is clear: the culture of misogyny and victim blaming is alive and well in Guyana.

Ever since Dutch colonists established a foothold in the jungle in 1616, there has been little urbanisation of the vast interior, a policy which remained unchanged when the territory was ceded to the English in 1814. Lethem is one of only a handful of towns south of the main coastal plain, and the 423 kilometres to Georgetown is via an unsealed road, which could be considered rough by any standards.

My fellow passengers in the robust Toyota Hiace each carry an impressive amount of shopping, having been taking advantage of the abundance of quality goods over in Brazil. As we pull away, the sun is

44 The New International Version of the Bible translates Romans 1:31 thus: "They have no understanding, no fidelity, no love, no mercy."

just a soft glow filtering through the leafy treetops to my left, and soon it collapses into the horizon leaving only stygian darkness. As the only Caucasian, the driver calls my attention to the remains of a wrecked RV at the side of the road, where a German tourist died after losing control of his vehicle. I think I discern a faint note of smugness in his tone, a satisfaction in his obviously superior driving skills, but I may be imagining it. I can only see a vague outline of the wreckage and assume it was some time ago, but I later discover the crash happened only four days before. The seventy-four-year-old driver and his wife had crossed from Brazil and were heading up to Georgetown. He was killed outright, but she was still in hospital in Lethem. Had I known this, I could have visited, shown her a friendly face instead of wasting my afternoon reading ignorant hate propaganda.

After only three hours, I'm surprised when we stop at a roadhouse to sleep. I must have missed that vital detail during the booking process. Fortunately, everything is taken care of—I'm led to a little gazebo with six hammocks, into one of which I obediently climb and sleep until 4:00 a.m., when we're underway again for the remaining, gruelling ten-hour leg. It's a good thing Dad isn't still with me, as this journey might have killed him! It's easy to transplant an image of him right here next to me. He's sitting with a good, straight back and eyes closed, hands clutching the water bottle in his lap, wisps of hair blowing in the breeze from the open window. Occasionally, his leg will perform a small, involuntary stamp, and his face will wince slightly in discomfort until it passes. Other than that, he waits, uncomplaining but slowly drooping, until the journey is over. He needs to change that t-shirt.

Our speed along the potholed gravel roads is too fast for my liking, but the most dangerous moment proves to be crossing the wide Essequibo River on a rickety pontoon ferry. As the boat nears the opposite shore, an impatient passenger hops down prematurely from the lowered vehicle ramp onto the slipway. He misjudges the distance and falls, leaving his torso directly between the approaching metal lip and the rough concrete. The unstoppable momentum of the craft looks destined to slice him neatly in two. Fortunately, he manages to scramble clear at the last second, whereupon the rest of us look at each other with raised brows and puffed-out cheeks, the international facial expression for "Shit, that was close!"

Georgetown is a wild, weird Caribbean city. Hot and humid, cheerful, bustling, messy, and chock-full of character, Guyana's only large conurbation has a distinctly African vibe: market stalls piled high with leafy greens, wandering hobos, evil sewers, and minivan traffic jams. I take a room in the YWCA, the only affordable accommodation in the city. It's a clean but run-down building with shaky bunk beds and threadbare sheets. While it's a fair distance from the city centre, walking is what I do best.

Designed by the Dutch in the 18th century, Georgetown has an easily navigable grid system laid out around a series of canals, which drain the below-sea-level city bowl. While there isn't much in the way of touristic highlights, I'm delighted to just absorb the culture. With its melange of South American and Caribbean influences, Georgetown is unlike anywhere else I've been. The people are welcoming but not overpoweringly friendly, and I'm content to stroll around the various slowly rotting colonial buildings. There is the Gothic St. George's Cathedral, a towering, whitewashed structure, which, at 43.5 metres, was once the tallest wooden building in the world. It's now situated in the centre of a traffic island. Down the road is another plank behemoth, the City Hall (1889), which boasts a front-and-centre billboard proclaiming "Responsible Sexual Behaviour is your Civic Obligation. Abstain. Be Faithful. Condomize."

The cultural highlight is the prominent statue of Cuffy, hero of the 1763 Berbice slave uprising. Guyana originally consisted of three separate Dutch colonies—Berbice, Demarara, and Essequibo—which were amalgamated into a single British colony. African slaves were imported early on to work the tobacco plantations, the local indigenous population having succumbed to European diseases or escaped to the jungle. Conditions were brutal and small insurgencies common. In Berbice, slaves outnumbered Dutch settlers by ten-to-one, and

Cuffy's revolutionaries held on to their liberty for over a year before being crushed by European troops.

After Cuffy, the city sights gradually diminish in stature, from the corrugated iron clock tower of the market to the final nail in the coffin—a public toilet with its price list daubed in large, crooked letters on the door. **Urinate: $20, Deficate: $100**[45] It's been a hot day and my feet drag on the way back to the hostel, not relishing another evening alone. After all, one of the side effects of holidaying in a place where no one else goes, is that no one else goes there.

Happily, it's not to be. Back at the Y, I'm no longer the only guest. Our numbers have doubled with the addition of another Englishman, Tom. I fail to hide my surprise when I see his sunburned neck on the back stairs, but I do manage to masterfully conceal my glee at having a potential companion. By now, the fear of loneliness has trumped any nervousness I may have in introducing myself. I once visited the small town of Quiriguá in southeast Guatemala, notable only for the presence of some very tall Mayan *stelae* at the nearby archaeological site. I'd been alone for several days and was dismayed to again find myself the sole customer of the only guest house in town. I was just wondering how I could possibly cope with my own tedious company for another night when a Kiwi traveller arrived. I almost ran up and hugged him!

I don't overwhelm Tom with questions but casually enquire whether he might like to pop out for a beer later, then I scurry away to my room so as not to appear too eager. As it turns out, we get on really well. Tall and fair skinned, an infectious grin permanently in place below impish eyes, Tom's got that laid-back attitude I only seem able to emulate rather than produce naturally. Of similar ages and backgrounds, I know I can fill my jokes and humorous observations of Guyana with cultural references from home. Tom responds in kind, and we strike up an easy rapport. I've finally clicked with someone!

Down at the market area, we sample the local beer, Banks Premium, at one of the poky cubbyhole bars. Friday night revellers lounge

45 $100 Guyanese is equivalent to about $0.50 US

around on cheap plastic furniture which encroaches onto the street, their raised voices vying for dominance with the neon-lit boomboxes belting out Caribbean pop music. We're inevitably befriended by some local chaps, one of whom insists on buying us bottle after bottle of Banks until I run out of fingers to hold them. We escape his slurring generosity for a cook-up, the traditional Guyanese rice-and-beans street fayre, and end up in the Rock Zone, a heavy metal club held, bizarrely, in the local Girl Guide Hut. At one in the morning, we stumble home, where the YWCA security guard gives us a lecture on temperance and good Christian behaviour.

The Surinamese embassy, source of our next visas, is closed until Monday so Georgetown must keep us busy all weekend. We walk out to the dilapidated seawall to gaze at the North Atlantic. We visit the botanical gardens, where families lounge with weekend picnics under the gazebo. The small zoo is home to a couple of manatees, only the second ones I've ever seen. Unlike the beautiful experience I had with Captain Chocolate on my first visit to Belize, these poor creatures are condemned to swim forever in bleak, inescapable circles. They bob around in the murky water, only surfacing to breathe and have their portrait snapped by camera-wielding muppets indifferent to their suffering.

I half-heartedly make enquiries about visiting Kaieteur Falls, an impressive 250-metre high waterfall in the interior. My enthusiasm is stunted because a flight is necessary to avoid the weeklong overland journey, and tourists need to book in small aircraft groups of about eight. Even if I did miraculously find a spare seat on a tour going the next day, I don't think I could bring myself to pay several hundred dollars just to see a waterfall, even the world's largest-by-volume, single-drop waterfall. I'm too much my father's son, and I indulge myself by imagining his reaction: "So, let me get this right," I picture him saying. "You want me to get on a small aeroplane, squeezed in with a crowd of sweaty people, and sit in the sky for several hours, just in order to look out of the window at a load of water falling off a cliff?" As well as causing me to spontaneously giggle into my fist, much to Tom's bemusement, this reminds me to reply to the old man's last email.

"I've finished all the really long bus trips," I write, "so if you've been faking the prostate thing to avoid those, you can come back now for the nice, relaxing bit on the islands."

His reply is swift and sarcastic: "You are right. I was so worried about Venezuela I had to find a way to get out of it! So, which will be your first island? Do you expect to fly or sail there? I don't recall you having information on hostels there." Bless him. He's worried I won't have anywhere to stay. I'll just find somewhere on arrival, as usual.

Monday comes, and with visas clutched in our hot little hands, Tom and I catch the afternoon bus east to the Corentyne River, the border with Suriname. In some ways the opposite of Guyana, Suriname was subject to the same Dutch/English tensions, but in this case, the Dutch held on to their colony after allowing the English to take a small island off the east coast of North America. That island was called New Amsterdam, now better known as Manhattan. Smaller and more expensive even than Guyana, Suriname looks to have some stunning colonial architecture, at least from what we can see through the thunderous downpour that envelops us as we arrive. Our hostel in Paramaribo, the capital, boasts wall-to-wall Dutch teenagers doing some sort of en masse state-sponsored voluntourism, and the new dormitories and coffee shop smack of European YHA chic.

To be honest, Paramaribo (Parbo for short) is not why I'm here. It's a nice enough distraction, but I'm more interested in French Guiana further east. I try to entice Tom to join me, but he has his mind set on a Jeep tour of the interior, so we'll be parting ways here. As a consequence of the rain, I spend much of the day planning and end up booking a flight to Trinidad, for which I'll have to return to Parbo after French Guiana. Trying to schedule flights beyond Trinidad is difficult, as I don't know how long I'll want to stay there, but I scribble down numerous possible itineraries by way of preparation.

With Tom gone, I finally have an opportunity to address the thoughts that have lain siege to my brain since the conversation with my brother. Could I really have Asperger's Syndrome? Surely not. Someone would have noticed. Still, there's no need to die wondering in the age of the World Wide Web, where I easily find some simple online tests.[46] The first involves examining a series of photographs of peoples' eyes in order to discern what emotion they're displaying. Apart from the eyes, only the top of the nose and the brow are visible, but it's surprisingly easy to pick which of the multiple-choice answers is being represented in each case. The emotions on display range from the basics, such as happy and sad, to more complex states, e.g. jealous or panicked. I score 32/36; so far so good.

The next test scores the reader's responses to a set of statements to measure their Empathy Quotient (EQ) and Systemising Quotient (SQ). For example, simple statements include "I am fascinated by how machines work" and "Seeing people cry doesn't really upset me." If the reader agrees or strongly agrees with either of those, it is posited they may be lacking empathy. Harder to define feelings are also gauged, such as "I find it difficult to imagine what it would be like to be someone else," or "I can tell if someone listening to me is getting bored."

My EQ measures 30/80, certainly below average, but then most Aspergians score lower, around 20. My SQ is also low, 30/80 again, meaning my systemising abilities are not as high as I'd thought. Most Aspergians score 40 to 50. Identical EQ and SQ scores indicate I have a balanced brain. From the EQ and SQ scores an Autism Quotient (AQ) is calculated. One must remember this is intended only as a guide, not a diagnostic tool, and of course, once one knows one is taking such a test, one's responses are already skewed. My AQ is 22/50. The average score for a man is 17 and a woman 15, whereas 80% of AS testers score 32 or more, cited as "clinically significant levels of autistic traits."[47] So where does that leave me? Further research has concluded that scoring less than 26 effectively rules out AS, although 22 is clearly further along the spectrum than the average male, just over halfway to AS.

While not a definitive result, I consider this a good indication that my brother was right—I've escaped the condition. I don't know

46 Autism Research Centre.

47 Baron-Cohen, *The Essential Difference*, 163.

whether to be relieved or disappointed, though. I was warming up to the idea of being mildly autistic. After all, it's just a label; it wouldn't change who I am. I wouldn't mind being considered highly intelligent and logical, if a bit weird. I like being weird. Plus, it might be a useful excuse for some of my more dubious behaviour. I guess I'll have to put up with being thought of as just plain rude, which doesn't really bother me either.

His sad eyes stare back at me, thin hair slicked back and a rough, backstreet rendering of a butterfly vivid on his upper chest. Resignation shows on the weathered face, or perhaps pity. Either way, the man's got a powerful, haunting gaze. He's looking right through me, and I through him.

Unlike its westerly neighbours, French Guiana is still in the hands of the motherland and is categorised as a French Overseas Department. As such, I now have to deal with the euro as currency and rely on the remnants of my schoolboy French. Some things are the same, though—the majority of the population live within a narrow coastal strip serviced by a single main road over multiple river mouths, and the interior is heavily jungled and expensive to visit. I'm not even going as far as the capital, Cayenne. My goal is a small city called Kourou about halfway across the enclave and, specifically, the small group of islands eleven kilometres offshore.

The *Îles du Salut* are three rugged rocks protruding from the waves of the North Atlantic like the knuckles of a clenched fist. From 1852 to 1953, they served as part of a brutal penal colony where the very worst of French criminals were transported. Translated as 'Islands of Salvation,' the name was optimistic; there was no salvation here, spiritual or otherwise. It's estimated that 40 percent of newly arrived detainees perished within their first two years from disease, overwork, punishment, or flat-out murder, and only a fraction of the eighty thousand inmates ever made it back to France. In fact, the islands were so called because they offered an escape from the terrifying conditions on mainland South America—heat and humidity, violent storms, and rampant diseases: dysentery, consumption, malaria, yellow fever, and leprosy.

For ex-con Henri Charrière, aka *Papillon* from his butterfly tattoo, the prisons, or *bagnes* of French Guiana were home for eleven years. Arrested in 1931 for the murder of a pimp (of which he always claimed innocence), he was sentenced to life. As a boy, I absorbed the exploits that rampaged through his 1970 autobiography, *Papillon*, with childish faith, and re-lived them in the subsequent Hollywood film starring Steve McQueen and Dustin Hoffman. Papillon's portrait on the book's back cover, his mournful expression staring forever into the camera lens, frozen in time, has never left me.

Although Dad, who introduced me to the book, found the tale fascinating, he had a hard time believing it in its entirety. It was a monster of a tome that detailed Henri's horrific captivity, adventures, and numerous escape attempts. At twelve years old, my impressionable young mind was captivated by the gory anecdotes, the courage of the protagonist, and an exotic land as remote to me as Disneyland or the moon. Now, some thirty years later, I'm on a day trip from the mainland to see for myself the setting of this story. I wish Dad could have been here, if only for today. I'm convinced this would have been another Panama Canal!

The three islands had, and still maintain, individual characters. While most of the penal colony was situated near the border with modern-day Suriname, the ruins of which I poked around on my way to Kourou, *Île Royale* served as isolation for the most troublesome cons. *Île Saint-Joseph* had an even more fearsome reputation as home of the *réclusion disciplinaire*, or solitary confinement cells, and diminutive *Île du Diable*, or Devil's Island, was initially a leper colony before being reserved exclusively for political prisoners. Landing there by boat was so treacherous that access was, for many years, by a basic two-hundred-metre cable car system from *Île Royale.* Escape from the islands was deemed impossible due to ferocious currents and shark-infested waters.

Charrière wrote graphically of his incarceration, the brutality of the guards, the years of solitary confinement, and his unbreakable will to escape. According to his account, he established himself as a hard man from the start: he feigned insanity, he fought sharks, he killed other inmates, he stole boats, and once got as far as Colombia before being arrested and returned.[48] As a young reader, I was with him all the way, rooting for his cause, suffering with him in the dark, and yearning for his escape from the physical and psychological torture.

Today, it's hard to reconcile Papillon's gruesome escapades with the tranquil scenery of *Île Royale*, where I and about twenty French tourists disembark from the tour catamaran.

Unfeasibly clear shallows around the landing dock reveal a languid sea turtle nosing among the weeds, and tall palm trees line the shore, waving in the gentle breeze. The sea is calm and inviting. Once the administrative centre of the islands, the near-equatorial sun shines down on well-tended gardens, handsome colonial stone buildings, and a modern cafeteria serving cool drinks. The central structures have been converted into a reception area, museum, and an *auberge* for those wanting to stay overnight. It's just a little *too* pleasant. In fact, it wouldn't be impossible to see the word 'paradise' used to describe this place in a glossy tourist brochure, but for the men who arrived here in shackles 150 years ago, it represented a living hell.

A short walk away sit the roofless ruins of the former prison blocks. The cells are eerie, some with metal shackles still attached ominously to the walls. Knowledge of the atrocities committed here lends the scene a grisly ambience, but open to the blue sky, most of the bleakness is cleansed, the flaking walls and rusty manacles are rendered harmless, and the morbid atmosphere disabled. These sanitised relics are fascinating, but there are darker places here; I can feel it.

Next, I make a circuit of the coastal path around the twenty-eight-hectare island, virtually alone since the majority of tourists stay close to the coolness of the café or the well-trodden paths of the free guided tour. From Charrière's memories, having replaced the ones I could never have had, I vividly recall the pig pens, the sanatorium, the lighthouse, and the chapel. A cemetery haunts this lonely stretch of shore,

48 Charrière, *Papillon*.

the headstones engraved with the names of long-dead wardens and their families.

"There was no cemetery for *Bagnards,"* explained Papillon. "When a convict died, he was thrown into the sea at sunset between Saint-Joseph and Royale, in a place that was infested with sharks."[49]

When I catch a glimpse of *Île du Diable* through the trees, I'm confused. Devil's Island is represented in Charrière's book, and especially the film, as being girt by fearsome cliffs and battered by waves, yet I see a low, forested hump with a rocky shore sloping gently into the sea. His escapology career apparently culminated in a final, successful attempt here, where he threw himself into the sea on a raft of coconuts, but it looks more like he could have strolled in to bathe. In fact, I couldn't find any evidence Charrière had resided on Devil's Island at all. I sigh, struggling to square the reality with an image that has existed in my head for thirty years. As a young lad, the privations Charrière was subjected to lodged in my imagination and blossomed to mythical proportions, although nowadays it's accepted that much of what he wrote was fabricated or borrowed from the experiences of other prisoners. When questioned on the accuracy of his memoir, Henri blithely stated: "I didn't have a typewriter with me."

Alone on the shore, among the graves and scattered ruins, I can feel the evil of the penal colony; I can see it when I close my eyes. *Île Royale* has whet my appetite, but I don't sense ghosts here. I don't feel the hairs sticking up on the back of my neck, the shiver of true misery, the echo of human suffering. Where are you, Papi?

I find him on *Île Saint-Joseph*. No restoration works here; the path from the jetty leads uphill into dense foliage, the canopy darkening the afternoon air to a dingy twilight. As my eyes adjust, I see the walls, looming outlines of the most feared structures in the colony—the solitary confinement cells which were the sole preserve of this island. This is *la mangeuse d'hommes*—the eater of men.

"It was hard to believe that a country like mine, France, the cradle of liberty for the entire world, the land which gave birth to the rights of

49 Charrière, *Papillon*, 252.

man, could maintain, even in French Guiana, an installation as barbarously repressive as the *Réclusion* of Saint-Joseph," wrote Charrière. "Those who planned this place must have been loathsome monsters, vicious and cunning psychopaths wallowing in sadistic hatred for the prisoners."[50] Here Papillon spent years of his life locked in the darkness as punishment for failed escape attempts, both the book and the film vividly realising the isolation and hopelessness therein.

The prison warden in the film told inmates the brutal truth: "The rule here is total silence. We make no pretence of rehabilitation here. We're not priests, we're processors. We process dangerous men into harmless ones. This we accomplish by breaking you, physically and spiritually. Put all hope out of your mind, and masturbate as little as possible. It drains the strength."[51] Silence prevails even now, the solid, incorruptible silence of densely growing trees. The rustling of agoutis in the undergrowth makes barely a dent in the stillness. You can almost hear the trees growing, their roots curling around the foundations of these ghost structures. With the slow-motion violence of time, they'll rip them asunder, their trunks filling the erstwhile corridors and tiny cells, life at last taking back the island from the squalid order of the colony.

Derelict and choked with jungle, the solitary confinement cells still exude an aura of cramped and gloomy claustrophobia. Each cell is five paces long, its thick walls, pierced only by a small, iron door, are three metres high with a ceiling made of iron bars "as thick as streetcar tracks," with guards patrolling walkways above the back-to-back cells. Little sunlight penetrated from the roof of the building, about seven metres above the ground, to the bottom of the cell, and even now, with the roof gone, my eyes struggle to make out details in the murk. The door was not to be opened for the entire term of confinement, sometimes several years long.

It's here I finally connect with Henri's ghost, in the whisper of rustling leaves, the squawking of macaws, and chattering of capuchin monkeys. Just like his spirit animal, he was hard to pin down.

50 Charrière, *Papillon*, 227.
51 Schnaffner, *Papillon*.

Charrière eventually admitted his autobiography was only about 75 percent accurate, although French journalist Gerard de Villiers claimed in his book *Butterfly Pinned* that the figure was more like 10 percent.[52] Undoubtedly, the reality is somewhere in between. While part of me is disappointed the tale I believed so passionately, the hero I rooted for as a boy, may not have been 100 percent *bona fide*, the rest of me is thrilled to be here, now, with his spirit beside me.

The moment is brief. Papillon stares through me once again, like he always did, from the garish Technicolor cover of the original paperback book. The butterfly on his chest, symbol of flight, escapes into the jungle with a flutter of iridescent wings. He's gone. After floating from the islands to the mainland, he sailed to Venezuela where, after a short term of further incarceration, he was eventually released as a citizen. After thirty years of freedom, gainfully employed as a restaurateur in Caracas, he died of throat cancer in 1973, a couple of months after I was born. Did you find salvation, Henri, or did you escape it?

"Hey, you bastards. I'm still here!" shouts Papillon in the final line of the movie. I know he is. I can feel him.

That evening I receive another email from Dad: "Hey! Four days and no reply from you. Where are you now?" It's unlike him to be so impatient, but he goes on to relate good news: "I'm told over the phone that the biopsy result is okay. Since the purpose of the test was to check for cancer, I assume that means there isn't any. Waiting now to see consultant again."

I shoot back: "I'm in French Guiana. Sorry if I forgot to reply. All is fine, flying to Trinidad day after tomorrow."

I must have caught him at his computer because he replies straightaway: "I thought we'd lost touch. You must at least let me know what I'm missing. What did you think of the Guianas? If you give me a hostel name or telephone number, I can call you on Skype, in Trinidad

52 de Villiers, *Papillon Épinglé.*

perhaps. Stay well." I'm too tired right now to type out adventures and plans. I'll reply from Port of Spain.

The wise thing would have been to book a seat on the 4:00 a.m. bus to Parbo, but 4:00 a.m. has always been a bit of a watershed for me. I refuse to accept it ever being necessary to be awake at this hour, never mind to climb out of a comfy hammock in favour of standing, shivering, at a bus stop. It's this stubbornness that sees me standing, shivering, at a bus stop on the edge of Kourou at 8:00 a.m. The thing is, due to torrential flooding caused by another outstanding tropical cloudburst, all post-dawn buses have been cancelled, and I'm left, drenched, by the side of the road with my thumb out. Vehicles are few and far between, and those that do pass elect to spray me with floodwaters rather than stop to pick me up. I don't blame them.

I'm acutely aware my flight leaves in less than eighteen hours from a different country, arguably a completely different continent since I'm technically in France, and this adds somewhat to my growing concern. With every passing minute, I become more frantic—and more wet—but eventually, a kind motorist does pull over and gives me a start. It takes three lifts and a fistful of euros to reach the Suriname border, from where, thankfully, a shared taxi delivers me back in Parbo with several hours to spare.

I book an airport transfer for 2:30 in the morning, obviating the need for a bed. The hostel where I stayed previously allows me to sleep on its chilly porch, where the driver will find me. To my surprise, I bump into Tom, who was supposed to be exploring deepest, darkest Suriname. He tells me cheerfully that one of the main rivers was so swollen by floodwaters it became impassable, and his vehicle was forced to turn back. With a whole evening in hand, Tom and I celebrate our unexpected reunion by heading to our favourite waterfront dive to drink Parbo beer with the locals.

Four hours, eight beers, and a short stagger later, Tom lets me inside the hostel to sleep on the sofa rather than camping out on the porch in the rain and wind. It's a great idea comfort-wise, no doubt, but one that wastes a fair bit of money. Although I do remember to set my alarm for 2:00 a.m., the gentle beeping fails to penetrate the blanket of fermented hops and soft cushions, and I slumber on. Failing to find me in the porch, the driver leaves without me. Thankfully, my brain has become conditioned, even in this state, to look out for me. An hour later, something buried deep within the ether of my soul clicks, and I jerk awake. A Sunday morning in Paramaribo is definitely not Kings Cross Station at rush hour, but I somehow manage to flag down a taxi and make it to the airport just in time.

"What can I do for you?" smiles the Trinidadian gentleman as he extends his hand. I've made the mistake of stopping briefly to examine the map in my guidebook, making sure I'm still en route to my chosen guest house, thus drawing attention to myself. I frown back, hunching my shoulders, but my innate Britishness cannot refuse his proffered palm, which I clutch as briefly as politeness allows. The Parbo vice currently gripping my head around the temples is not helping my sociability either.

I've inured myself to hustlers the world over, become accustomed to peremptorily brushing them aside, but this time, I hesitate. He's only the second person I've met in this country, the first being the taxi driver who brought me to Port of Spain from the airport. I've only been here an hour and the Caribbean is already depleting my resources exponentially, but apparently, airport buses don't run on the Sabbath. I've barely had time to get my bearings in Independence Square before this character is on to me, but I shouldn't pre-judge the poor man, hustler or not.

"I'm fine, thanks," I reply as courteously as I can, while intimating he can leave me alone now. I do this by studiously examining my guidebook and comparing it to the surrounding streets. There is a preponderance of litter, fried chicken shops, and pedestrians, some in their church best and others, like this guy, in well-worn but clean attire. He's still here.

"I can help you find anything at all." He grins. "No charge. Are you looking for a hotel?"

"I've already got one," I reply. "Pearl's." It's the cheapest place listed in the Lonely Planet and is only a few blocks away. I march confidently off in the right direction.

"Ah, Pearl's," he agrees, matching my stride. "Good choice. I'll take you there."

"There's no need," I say, my tone getting increasingly brusque. I imagine that once we arrive at the place I was already going, he'll either ask me for a tip or enter with me and imply to the owner that he brought me and is deserving of a cut from them. Or both.

He smiles. "Oh, it's no problem. There's no charge. My name's Marcus. What's yours?"

I give in, too hungover to resist. There's no law against walking with someone, and he seems friendly enough. I tell him my name and answer the barrage of questions that follow; by the time we arrive at Pearl's, I'm surprised at how much I've shared with him.

"They don't allow non-guests inside the hotel," he advises as we arrive, "but, please, if you need anything else while you are in Port of Spain—a tour, a taxi, anything—please call me!" He presses a piece of paper into my hand, his scribbled phone number, and saunters away down the street.

Well, he seemed nice, I think as I check in. I desperately need a shower and a nap but also to plan my Caribbean odyssey. I have just two weeks to reach Cuba and have been tearing out my hair trying to formulate an itinerary encompassing a reasonable number of countries with enough time at each. There are twenty-eight nations, states, and overseas territories in my path, which equates to about half a day apiece, excluding travel time, should I visit them all. Of course, that would be ludicrous, so difficult choices must be made: Barbados or Dominica? Haiti or Jamaica? It's a painful process.

Then there is the hassle of aeroplane tickets, ferry schedules, limited accommodation, and "island time"—the built-in lateness factor applicable to anywhere that reveres Bob Marley. Out of my natural element of off-the-cuff dorms, buses, and street food, the whole process is absolute anathema, but I know if I don't book ahead, airfares will double, and I'll be forced to pay through the nose for accommodation. Just thinking about it doubles my headache, so I lie down and try to close my eyes for a while.

I fail. Crapulence still thumping in my ears, I shower and get busy with a razor. I'm just wiping the shaving foam from my ears when I hear my name called from the corridor. The manager must need some detail or other from my passport, I reason, but I wouldn't have expected him to call me Dan. He sounds different, too. I open my bedroom door and step into the corridor, but it's not the manager at all.

A few years ago, I played an evil trick on my sister. I was living in South Africa when her thirtieth birthday came around, by which time I hadn't seen her for a couple of years. Gerda and I hatched a scheme to gate-crash her party and surprise her, and to that end, we secretly bought flights to the UK. Frustratingly, though, she decided on an extravagant weekend in New York in lieu of a birthday bash, completely stymieing our plans. This left us spending most of our holiday without her, with no alternative but to drop the bombshell when she landed back in Birmingham.

With Christmas approaching, I got even sneakier—I donned a cheap Santa Claus outfit and accompanied my parents to the airport. As she appeared in the arrivals hall to greet them, I approached like a beggar, hiding behind a face full of white, nylon beard, and proffered my festive cap.

"Spare any change?" I mumbled.

She politely refused and turned back to her husband who (along with airport security) was in on the stunt. I persisted in my shuffling and muttering routine, and only on the third pass did she twig who was behind the disguise. Then she cracked, flung her arms around me and wept for several minutes. At the time, I was bemused at this outpouring of emotion; I was expecting surprise, a double take, a laugh, and a punch on the arm, but not this. Now, however, I understand it completely.

The last thing I ever expected to see in that Trinidadian hotel corridor was him, my old dad, standing there as if he'd been with me the whole time. My step falters as my eyes lock in their sockets, like steel balls transfixed by electromagnetic saucers in a pinball machine. The scene is so improbable that I assume someone's placed a life-sized cardboard cutout of him there for a joke, complete with unfashionable sunhat tied tightly under the chin. The hint of a mischievous twinkle in his eyes is moderated by a couched nervousness that lingers only until he's definitely sure it's me, then he raises his brow as if he just popped round to borrow a cup of sugar.

When I finally believe my eyes, I run forward to embrace him, utterly overcome with emotion. I sob uncontrollably, clutching tightly at his ridiculous fishing vest, my face buried in his grizzled, dandruffy beard. I can't explain why, but I feel like I've been hit with a tear grenade—my brain just collapses, giving way totally to the urge to blubber. "It was the shock rather than the emotion," he'd said of the death of his mother. "It was out of my control." I'm experiencing something similar right now.

I can't speak for minutes, rendered mute in this mingled shock and relief. Half-formed words escape my mouth like an exhausted athlete. "Wha . . .?" I gasp. "Wha—How . . .?" His face mirrors my bemusement at my Christmas trick, but he stands there and gamely tolerates the grown man shaking in his arms. Oh, yes, he's stitched me up good and proper.

"About a week ago you sent me an email update, casually joking that if the whole episode had been a hoax to escape the hard bus journeys across Venezuela and Guyana, I could come back now," he explains once I've recovered. "Then on Friday you happened to mention you were flying to Trinidad on Sunday morning."

This seed of information germinated into an idea, and he began to think to himself, *I could, you know. I could do it!* He must have booked his flights immediately and gone straight to the airport, without a word to anyone.

"I came to keep you company," he adds. "That's my job!"

What a guy! I start blubbering all over again. That's twice he's done this to me in a month! But isn't he still sick? What about his prostate? He can't possibly have had surgery and recovered already. Apparently, his doctor has set a date for the operation and fixed him up to be much more comfortable until then. He now has a long-term catheter with a tap arrangement to drain his bladder, and he can move about almost normally. It's actually better than before the yacht trip that broke him.

Now, for the big question: how the hell did he find me?

"I arrived last night and stayed near the airport," he explains. "I'd planned to meet your flight, but I was still on UK time, so I got up late and missed you. I came to town, determined to find Port of Spain's cheapest hotel, for that was where I knew I would find you." I chuckle inwardly. I guess I'm that predictable.

"That wasn't necessary however, for as soon as I arrived at Independence Square, I was approached by a friendly fellow. 'What are you looking for?' he asked. 'My son,' I replied. 'And what is your son's name?' asked the man. 'Dan,' I told him. 'Dan?' repeated Marcus (for it was he). 'Studied Chemical Engineering? Cricket fan? Follow me.' "

Dad was flabbergasted. He's always been proud of his ability to locate people, but this was a hole-in-one in a city of fifty thousand people. Marcus duly brought him to Pearl's, received fifteen American dollars for his enterprise, and went his merry way. I can't communicate how happy I am to have humoured him instead of brushing him off. There might be a lesson there, somewhere.

When I manage to get myself under control, we check Dad in and I call Gerda, waking her in the middle of the night to tell her the news. I'm just so overwhelmingly happy that I have to share it with someone, but as soon as she answers, I dissolve into sobs again.

"What's the matter?" she asks immediately, panic strong in her faraway voice.

"You won't believe—" I choke on the words. "I can't—the most unbelievable thing . . . just happened," I squeeze between sniffs and gasps. "I—I can't believe someone would do that for me." My breath shudders. "It's just . . . s-so amazing!"

"What?" she asks, urgently. "What happened?"

"He—he came back!" I blurt, and eventually manage to stutter out the basic facts of the tale.

She gasps when I'm done. "Oh my goodness, that's incredible! I'm so, so happy for you!" Sharing the news seems to calm me down a little, and, of course, it's lovely to hear my wife's voice. My breathing has almost returned to normal by the time we say our goodbyes, and I turn back to Dad, reassure myself I wasn't hallucinating, and take a deep breath.

"So, what do you want to do now?" I ask, wiping the last tears from my cheeks.

"Whatever you want," he says. "You're the captain."

And that sets me off again.

Part III

Hello, Again

Chapter 12

Retrouvaille

It's as though he'd never left. We venture into Port of Spain to find him a latte and talk about the price of gold. As we walk, I find myself swiftly reprogramming my head. I can't believe he's back!

Apart from the obvious benefits of companionship, what logistical impact will his return have? Pretty much none at all. With no pre-booked accommodation and only a single onward flight, my travel flexibility reigns supreme. All we need do is purchase a second ticket to Grenada and we're good.

"I've left a few things behind this time," he announces, sashaying his hips as he walks to some private music in his head. "Some paperwork I never needed, the cotton sleep sheet and mosquito net, and my old shoes." He's had his dodgy toenail fixed and finally admitted that the shoes I made him buy before we set out are comfortable enough to trust.

"And . . ." He pauses for effect. "I'm happy!"

I stop in my tracks, unsure I've heard correctly, as he gives me a too-big smile that would look outright fake on anyone else. "Pardon?"

"I'm happy," he beams, like happiness is something he's only seen in films and never thought would apply to him.

"How do you mean . . . happy?" My brain is still struggling with the concept.

"The magic pills! The Sertraline! It's working. I'm no longer depressed!"

I recall now the tablets had a lead time of six weeks, but our Colombian disaster happened before they had time to fully kick in. Of course!

"Wow, when did this happen?" I ask, feeling the warm glow of happiness myself.

"Well, it didn't start on a particular day," he replies as we resume walking. "It builds up as you take it and you just don't feel so bad so often. It's a gradual thing. Also, I've discovered an ability to spend money! It's probably another effect of the pills, but I had no trouble buying this last-minute flight to Trinidad." He doesn't mention how much it cost, and I don't ask.

"Actually, I've realised where we inherited our stinginess genes—from my grandfather on my mother's side." My great-grandfather Walter,[53] a pattern maker for industrial equipment, served as a machine gunner in WWI. I've never known anything about him except his name. "Whenever he visited us, we would have to turn the electric fire off, because if he saw me and Michael playing in the front room with the fire on, he would consider it a waste of money. 'Your mother can't afford this,' he'd grumble. When he had to go to hospital, I believe they took him on the back of a lorry because he wasn't prepared to pay any expenses to get there."

Sounds like one of us, alright! Discounting the gene theory, though, is my own miserliness purely a result of my low-income lifestyle, or is it something deeper? Did I, throughout childhood, witness Dad's thrifty ways and subconsciously absorb them as a behavioural model? It seems possible. After all, many young people with poorly paid jobs spend money as if they expect to be hit by lightning tomorrow. Most of them buy on credit: cars, phones, computers, homes. I've never had a credit card, let alone a mortgage. I haven't used an overdraft facility since I graduated.

"I'm very careful with money nowadays," Mum told me once. "And I'm grateful to Peter for that. Whenever I'd suggest buying something or getting work done, he'd squawk, 'How much?' just

53 As distinguished from my grandfather, Walter, on my father's side.

like Arkwright in *Open All Hours.*[54] 'Do you know how many hours I have to work to earn that much money?' he'd splutter. And sometimes he'd even try to calculate it!" I must admit, I've had a similar influence on my wife's spending habits, and I don't consider it a bad thing.

Now that I know AS can be hereditary, I take the opportunity to ask Dad if he thinks his father might have been affected.

"Yes, he would have been one undoubtedly," comes the reply. "A very remote figure, not good with children, never showed any emotion. He's another one who should never have got married, but that's what people did in those days."

On finding a café, he offers to buy me breakfast, and caught up in the joyful mood, I agree. Of course, it turns out he doesn't have any Trinidad and Tobago dollars, so I end up paying for us both. I roll my eyes. Ah, yes, it's good to have him back.

"So, what shall we talk about?" he asks, unfolding his arms and arching his back with a grunt. Where to start? I'll give him a rundown on my South American adventures later. Right now, I'm curious to know how he coped with the temporary adjournment of our voyage.

I begin cautiously, "How did you feel—"

"Wait!" he interrupts. "I can't hear when I'm yawning. Hang on, I'm not yawning. I'm stretching." It's true. He is.

"Can you hear when you're stretching?" I smirk.

"No."

"Right. I'm glad we clarified that." I wait until he's finished doing whatever it is he's doing. "So, how did you feel having to leave Colombia?"

"Well," he says, after the usual pause for thought, "you're talking emotions now. An emotional response would be disappointment. I can't remember feeling disappointment. It was just a fact. Leaving was what I had to do. That was the process. 'Oh, dear, now I've got to go.' "

54 A well-known 1970s UK sitcom.

"Ah-ha," I pounce. "If you thought, 'Oh, dear,' then surely that's a display of emotion?"

He shakes his head. "It was a disruption in what you had expected the sequence of events to be, an inconvenience to you to change your plans, hence 'Oh, dear' on your behalf."

"You apologised to me, though," I point out. "Doesn't that mean you were sorry?"

"Not exactly," he hedges. "I had told you I was going to spend three months with you, and then I wasn't going to. That merits an apology, doesn't it? I apologised because I'd said something and not followed through with it. Whether you were disappointed or not is neither here nor there."

I persevere, propelled by optimism despite his inadvertent bluntness. "Could you tell I was disappointed?"

"No, I don't remember you expressing great disappointment," he decides.

I was blinking back tears when I met him in Cartagena. Can he not have noticed that, or has he forgotten?

"But then Aspergians are notoriously selfish," he continues. "We don't think about other people; we only have interest in what affects us directly and at that time. If something doesn't directly concern me, I'm not even listening. Look at your brother, Matthew. He's only ever concentrating on what's about to happen to him in his little world, which is a typical AS characteristic."

By now I can't hide the hint of supplication that gilts my voice. "But you seemed like you were genuinely sorry for me."

"I can't remember." He shrugs. "Yes, I am capable of being genuinely sorry if I've done something to inadvertently offend somebody, definitely more so if it was an error on my part. If something is totally out of my control, then I'm not going to feel as sorry as if I did something accidentally or made a wrong decision."

"Oh. Like going on a long boat journey, you mean?" My tone is so pointed we could skewer a goat on it and have ourselves a nice spit roast, but it's tempered with a grin.

"Yes."

"So maybe you felt sorry for that decision?"

"No, I didn't feel sorry for that. It was a bad decision in hindsight, but not in foresight."

I sigh. I don't know what to say. A man prone to seasickness going on a five-day yacht trip over rough seas seemed like a bad decision to me from the very beginning, but I decide not to pursue it.

Dad's inconsistent statements about his own empathy and emotion are frustrating. Most of the time he claims not to understand or feel emotions, yet sometimes he clearly displays them.

"I don't express emotion but that doesn't mean to say it's not there," he says when I press him. "It doesn't mean I'm not enjoying something just because I don't express it."

Similarly, sometimes he denies having empathy, and other times he admits he does but doesn't display it. He gives money to charity, clearly an empathic reaction, and sometimes in considerable amounts. I remember once standing with him in a train station when a scruffy man approached and asked him directly for some change.

"Oh, of course!" he replied without hesitation, digging his hand into his pocket and retrieving a handful of coins, which he handed over without counting. He made it look so natural, like it was the only reasonable thing to do. He explains this away as common sense: "It is logical that those who have little should value small amounts of money more than me. It's no problem to part with a sum I won't even miss."

One explanation is that he displays deep or 'emotional' empathy, but not shallow or 'cognitive' empathy.[55] This would explain why he claims to feel empathy, for instance, for sad people and characters in films, but consistently displays a non-understanding of reading the emotions of other people in the room. Armed with this theory, I ask him again, straight out, whether or not he feels empathy.

"The problem is that I don't know whether I've got what other people have got. If I think I'm empathising with a situation, I don't know whether another person might feel stronger or different about

55 See Appendix IV

it. Tears come more readily now that I'm old, but it's usually not to do with real situations, more fictional ones. It's sadness that causes me to be sad for other people."

"But that is empathy!"

"Then I'm telling you that I do have empathy," he concludes, his inflection drawing a line under the debate. "Today, at least." It occurs to me his ability to empathise may have improved with age, although I wouldn't have thought that was something that could evolve after the initial childhood learning phase. I suppose it depends on the individual. Maybe if he lives long enough, he'll eventually pass for a normal human being.

On a tedious Monday afternoon in June 1994, I came home from university and switched on the television to see sporting history being pummelled for six. I'd told Marcus the truth about being a cricket fan. My home team back then was Warwickshire, and their ground at Edgbaston was a short bus ride from my digs. I used to go regularly to Sunday games. In fact, I'd been only the day before. Warwick had recently signed the already legendary West Indian batsman, Brian Lara, as their prime overseas player, and I was excited to catch some of the fireworks that had earned him the highest ever test match score of 375 a couple of months previously.

I'd been disappointed. Although my team won the match against Durham, Lara had scored a dismal six runs before being dismissed. Maybe all the fuss was unjustified, I thought. The Sunday league games were played as a break from the more important four-day county games that ran from Thursday to Monday. The result of that Sunday match, also against Durham, would certainly be a draw due to rain on Saturday, but Lara used the dead time to build his overnight score of 111 into a towering plinth to support his life's work. When I slumped onto the sofa after a hard day of engineering chemicals, Lara had topped 400. The record for a first-class inning was 499 by Pakistani, Hanif Mohammed, in 1959, and it looked like the diminutive

Trinidadian might go all the way. I was torn—should I stay and watch on television or race to the ground to see it with my own eyes? He might be out any ball, and if so, I'd have wasted my money and missed the dismissal. On the other hand, I could be seeing history made.

Laziness won out and I stayed at home, a decision I'll forever regret as Brian went on to become the only batsman ever to reach, and exceed, a quintuple century. His score of 501, not out, achieved on the penultimate ball of the match, is a record that still stands today. I mention all this because although Port of Spain has little in the way of tourist attractions, the undoubted highlight is the bronze statue of local legend Lara, one of the greatest batsmen ever to smack willow against leather.

After 'meeting' Brian, the rest of the city pales in comparison. Trinidad was first claimed for the Spanish by Christopher Columbus in 1498 and remained in their hands until Britain wrangled control in the early nineteenth century. Consequently, most of the places of interest are dilapidated colonial buildings. Port of Spain is also the country's industrial hub and suffers from the attendant poverty and crime issues, although I can imagine the streets transforming into epic party zones come the famous Carnival. Unfortunately, we're a couple of months late for that particular shindig.

It's back at Pearl's where the real interest of the day lies, in unfolding our path to Cuba. The route is largely determined by the scarcity of flights into Cuba and the LIAT (Leeward Islands Air Transport) airline schedule. Barbados is discounted as too expensive, and I'm sadly forced to ditch Haiti, the most intriguing country en route, and Dominica, a hiker's paradise. Our final itinerary will be Trinidad, Grenada, St. Vincent and the Grenadines, St. Lucia, Antigua, Dominican Republic, then Cuba.

Booking the flights, however, is easier said than done. The lumbering LIAT website, combined with my bank's online Visa security check, refuses to accept my debit card more than once. There are rare occasions when not counting a credit card in my arsenal of payment options does cause frustration, such as when I need to hire a car and the rental company refuses to accept a deposit from anyone who doesn't conform to society's ridiculous addiction to living on other people's money. Today is another example, but in this case, Dad's impressive array of bank accounts comes to the rescue. And fortunate we are that he has such a gang of flexible friends, for each one is only accepted once by the LIAT website. We need four separate cards to complete the string of bookings, but in the end, we're successful. Presumably, there is a LIAT agent somewhere in Port of Spain, but without this man and his prial of plastic, my job would certainly have been harder. Hooray once more for his unexpected return!

The ground before me gives way to an oily, bubbling, glutinous pond; a wide, wet vat of sticky liquid, its black surface absorbing all the light and heat of the day. This patch of goo, otherwise known as Pitch Lake, appealed to me as the most interesting sight on Trinidad, and we've come from the other end of the island to have a gander. I also judged it would appeal to Dad's scientific nature, and, indeed, he was curious enough to come along.

I'd never really wondered what asphalt was or from whence it came. I guess I assumed it was some icky substance made by humans out of oil for the purpose of road building—so I'm surprised to discover much of the world's natural supply actually seeps from the ground around this small hole in the Caribbean. Although now synthesised from petroleum, for a long time this very place, along with a handful of smaller sites in the Americas, was the source of all pitch.

As we approach the natural oddity from the car park, it resembles nothing more than a thick, matte-black skin, wrinkled and lumpen like the hide of an elephant, accompanied by a sulphurous odour. To say it seeps may seem misleading, as the semi-liquid substance is actually quite stable. The University of Queensland in Australia has been running their famous Pitch Drop experiment since 1930, in which pitch is left to flow from a funnel into a beaker below.[56] Such is its

56 The University of Queensland.

viscosity (230 billion times that of water), it takes approximately fourteen years for each drop to form and detach, and nobody has ever been around to see one fall.

The pitch here can actually be walked over in some places, although clambering around without the knowledge of a local guide to steer one away from the softer spots would be foolhardy. After all, the lake has swallowed trees, livestock, and even vehicles over the years, and has in turn spewed forth precious artefacts including the bones of a prehistoric giant sloth and the tooth of a mastodon. I wouldn't want to be the first tourist to prove his stupidity by sacrificing himself to the underworld. In pre-colonial times, the Amerindians believed the gods created the lake as a punishment for wrongdoers, and legend tells of an entire tribe that was swallowed by the earth after they dined on hummingbirds, believed to be the souls of departed ancestors.

But seep it does, in a circular motion in a vertical plane, rising up from the bowels of the earth in the centre of the lake, then slowly creeping outwards to the edges before being sucked back under. This we learn from the man who furtively emerges from the bushes around the car park to offer his services. Through an awesome white beard, which contrasts beautifully with his shiny black head, he explains the details of the lake in a Caribbean accent almost as thick as the soup of tar itself. He tells us the history of the site, the uses of the product, and its current extraction and refinement by the state-owned Lake Asphalt of Trinidad and Tobago.

The largest of the world's natural asphalt lakes was shown to Sir Walter Raleigh by the local Carib indigenous people in 1595. He used it to re-caulk his ship before going on to capture the island from the Spanish garrison stationed here. In his diary he wrote about "the abundance of stone pitch, that all the ships of the world may be therewith laden from thence, and wee made trial of it in trimming our shippes to be most excellent good, and melteth not with the sunne as the pitch of Norway, and therefore for shippes trading the South parts very profitable,"[57] meaning it was a valuable resource for a seafaring

57 Abraham, *Asphalts and Allied Substances,* 42.

nation seeking to conquer the New World. Although the days of wooden tall ships and conquistadors are long gone, the lake found new value in the late nineteenth century as a source of asphalt for road building, a use which continues to this day. Currently over three hundred tons of the black stuff are extracted from the lake every year. The total volume of the seventy-six-metre deep site is estimated to be ten million tons.

"Wasn't that interesting?" I declare, hustling Dad aboard the minibus back to Port of Spain.

"Not particularly," he replies, taking his seat.

Charming, I think, but he gets his comeuppance minutes later when the driver is collecting the fares and he drops loose change all over the floor. I sit back and chortle as he kneels creakily down to retrieve it. "Wait until I tell Gerda you had me scrabbling around in front of all these people for one cent!" he threatens from shoe level.

"What?" I straighten my back. "But that's not true!"

He grins. "Yes, but she'll believe me."

She would as well. In public, she'll side with anyone against me, but I don't mind because in private she's all mine. I still find it hard to believe I was chosen among all her other suitors. I just can't fathom it out, and neither can my friends or family who regularly remind me that I'm "punching above my weight." On the face of it, we're very different. She loves dining out and appreciates fine wines; I drink beer and prefer to cook. She's a churchgoing Christian; I'm a confirmed atheist. She's a proper lady; I still dress like I'm a teenager. Somehow, though, it works, and brilliantly at that.

That evening we decide to work up an appetite in a bar. I don't remember him being a big drinker in my childhood, he certainly never spent any time in pubs, but if it wasn't white wine, he'd be on the scotch. I credit him with putting me off whisky for life. When I reached that age of curiosity, as every child does, and asked if I could taste his drink, he consented. When the first sip of that vile, burning liquid hit my throat, I ran to the sink to suck down as much humble Birmingham tap water as I could fit in my belly, while he stood at the mantelpiece, laughing his socks off. I haven't touched it since. Well played, sir, well played.

Tonight, though, his eyes widen in alarm on scanning the drinks menu. "I don't like whisky anymore," he announces, his wallet shrinking from the prices listed within. "What shall I drink?"

My suggestion is rum, which is cheaper by half. We're in the Caribbean, after all, not Scotland. Once served, my ears tingle at the prospect of an evening in his company. Dad told me early on that he craves intelligent conversation, and I'm one of the only people he knows who can supply it, which made me smoulder with pride. I, too, have sorely missed our discussions, but tonight, I'm content to listen to him expound on a variety of topics. Most of them I already know by heart, but I don't care; I just insert a key word and stand well back.

Film censorship: "I hate these modern films filled with sex and car chases." He grimaces. "They influence people towards casual sex. I mean, when every other film shows the main couple having it off straight after they meet, young people are going to accept that is the done thing, that it's okay. They can't, or won't, differentiate between film and real life."

Education: "I don't think education should be compulsory, it should be voluntary. If children don't want to behave, send them home. That would be better than having them in the class, being disruptive and preventing the ones who want to learn from learning. It's not going to make them worse off because they don't go to school to learn anything anyway. They go to have fun with their friends and cause trouble. What you would have instead is the facility for adults to complete their education when they realise how useful it is and decide it needs to be done. Give it to them when they want it, not by forcing it down their throats."

Fashion: "Of course I'm a follower of fashion," he protests when I scoff at his corduroy trousers and Willie Nelson t-shirt. "Otherwise, I would wear a dress."

Social psychology: "A lot of people are too lazy to think for themselves, so they just follow everyone else. As apes, our learning was based on copying, and in today's society, people do the most ridiculous things that are totally illogical and unnecessary just because other people do them. A need to conform was part of evolution and is why human beings have successfully evolved on the planet. Fitting into communities was part of the success of the human race, but nowadays, it's not logical. Generally speaking, grouping together for protection is not necessary anymore, and I'm thinking more and more that I'm not going to do something just because it's expected of me."

Religious devotees: "I envy them their faith in the afterlife and ability to endure any misery while awaiting paradise. You may label them gullible, but ill-education is usually the explanation. In small villages in Africa or the Middle East, people have no education other than what they get from their religious leaders who can tell them whatever they like. I once asked someone why he believed in God, and the answer was, 'Because everybody else does.' That's how religion survives. There are so many people who can't believe that so many other people are wrong, that they believe it, too. People don't want to stand out. At one time, they were persecuted if they denied believing in God, so they'd be very foolish to admit it. I don't look down on them. Remember, it wasn't that long ago that everyone believed the world was flat."

Age: "I'm losing the ability to process information. I can't hold facts in the air for any length of time. I'm starting to realise how stupid people must feel, all the time. Is this how they live, looking to other people to see how they should react, like sheep? I'm finding it harder and harder to structure my thoughts. It's sad, yet at the same time, I have never been happier, free from the responsibilities and pressures of youth."

Politics: "Any government's most important responsibilities are defence of the realm and law and order, leaving people to live their lives freely," he states. "However, man being man, the rich and powerful are able to take advantage of the poor and weak, so it becomes desirable to exercise some control of the situation. This is best done with legislation which limits the exploitation of the poor.

However, since the government consists of many of the rich and powerful who do the exploiting, it's easy to understand why this does not work.

"Instead, you have the advent of socialism, this ridiculous system of taking money from one class of society and giving it to another, leaving a loophole for a third class, the very rich, to slip through unscathed. This results in one group who are discontent at having their earnings stolen from them, and a second group who are deprived of the satisfaction of earning their way in life and are actually encouraged to rely on state handouts for their existence. I think it is bordering on cruelty to force people into a state of dependence." As someone who leans towards socialism, I can't sanction his viewpoint—of course we should help those less fortunate members of our society—but this new perspective is making me think deeper about something I'd always considered a simple issue.

"Just as I disapprove of inheritance and the ability to catapult young people into immense riches, thus depriving them of the satisfaction of achievement, so I disapprove of rewarding them for doing nothing. If somebody hasn't got a job, they don't make any contribution to society at all. That person is worthless." I'll charitably assume he isn't including stay-at-home parents, people on disability pensions, retirees, etc. in this bracket, but even so, one couldn't exactly accuse him of being a bleeding-heart liberal. I don't doubt AS is partially to blame for his unsympathetic opinions, plus he is an old man, and the older generation is generally more conservative in their views, so I make allowances when hearing these tirades.

"Socialism doesn't work," is always his conclusion. "It's a good idea, but it is not in people's nature to want to be equal. They will always strive to be better than somebody else."

By this time, we've demolished five rum concoctions and a couple of bowls of potato wedges. Music is filtering through from an adjacent room, which appears to be hosting a karaoke night. What happens next is one of the greatest revelations I've experienced in this entire shambolic escapade thus far: my grumpy, anti-social, semi-autistic father tells me how much he loves karaoke. Apparently, he owns a karaoke machine at home in Spain and spends hours singing to himself. If he'd admitted to dressing up as Spider-Man at superhero conventions, I couldn't have been any more surprised. This is a side of him I'd never suspected.

"It's a nice little diversion," he explains, drumming his fingers on the tabletop. "Something to do. For me to actually go out and do it in public would be a great achievement. It's a task I've set myself: other people can do this, so I need to be able to do it, too." His ears prick up when Elvis Presley becomes audible through the doorway, and he ushers me through.

Karaoke isn't my cup of tea. I love music, but self-consciousness and the inferiority of my singing voice keeps random punters safe. I've performed a couple of songs in my time, most notably in an incongruous, neon-lit venue in the Himalayan Kingdom of Bhutan, but only when well on the way to intoxication. On that occasion I recall belting out the '80s standard "Big in Japan" by Alphaville to the clients in my tour group, cunningly changing the lyrics to "Big in Bhutan." I thought it hilariously clever, them less so.

Confronted by a decent crowd and talented local singers, Dad shrinks back into his seat. He seemed close to putting his name down but now plainly feels intimidated. It's a shame; witnessing him on stage crooning, "Maybe I didn't love you quite as often as I should," would have been something to see. I've heard him sing it many times, even in the last two months, and he'd have killed it. In the late stages of my parent's marriage, in an uncharacteristic but, I thought, touching olive branch gesture, he created a framed collage of photos of my mother in her youth with the words to Elvis's "Always on My Mind" printed across it.

"Too little, too late," was all she said when I told her how lovely it was, yet she kept it on her bedside table for years.

We sit for a while in silence, while a feisty woman belts out a Tina Turner number, much to Dad's admiration. I'm content enjoying his enjoyment until the next singer begins a song I've never heard before, but which strikes a chord deep inside me.

If I could get another chance,
another walk,
another dance with him,
I'd play a song that would never ever end.
How I'd love, love, love
to dance with my father again.

I listen, captivated by the lyrics. They express such beautiful emotion that I feel myself tremble. The more he sings, the more my eyes begin to prick with fluid. The song, "Dance with My Father" by Luther Vandross, is a man's paean to his deceased parent—a bittersweet ballad which combines touching memories with a soft regret that they'll never be able to spend time together again. The message hits me loud and clear—don't waste a single day. I've been blessed with a second chance here, and I'm going to appreciate every minute of it.

It's not like we danced together often, but I remember a rare party at our house in Cornwall when I was about fourteen. We had guests down from Birmingham, and after dinner we cleared a space on the slate flagstones of the kitchen, plugged in the twin cassette deck, and danced around to the best the '80s had to offer. I was bounding around like an idiot, trying to impress the slightly-too-old-for-me daughter of the visiting family, when he approached me, smiling.

"I'm glad you've got the music, son," he said simply. He could see I had rhythm and knew how to use it, unlike my hapless brother. It was a moment between us, an instant when I felt connected to him. It made me happy, and I recommenced bouncing with renewed vigour.

"I like most music," he tells me, stumbling a little on the walk home. I take care to guide him up the kerbs, although I'm not too steady myself. Did we end up eating dinner in the end? I don't remember. "I don't enjoy heavy rock, which is just loud noise, poor lyrics, and often offensive language. I don't like rap, which sometimes has fair lyrics but fails in the music department. I have a problem with pop music that again fails with the lyrics, having one or two lines repeated and repeated, sometimes only to extend the length of the recording. You may gather that lyrics are important to me. I've discovered that many people don't listen to them and only absorb the recording as a whole. Even the singers don't bother to articulate the words too well. One has to Google the lyrics to discover what they were warbling about."

It's been a really good day, experiencing the pitch lake together, spending time chatting over drinks and then the beautiful coincidence of that song. I write its name in my notebook before I doze off. I never want to forget it.

Chapter 13

Thelemite

It begins innocently enough. "Would you like me to tell you about the old days?" he offers, and my head swivels his way. It's not as though I'm plying him with the Caribbean's finest duty-free rum purely to encourage a disclosure of his innermost secrets, not exactly, but I'm eager to hear the next part of his life story, and I don't mind topping him up while he tells it.

Our holiday apartment outside St. George's, Granada, is cheap as chips in the off-season. It's late afternoon when we arrive, so I crack the seal on our bottle of Trinidadian Angostura rum, pour a couple of measures into some faded mugs I find in the kitchen, and we sit on the porch, watching the blue sky fade to purple.

"When I was a boy, I wore short trousers all year round."

Ah. This isn't *quite* the information I was after; this sounds more like the inane ramblings of an old codger.

"I had to wash my knees every morning before school. I was eleven years old before I got my first belt." My face must look particularly crestfallen because the moment he glances at me after this verbal equivalent of juddering, black and white news footage, he bursts into laughter, clapping his hands in glee.

I allow him to enjoy the moment, drawn into smiling along with him. The hooting, cartoony sound of his delight has been as rare as the dodo's mating call, and I've no wish to interrupt it for anything. After another sip of amber fluid to calm the mirth, he relents and tells me what I really want to hear.

On his return to England, Dad had immediately felt himself slipping back into depression. "I had been out of it while abroad, but then I started to get the shakes every time I drove to work," he tells me. "I knew I couldn't stay there." He'd given up his dream job in Spain for a subtle, drawn-out form of suicide.

Fortunately, not long afterwards Mike decided to relocate his family to Cornwall. He took most of his machines with him, and his best client, and pretty much started from scratch. Dad encouraged the move and helped out enormously when the time came. It was winter, and one weekend he was so worried about his brother's family in the bitter southern cold that he bought a portable heater and drove all the way down there to deliver it. With the move complete, however, Dad took the opportunity to get out once and for all.

Mike wasn't happy with Dad's departure, which he seemed to consider tantamount to a betrayal, especially when Dad finally took the plunge and opened his own injection moulding business. Nevertheless, Dad didn't hesitate to use his new company to help his brother. "I bought a machine off him, ten thousand pounds for a seven-thousand-pound machine, and took over all the crap jobs he didn't want. Then I took another of his machines, which I paid him two pounds an hour to use, and I took his entire shed full of sprues, ground them up and paid him 90 percent of the virgin value. I warehoused his goods in Birmingham and continued to run his business on paper, doing the accounts for free and arranging all his local deliveries. And I seemed to be his spares department—anytime he had a problem, he came to me for machine parts."

I swat at one of the insects drawn to the glow of the porchlight. "Why did you do all this when he'd treated you so badly before?"

"Because he's my brother." He shrugs, swilling the thick liquid around his mug.

"Did he appreciate it?"

"Apparently not. That move was very successful for him, but all he ever said was, 'You should have told me you were thinking of leaving.'"

Maybe Mike had some sort of suppressed adult sibling envy, unable to admit to himself that his little brother had helped him so effectively and selflessly. Even today, he contends that Dad acted purely for his own benefit.

"He tells his sons I let him down." He sighs, setting down his drink like he's lost the taste for it. Of course, I'm only hearing one side of this story, but I want to believe it. I don't want to think his memory is defective or that he did somehow act selfishly.

"Was this a major falling-out?" I ask, topping up our glasses. I feel like the world's worst doctor prescribing alcohol as an antidepressant.

"I don't think so. I don't really bother with him anymore. I don't treat him as a brother. He wants to be all family oriented now, but I don't. But there wasn't a fallout or a rift."

Although he delivers these words confidently, his slumped shoulders and downcast eyes tell me the rift does exist. His mood has deteriorated following this line of questioning; the hollering, hand-clapping Peter is nowhere to be seen.

"You're pulling me into the past," he says, suddenly serious. "It's not a nice place to be. The present is much nicer."

I stop my interrogation immediately, concern quashing my curiosity. I shouldn't be pushing him to these dark places. It's late anyway. I'm a little drunk, and I can tell I'm not the only one. Later, after retiring and switching off the lights, his tossing and turning culminates in a hurried dash to the bathroom where I hear the unmistakeable sounds of retching and vomit hitting water. I cringe into my bed sheets.

Over breakfast the next morning, Dad grumbles, "What rubbish was I talking last night? Your alcohol loosened my tongue." He's feeling a little the worse for wear, although only an expert would be able to tell the difference. His glasses sit askew on his face after he fell asleep on them, breaking off one arm, and I'm ashamed to register he smells faintly of urine, that clichéd old-person odour. It's hardly surprising with his tap and bag arrangement, which makes it hard for him to shower properly.

Apparently, this is an appropriate time to inform me he hadn't drunk alcohol for eighteen months before we met up in Cancún! What? Why didn't he tell me at the time? We had margaritas the very first night. Did I push him off the wagon? I silently berate myself and swear last night's incident will not be repeated.

I waggle a pantomime finger in his face. "I'm not going to let you have any more than two drinks from now on."

"Nonsense," he replies, brooking no argument. "I'll drink what I like."

Initially formed as an underwater volcano a couple of million years ago, and subsequently inhabited by Arawak and Carib people, Grenada's history followed the usual Caribbean template: discovery by European conquistadors (in this case Columbus himself), tag-team colonisation by English and French, independence, and a slew of internal coups before achieving stable government. The country deviated from this pattern briefly by being invaded by the US. Ronald Reagan was paranoid that the pro-communist government was building an airstrip to support Cuban aeroplanes, and so, with no evidence and in violation of international law, he barged in and demolished the political structure.

Our wanderings have brought us here on May Day, a public holiday, and consequently the streets of St. George's are deserted, the shops closed. The rest of the island is a pleasing combination of green jungle, low hills, craggy coastline, and well-maintained roads passing through tidy villages as we discover by hiring a car for the day. Most of the sights our driver points out are of only passing interest—the National Cricket Stadium, a waterfall—but I'd recently heard about a fascinating underwater museum created by British sculptor Jason deCaires Taylor. Seven years ago, on the bed of Molinere Bay just north of the city, he installed a series of eerie statues. At depths of between four and eight metres, life-size figures cast from the bodies of local Grenadians now decorate the sandy bottom.

I'm eager to view these sunken artworks, but due to the public holiday, I can't locate a dive shop. At short notice, my only option is to hire a man with a boat to shuttle me out into the bay with an elderly dive mask and snorkel. He positions us roughly above the area of the sculpture park, and I hop in, kicking down inefficiently with my finless feet towards the murky shapes below. Patchy cloud cover and wind-whipped waves have reduced the visibility and warmth of the normally glass-clear water of the bay, but they're still there, waiting for me.

Coming face-to-face with the rough features of Taylor's creations, fashioned from concrete and rebar and intended to double as artificial reefs for marine life, is as spooky as I'd hoped. The most prominent sculpture is a ring of standing figures facing outwards and holding hands like a group of religious fanatics braving the apocalypse armed only with prayers. Weightless and silent, I can devote my entire focus to these drowned creatures, their haunting expressions obscured by a gentle accretion of algae, lichen, and coral. Inscrutable at first glance, I gradually detect a sadness in their body language—their unsmiling mouths, the melancholy tilt of their heads. Like the weather-stained tears of a centuries-old stone angel in a forgotten corner of a cemetery, it's impossible to discern any fragment of happiness in such a face.

There are other pieces—a man sitting at a desk, immobile before a typewriter; a row of faces peering out of a rock face; a lone figure riding a bicycle along the seabed. I can't hold my breath long enough to examine them as closely as I'd like, and numerous trips to the surface and back eventually tire me. This was Taylor's first underwater sculpture park; he's since designed a bigger and more famous one in Cancún. Had I but known it when I was there!

Here I go again, entering a country by the back door. Last week, it was a barely used jungle border, and today, a creaky wooden mail boat across a bumpy stretch of water. I'm dubious at first, not because of the seaworthiness of the craft, or lack thereof, but because the last ocean journey I took with my travel companion was an unmitigated disaster. He assures me he'll be fine this time, though, and as I really want to go this way, I pretend to believe him.

It'll only be an hour long crossing anyway, and he was fine this morning when our small, yet sturdy, ferry chugged away from St.

Georges' picturesque waterfront promenade, the Carenage, and out to sea. Behind us, an abstract canvas of colourful buildings spread up the steep hillsides of the harbour, a curious double horseshoe bay formed by collapsed volcanic craters and petered out along the forested hilltops. The short passage and calm seas left us unscathed as far as Carriacou, fifty-eight kilometres northeast of Grenada and the largest of the island chain known as the Grenadines. From here, we'll cross to Union Island which, along with the larger St. Vincent and all the scattered rocks in between, makes up the West Indian nation of St. Vincent and the Grenadines.

While we wait for the *Lady JJ*, the aforementioned mail boat making the run across the strait, Dad is quiet, content just to read. Last night we barely spoke at all. I hope our last history lesson hasn't raised dark shadows in his mind, inviting the depression to return. I don't think I could live with myself. I offer him the book I'm reading as a change from his Kindle, and he squints at it, brow furrowed.

"How do you make the print bigger?" he asks, only half joking. He follows with a sigh and a small shake of the head. "I don't know why I bother reading anything anymore. I read the other day which country first used the dollar as currency. 'Oh, that's interesting,' I thought . . . *whoosh*, gone," he says, whipping a palm over his head like a low-flying aircraft. "No idea now."[58]

I leave him in a café near the jetty to get our exit stamps from the passport office. I'm only gone ten minutes but return to find him in a state of near panic. "I didn't know where you were!" he exclaims. "I looked up and you were gone. I was just sitting here trying to work out where, but I couldn't remember." I'd told him exactly where I was going. I suspect the Sertraline may be hampering his general awareness, at least I hope so, as any other explanation would be more sinister. Either way, he doesn't seem as 'with it' as before. I'm going to have to keep a closer eye on him.

58 It was the Kingdom of Bohemia in 1520. The currency was called the *thaler* after the word for valley, or dale.

Despite my concern, the *Lady JJ* goes well. She's a tiny little thing with room for only ten passengers and some cargo, but at least she has a roof and a motor. I'm careful to hold on to the old man as he steps aboard, but he seems stable enough and the journey passes uneventfully. He admits to feeling a little nauseous but doesn't need to lie down, and we arrive in the cute town of Ashton in the late afternoon.

Union Island displaces nice square kilometres of the Caribbean Sea and is host to only two small towns. Ashton, the smaller one, has a population of around a thousand and a high street barely five hundred metres long lined with colourful wooden buildings and crowned by a tangle of power lines and fluttering bunting. The asphalt road (made from Trinidad pitch, perhaps?) is busy with pedestrians, children walking home from school, and a slow-moving hand-cart filled with bananas, mangoes, and pineapples pushed by a white-bearded Rasta. There are even a couple of cars. On one particularly bright pink and blue shack is daubed the legend 'It's Kathy's Local Handmade Souvenir Shop,' although it's unclear whether it's the souvenirs which are handmade or the shop itself. A tall man, presumably a council employee, is using a string trimmer to tidy the sandy grass of the small playground near the jetty. He's wearing a ludicrously tall woollen beanie, underneath which is a considerable mass of dreadlocks. He looks so Caribbean—I love it.

The surrounding reefs are world famous, especially those of the Tobago Cayes, a cluster of five small islands poking their heads above water around five kilometres off the coast. I'm excited to spend the day there, until I remember I haven't brought my personal ocean-going yacht, the vehicle of choice for most visitors. Instead of hiring a boatman at exorbitant expense, I visit the office of the Marine Park rangers, whose job it is to administrate mooring fees. For a few thalers the nice lady on duty agrees to ferry me over to Baradal, the third largest island, where I can chill for several hours while she collects the yachties' money. Dad opts to stay in Ashton for the day, away from the nasty saltwater and sand grains.

Chugging out, I feel utterly captivated by the idyllic scene that greets us as we round the headland—the turquoise water and azure sky are indistinguishable save for the low humps of the cayes separating them. My morale soars at the sight, and I'm drenched by a wave of vivacity and delight. How fortunate I am to be in this place, or more accurately to have a life which allows me to travel to this place. I spend the day snorkelling among sea turtles and playing on the golden sand. I'm not sure whether to be worrying about the old man or not. I'm confident he's content, possibly even, as he claims, happy, but I'm still concerned he might not remember where I am or who he is.

"I've enjoyed doing nothing today," he confirms when I find him relishing the late afternoon ambience of *Sweet Sailing*—a wooden boat casually resting alongside the High Street. She's painted red, blue, and yellow, and decorated with queen conch shells; up a short flight of steps is the wheelhouse, now converted into a kitchen for the preparation of juices and ice cream.

"Coffee, fruit, reading; I've had three lie downs! I must be getting old," he concedes.

His streak of contentment continues into the traditional nightly hunt for sustenance. Sometimes I'm apt to wind myself up about food, punctiliously sticking to my budget for no appreciable reason other than internal legislation, and try as I might, I can't find anything both appetising and affordable this evening. The only real option in town, beyond smoothies and fried chicken, is a resort restaurant way beyond my budget. When Dad sees me beginning to stress about this non-problem, he intervenes. "I'll pay. We'll call it an early birthday meal," he decides, cleverly circumnavigating my rules. I resist, as nine days still remain to the anniversary of my fortieth trip around the sun, but he goes for the coup de grace: "I'll have forgotten about this by your actual birthday, and we can do it again!" he jokes. I admit defeat and order a steak.

My vacillation is replicated the next day when searching for a reasonable hotel in Kingstown, the capital of St. Vincent. "Don't worry too much about the price," cajoles Dad as we traipse around the unforgiving streets of the scruffy port town trying to find a room under seventy dollars. "I can afford it."

It looks like he spoke the truth on his triumphant return from Spain—he really has discovered an ability to part with money. If only he could pass it on to me!

"I don't want to take advantage of you," I argue, unconvincingly.

"I'm trying to spend my nest egg," he insists. "I need help to do it!"

We're lucky to have made it to Kingstown at all. The morning ferry from Union Island took five hours to hop between the remaining Grenadines, passing such exotic-sounding paradises as Canouan, Baliceaux, and Mustique, playgrounds of the über rich. Thankfully, it was a large vessel which ploughed through the waves with nary a shudder. I'd left Dad outside on a bench and gone inside to rest my head on a table, and the next thing I knew, he was shaking me awake, saying we had to board a small dinghy to the island. That didn't ring true, even through the fog of drowsiness, and a brief investigation revealed the current stop was Bequia, not St. Vincent. Somebody had asked him where he was disembarking, and he couldn't remember. Panic over, he assured me he would've been paying more attention to his destination were he alone. I hope so.

Our timing is good for once: tonight is the launch of Vincymas, the country's annual carnival. Trinidad may have the best-known party in the region, but Vincymas boasts longevity. From its awakenings in early May, various street functions continue over the next three months until climaxing in July with the main parade. Tonight may only be the forerunner to the real action, but it'll give us a taste of what carnival season in the Caribbean entails.

It begins with a parade of sponsored vehicles along the main street, packed with revellers waving flags and advertising LIAT, Carib beer, and Digicel. Little more than trucks with plastic banners hanging from their sides, they aren't quite the floats of Rio Carnival, or even Notting Hill Carnival for that matter. Tables line the route selling cheap plates of tasty roast pork with rice, and rum drinks in plastic cups. Of course, Dad shies away from the sensory overload of large crowds, but I can see he's struggling with his natural inclinations, as he's enjoying the costumes and the music.

The situation improves when the action moves to a stage erected in a car park. Various groups of costumed dancers take turns to shake their stuff while an MC stirs up the crowd to the sound of a steel pan band. The performers' outfits are dazzling. A swarm of butterflies with shimmering wings gives way to skimpily dressed Zulus with flaming headdresses, followed by a troupe of young boys dressed as glittering green dragons complete with scales, pointy wings, and gaping maws of huge, pointy teeth. There are strutting pink peacocks with golden helmets and what look like bejewelled Aztecs with bamboo clubs and windmills on their heads. The amount of effort that has gone into these ensembles is remarkable.

Dad somehow manages to fall into discussion with a local man, admirably holding up his end of the conversation. He asks questions and everything! He must make a good impression because when his friend leaves, he clasps his hand African-American style and calls him a "White Rasta."

"Look at me," he beams, doing his little happy dance. "Socialising!" Contrast this with the man who was horrified when our Costa Rican pension owner befriended him. He laughs. "These magic tablets." He's like a one-man theatre company that's switched its tragedy mask for the comedy one. As the inspiration for his renaissance, I glow like a proud father.

The change in him has been remarkable, but by 9:00 p.m., he is physically tired. It's as late as he can last any night nowadays. "I'm alright to get home on my own if you want to stay," he offers. I'm tempted to linger a while, but I don't feel the confidence to strike up a conversation with a stranger tonight. The Jackdaw of Diffidence sitting on my shoulder is threatening to peck me on the ears should I dare. I don't dare. It seems the old man has outperformed me tonight. Oh, how the tables have turned.

I knew as soon as I saw a picture of the Gros Piton—a craggy, 798-metre-high volcanic plug—that if I did only one thing in St. Lucia, it would be climbing this, and due to our hectic schedule, one thing is pretty much all I get to do. I don't mind too much though, because in terms of highlights, our hotel location will take some beating.

As a confirmed hater of overpriced airport transportation, few things make me happier than strolling casually past the queuing taxis and surcharged public transport and directly to my accommodation. In this case, although the capital, Castries, was only a couple of kilometres away, a distance I'd normally have skipped without thinking, I feared my passenger's skipping days were over. I'd already tricked him into hoofing the same distance to St. Vincent Airport that morning. Still on a high from that success, I decided there was no harm in going at least as far as the airport roundabout to see what we could find.

After a mere seven hundred metres of slow pacing, we spied a hotel sign by the roadside. Bingo! Initial investigation revealed the building was closed in preparation for the upcoming season, although there were a couple of staff present doing odd jobs. Undeterred, I faked my most disarming smile and politely suggested we be allowed to stay there anyway. We wouldn't mind the mess, honest; we'd be no bother, etc. Lo and behold, the nice lady agreed, even charging us below the regular rate on account of the lack of amenities. From our third storey balcony, we could peer right down the tarmac runway. We'd done the double!

The morning after, I bus down to *Soufrière*, a stunningly set town on the island's southwest coast. St. Lucia has more French flavour than most Caribbean islands due to its Gallic invaders holding out slightly longer than usual before submitting to Rule Britannia. A smattering of colonial-era buildings are nestled around an emerald cove, trailing back into a valley between equally green hillsides. Standing guard to the south are the twin peaks of the *Petit* and *Gros Pitons*, pointing skyward like a matching pair of Caribbean Matterhorns.

It's mandatory to hire a guide up the rough spire composed of an igneous rock called dacite, and mine is a teenage mother working on her birthday. We have a pleasant chat on the hour-and-a-half ascent, the track steep but easy to follow, until she tires, and I leave her behind. The view from the summit is excellent; in truth, *Petit Piton* is the more beautiful of the two, but *Gros Piton* is slightly higher, meaning I get to gaze upon the one from the other. I enjoy the exertion but for me, the euphoria of standing atop such a beautiful pinnacle is the main attraction. Like Julie Andrews in *The Sound of Music*, I feel the urge to scale every mountain I come across. It can be quite a time-consuming obsession.

"Three hours overdue!" exclaims my father on my return, for I'd plucked an ETA from thin air before leaving. "I was just writing you a note before going out to make enquiries."

Oops. I guess I have been away most of the day, but even considering the six and a half hours spent travelling for a two-and-a-half-hour hike, I'm content. I got to see life from the minibus window, observe St. Lucians' going about their daily business, exchange words with a few of them, and generally soak up the vibe, which is a huge part of the pleasure of travelling. This is a beautiful island, one I'd relish returning to. When it comes down to it, though, I almost always choose to go somewhere new rather than re-tread old ground.

Dad has actually been to St. Lucia before, on an improbable week-long holiday with my mum in late 1984. As far as I could remember, they'd never previously been on any vacation that could compare to those advertised on television or in glossy tourist brochures. Until that year, the only two overseas holidays we'd ever taken were to Brittany in France, driving via the car ferry and staying in self-catering chalets, and back to the town where we'd briefly lived in Spain. I'm not complaining—they were still summer holidays in exotic European countries and very enjoyable—but at the age of eleven, I was faintly shocked when my parents declared they were jet-setting off to the Caribbean, and without us! Mum's sister, Jean, and her husband, Brian, babysat the three of us for the week.

"It's all a distant memory now," says Dad unhelpfully when I ask how it came about. "Best ask Brenda the why and when of it all. Maybe I enjoyed it—my brain deleted most happy memories during the depression. I do remember the frogs, though." Their flight arrived in the early evening when the dark air was filled with a deafening chirruping. "I could scarcely believe a frog could make such a racket!"

According to Mum, St. Lucia was one of his random extravagances, albeit more extreme than usual. "It was the year of my fortieth birthday," she told me during our next catch-up. "Maybe that had something to do with it. 'Go and choose a holiday,' he said to me. I was back with an armful of brochures before the end of the day! It's difficult to know if he enjoyed himself." I imagine her shrugging over the phone. "I think so. He was never happy being away from work. The family holiday we took to Spain in 1978 was a nightmare! He couldn't keep still. He was pacing the streets for the first two and half weeks, then five days before we were due to return, he finally settled down, happy he was almost home and back in his routine. On another holiday in Menorca, when you had all grown up, he really didn't like me talking to other people, specifically the lady in the room next door. 'Why are you talking to her?' he'd demand. I was just being friendly! Yes, he felt trapped on an organised holiday."

Apart from France and Spain, I can barely remember any holidays we took as a full family. Five years after St. Lucia, Dad took the three children to Lanzarote for a week. Mum stayed at home. Why? Her memory is unclear. "I think maybe we'd fallen out, and I was just being contrary," she ponders. "A lot of the holidays he suggested would be in self-catering units, and who did he think was going to be the 'self' that did the catering? Me, of course. So, I often refused unless we got at least a bed and breakfast."

Dad can't explain the situation any better. "She refused point blank to go to Lanzarote, and I never really knew why," he admits, "so I took you on my own." Here again, we see his inability to read his wife. He may not even have known they'd fallen out unless she explicitly said so. Black looks, sarcasm, and terse silences don't work so well on Aspergians.

After I left home, Dad took my sister, Vicky, then sixteen, on a tour of the Greek islands, again without Mum, who again can't recall the reason. She does have fond recollections of their absence, though: "I remember waking up the day after they'd gone and noticing the dial on the radio beside the bed was a bit grungy, so I cleaned it out with a tissue. Then I saw the rest of the radio was dusty and dirty, so I cleaned the whole thing. From there I did the bedside table, the lamp, and went on to systematically clean the entire house, with no interruptions. It was wonderful.

"Don't forget though, I took you on lots of holidays because he was too busy!" she adds, keen to impart her contribution to our vacations. "We went to London several times and to holiday camps like Butlin's. That was where I made the horrific discovery that holidaying couples don't want to chat to a woman alone with children. I'd expected to interact with other people, but apparently, I was not welcome to socialise. I was shunned! Presumably the females saw me as a threat, but short of wearing a sign on my chest saying 'I do have a husband actually, so I'm not interested in yours,' there was nothing I could do. That was a three-day weekend, one I thought he could've spared, but he decided to stay and work. It was a lonely weekend without any adult company."

I have to wonder why Mum reports him as being terribly anxious about work during their holidays together, yet I have only happy memories. Were we blissfully ignorant in our youth? Did he try harder to please us than please her? Or was the mere presence of his wife the stress factor?

"No, I wouldn't say that," he disagrees, when I approach him after digesting my conversation with her. "I wasn't always worried about work. Sometimes I was in a good position to get away, but I've never really liked going on holidays, package holidays especially. Going away for a fortnight is not something I've ever been attracted to, because as soon as you go, you know when you're coming back. It's not like embarking on an open-ended trip. In fact, it's almost more stressful than stopping at home." His last sentence is preposterous. Were that true for everyone, the global tourist industry would collapse.

"On package holidays, you end up doing things that someone else has chosen for you," he pontificates, getting into his groove, "often the activities on which the rep makes a commission. The money you spend goes to the airline and the tour operator, and their shareholders, and to the owners, probably foreign, of the hotel. Travelling as we are now means you don't see the tourist façade of the country you're visiting; you see the people themselves and experience more of their culture. The money you spend, though it may be less, goes straight into the pockets of hard-working natives, into their restaurants and hostels. If you choose to help the poor begging at the side of the road, though they may not always be as poor as they convey, you can be pretty sure they're not rich, and it's unlikely they've got shareholders. So, this is just the sort of trip I like, but without the inconvenience and worry of the planning, research, and organizing." I love that we share this philosophy of travel. I can't imagine many septuagenarians enduring my low-budget style.

Yes, Mum's sad experiences are in stark contrast to our relaxed meanderings. Nowadays, Dad doesn't want control of anything, or any routine at all except for morning coffee. He no longer has the stress of work or the burden of children and has given up pretending to be a normal person. He's determined to be himself and is more comfortable and happier for it.

Chapter 14

Ergophile

"I blame the others," he declares over the gentle bobbling of the steel pan band. "It was they who arranged that on the day my elder brother was to be married, so was another of our friends, and I'd also been invited to a third party. What was a young guy to do? I had to somehow accept all the invitations. It was only polite to do so."

We've caught a bus a little way up the coast to Rodney Bay, where there's some sort of Jazz Festival in progress. "Which 'others' do you mean?" I ask once we've caught the attention of the barman. "Some mutual friends? Or Clotho, Lachesis, and Atropos?"[59] He's telling stories of times in his life when he was overwhelmingly, excruciatingly inebriated, and I'm rubbing my hands together in anticipation, ears eager for nuggets of comedy gold.

"Yes, them," he answers brusquely, as if the Fates were the only possible culprits. "The ones who always contrive to arrange these things on the same evening." He rushes back into the thrust of his tale. "Anyway, my means of transport those days was my BSA Golden Flash 650cc twin motorcycle along with its Avon sports sidecar, the E-Type Jaguar of the extremely poor. With this sturdy steed, I could rotate around the celebrations and not miss out on anything, particularly all the free bars offered."

59 The Morai of Greek mythology were three sisters who controlled the destiny of every human being. Between them they spun, measured, and cut the thread of life.

"Oh," I say, disappointment washing over me. "You were planning on drinking and riding?"

"Well, yes." He shrugs, his annoyance at the interruption eclipsed by the opportunity to educate a young 'un in the superiority of the golden years. "You have to understand that standards were different in those days. One was either drunk or not drunk. If someone could stand without aid and walk along a straight line—the police test—then one was 'not drunk,' and if one was 'not drunk,' one could drive."

A gentle snort echoes around my sinuses, part amusement and part wonder at the naïveté of the olden days.

"With these guidelines, I toured the venues, ending the evening at my brother's wedding. At this point, I was still *compos mentis,* and I remember asking someone to drive me home if I had one more whisky. They refused. I had it anyway. I remember little thereafter."

My mouth broadens into a grin. We've all been there.

"It seems I transported cousin Frank back home in the sidecar," he continues, really hitting his rhythm. "I have a single frame image of the journey home: we were passing the local library and I was lying on my back along the motorcycle seat with my legs in the air. I suspect there was a 'whoopee' noise accompanying the move." The dryness of his delivery brings little involuntary twitches to my shoulders. "It can only have been for an instant, though, motorcycle combinations having a great reluctance to travel in a straight line unaided.

"The next memory I have is in the kitchen at home," he continues, feeding off my reaction, "which was full of visitors. I was crawling around the floor in between everyone's legs. I thought it was hilarious."

I can't hold back any longer: the twitches become shudders and I finally laugh out loud. This story resonates on another level because I went through a period of crawling through strangers' legs in night-clubs, although I was considerably older than seventeen at the time!

After we've had a good chuckle, he brings the story to a close. "And then the following morning—oh dear! That hangover lasted well into the second day. It was more than ten years until I could tolerate the smell of whisky again."

Oh, yes, I know that sucker punch to the frontal lobe, the memory that hits a few seconds after recovering consciousness and makes you cringe into a ball. Thanks, brain!

That something as silly as a drunken anecdote can bring people together is basic psychology, but all the same, I feel another faint barrier has been pushed aside. I refrain from telling him my worst stories, though, out of a fear of losing even one iota of the respect he may have for me, and while there are some embarrassing ones, they could have been a lot worse. Instead of prowling the vast and dingy urban precincts of Birmingham, as I'd always expected, my formative years were spent in a small, ten-pub town in Cornwall, where I prowled the car park behind the supermarket or the post office frontage, wasted on cider. I'd always wondered exactly why we had to make that move.

Working for himself was a huge relief for Dad. "I have always been better self-employed. It seems to be one of the things AS are better at. Matthew doesn't take orders. He doesn't work for people and do as he's told. He's got to do his own thing even if he doesn't get any money for it. So, I was happy, yes, but working eighteen hours a day." He called his company Victoria Plastics after his new daughter, and with his single-minded devotion and excessive work ethic, it was successful. However, this became something of a curse because it meant he needed help to run the machines.

He sighs. "The first few were alright and then, suddenly, I ended up with sixteen employees." It may have seemed sudden to him, but this happened over a period of six or seven years. "Sixteen employees, and I hated them all, every last one. Animals." His eyes defocus as his nemeses drift across his vision. "They were mostly men with whom I had nothing in common. I despised them and they me. My opinion of them was clear on my unsmiling face, and in return, they cheated me when they could and stole from me during the night shift when I wasn't there to see. I was a poor people manager."

The whole horrible venue springs up before my eyes, pieced together from childhood memories of the factory and the new knowledge of this man in front of me. Huge, noisy machines, oily floors, acrid smoke from burning plastic, grubby communal areas. When I visited, the workers mostly smiled and treated me well, but when I place my father in the background, tense, unhappy, radiating distaste, the scene becomes ugly and uncomfortable. I see narrowed glances cast in his direction, hear whispered comments in his wake, feel the aversion in the air. A flicker of indignation on his behalf immediately cools to sorrow for his intolerable existence.

"I had to get out of that situation because it was driving me crackers," he tells me, breaking at last from his factual account with an admission of weakness. "One night while driving home from work, I stopped my car and screamed out of the window."

I say nothing, unwilling to acknowledge he'd been so desperate, so close to another breakdown. I imagine he was screaming at his life, screaming at the world he couldn't handle and that didn't understand him, screaming at the curse of being an irregular piece in a homogenous puzzle. He screamed out of frustration and anger and impotence. Something had to change.

"My brother was encouraging me to follow him down to Cornwall, and it seemed like a good idea."

I clearly remember sitting on the floor of the front room, reading, when I was told the news. By then we were living in a huge, three-storey, semi-detached house in the north of Birmingham, and our front room may have been the smartest in the whole city. It was where we kept the good tableware and the plush chairs, my mother's writing desk, and the fireplace where we hung Christmas cards. Like a drawing room of old, it was always kept immaculately neat and tidy should the occasional visitor appear.

Dad entered and asked me to put down my book. He had important news. "You know that broken-down old farmhouse we saw in Cornwall," he began. "The one where you said, 'Who on earth would want to live in a dump like this?' "

"Yes," I replied, obediently, too innocent to guess the somewhat predictable news that was coming. That summer we'd been on holiday to Cornwall to visit Uncle Mike, the third time in as many years. My parents had talked about the possibility of relocating and had looked at a few properties. To me, the idea of leaving our gorgeous home in Birmingham, the only place I could ever remember living, to move to a pile of rubble on a windswept hilltop so far away was simply inconceivable. I'd treated the viewings as an opportunity to explore some interesting and creepy new places, to wonder at the damp stone and stink of cow manure that comprised this county, and laugh at the thought that anyone would willingly live here. I forgot about the prospect as soon as we left, and here it was, rearing up in front of me.

"Well, we've bought it," he continued gently. "We're going to go and live there."

It took about three seconds for me to realise he was serious—then I burst into tears. I couldn't believe it. I was happy where I was. I had friends. I even liked my school. Cornwall had nothing for me. At eleven years old, I couldn't look far enough into the future to see past the immediate desolation, both social and geographical. Instead, I felt it open up before me like a void, black and empty, and I hated it.

He started to explain, listing the reasons for their decision, but I wasn't listening; I didn't care. All I could think about was my friends and this big old cosy house and starting anew in a horrible, cold, stone ruin.

He drew me to him, sat me on his lap, and hugged me. "I'm sorry, Sunshine," he said, rocking me. It helped, a little.

"I was also worried about the growing violence in the city," he says now. "Cornwall would have been safer for you as teenagers." One troupe of musicians is being replaced by an almost identical one, differentiated only by the hue of their brightly coloured shirts, and we throw a few hand claps in the direction of the stage. Then there was the economy: he thought it important to own land where we could grow our own food if necessary. He even mentioned the threat of nuclear war and how we'd be more likely to escape the fallout there (this was shortly after Reagan and Andropov had brought the world to the brink of self-destruction). "The main reason we hesitated, though, was your education."

I was enrolled in King Edward VI private secondary school (est. 1552) in Edgbaston, reportedly the best school in the country. King Edward's didn't take boarders, so after the move, I stayed with my best friend and his family in Birmingham for two terms. In some ways it was great, but after a while I started to miss my own kin.

"You wanted to come home, and I should never have allowed that," he says, berating himself. "I should have insisted you stayed attending that amazing school, and for that, I apologise now. I should have put my foot down. It was a bad judgement and one that influences me even today on how my grandchildren should be treated."

"Don't beat yourself up, Dad!" I protest. "I turned out alright, didn't I?" From my third year onwards, they sent me to the best school within reasonable travelling distance, which was in Plymouth. It was still a private school with a tough entrance exam, but it wasn't of the same calibre.

"You said it yourself," he argues. "You would almost certainly have gone to Cambridge University had you stayed in Birmingham, which would have meant a better and easier life for you." It's true; every single student in my year at King Edward's continued to either Oxford or Cambridge.

"How could my life be better than it is now?" I ask, primarily to make him feel better, although I think I may actually believe it.

"Well, you don't know, do you, because you haven't led that other life." He seems to have got used to the switch to rum easily enough, and his next swallow somehow reminds him of the topic at hand. "Anyway, I was earning reasonable money from the business by that time, but I was accruing more and more employees, more and more stress, more and more worries. The decision to move was very sensible—dump all the trade moulding work I'd inherited from Mike, concentrate on making cable ties, cut down on the employees, and live in sunny Cornwall."

"And how did Mum feel about it?" I ask, temporarily wrong-footing him.

"You'd have to ask her," he replies diplomatically as our jerk chicken arrives to displace the words in our mouths. "I think she was a bit discouraging, but I can't remember her giving me much trouble. Well, not until she discovered we'd be living in the yard the whole winter . . ."

Seizing the day, I phone Mum via Skype in an internet café while Dad is having an afternoon nap. "Cornwall was very nice and seemed to be going quite well for Mike and his family," she says, her face pixelated over the slow connection like a deranged 8-bit cartoon character. "We went down and had a look at some properties, mostly beat-up old farmhouses with barns and outbuildings that could be converted into a factory." She seems willing enough to discuss it, almost relishing transporting herself back in time. "Peter wanted to make an offer, but I told him I really didn't want to go. I had all my private chiropody patients in Birmingham and two or three part-time jobs, from which I was earning a lot of money. I'd got friends there and my only family. Well, he quietened down, and it must've been four or five months later that he told me the farmhouse was still on the market. At that point I relented. He obviously desperately wanted to do this, and I thought downsizing would suit him." I can hear the note of tenderness in her voice, even through the muffled delay of the VOIP connection.

Her face jumps and jars as the video tries to catch up with reality, the static frames displaying surreal approximations of her face. "When he'd hire employees in Birmingham, they'd be all good for a while, but gradually, over a few months, he'd come home complaining about them. There'd be more complaints and more things they weren't doing right, and they'd go out of fashion. Soon he'd be really against them. When Brian[60] was between jobs, Peter employed him, and after a while, he'd come home complaining about Bri, too, about how he'd stop to talk and not be working hard enough. Well, I wasn't happy about that. Bri's a nice bloke and he expects to work for his money, and that's when I started to see a pattern. The next thing I thought was, 'Well, so far I'm still in favour, but how long until he starts complaining to himself about me? When that happens, I'm done.' I actually remember thinking that." The tenderness has gone, replaced by a mixture of indignation and wonder.

"Many years later, Bri spoke to me about it," she continued. "'Oh, he always wanted more,' he said. 'You'd be working all the time, but

60 Mum's brother-in-law

he'd always want you to do more. If he could've put a broom up my arse, he'd have had me sweeping the floor at the same time.' " As tinny and distant as her voice is, I can still discern the faint edge of disappointment. "Nobody lived up to his expectations. He wanted as much from his employees as he gave himself, yet he should have understood that a hired hand will never match the effort of the business owner."

Her words make we wonder about the times I worked for him myself, more as an adult than a child. Proper factory labour wasn't about sticking bases on adhesive strips, it was about doing the job you're being paid to do without stopping for unnecessary breaks, making endless cups of tea, smoking and chatting to fellow workers. He always seemed happy with me. Maybe, as the fruit of his loins, he could forgive me more readily than strangers, but I'd like to think that wasn't the reason. I'm proud of my work ethic; I don't stand gossiping, and I don't smoke or drink hot drinks. On the moulding machines, I'd work for eight hours with only a lunch break, and I think he appreciated that.

My sister suffers the same legacy. "I still work as if I'm doing piecework," Vicky told me once. "I couldn't take a break if I tried. I always have to make sure whoever is paying me is getting their money's worth, and that comes from working for Dad." I've never had employees of my own, but I know I'd struggle to respect those I considered to be slacking. Workmates frequently present me with this dichotomy: I like them as people but dislike working with them, as I don't respect their work ethic, and it's not even my money they're wasting. I'd be a terrible boss.

With the move, Dad's new factory was to be in one of the derelict barns that sat across the main yard from the farmhouse, and that first needed to be rebuilt. The whole roof and one of the beautiful slate-faced walls needed replacing, so he hired tradesmen to do the job. If it was raining, though, which it does rather a lot in Cornwall, they'd sit in their van until it stopped. They wouldn't move their mealtimes either; if the sky happened to clear exactly at lunchtime, they'd stay in the van and eat through the only sun of the day. He used to rant and rave about them because he was desperate to move in his machinery and start production.

"I hadn't realised the barn was the priority," Mum finishes. "I thought there'd be some work done on the house first, as it wasn't fit to live in, but no." Our whole family was squeezed into a static caravan in the front yard for half a year, a cramped and claustrophobic existence compared to our former residence. "That was obviously another miscommunication."

I rather think she assumed one thing and he assumed another, and there was no actual communication. I ring off, leaving her thinking of happier times, maybe not the happiest ones but at least ones in which she still had a husband.

With no machines running and stock levels rapidly depleting, Dad had to sub-contract his two big jobs to other firms. It would've been hard for him to give up control of production, but he had no choice, so he located two supposedly experienced moulders in the West Country and trusted each with one mould. He was right to be nervous—both were soon damaged by careless operators. After two lengthy and costly disputes, he got them back, but neither ever functioned properly again. Meanwhile, he had two other moulds he could use to make cable ties, and when the factory was eventually up and running, that's what he did.

For a couple of years, he worked hard to run a business on half his product. We all helped out, myself included. This is when I operated the huge moulding machines, a fourteen-year-old boy playing with pneumatic presses and hot, spitting plastic. It was like something from the industrial revolution. I'm surprised he didn't have me sweeping the chimney, too!

Ultimately, though, despite all our best efforts, the business ceased to be fully functional and he was forced to shut down and sell all his equipment. The only job that remained was sticking cable tie bases onto the adhesive backing, the same process at which I had failed so spectacularly half my life ago in Birmingham. Fortunately, my concentration and accuracy skills had improved in those seven years, and I spent many long hours in the second barn, which was still furnished with old cow stalls, sticking bases for pocket money.

A new mortgage, two children at private schools, and living in a tumbledown property on a lonely hilltop—for any normal provider this would've been a period of extreme stress, but not so for Dad. He was still free of the pressures of social interaction, and the rest of the situation was just a problem that required solving. With no other source of income, his first instinct was to seek work as an electrician again, but technology had moved on considerably in that industry, and he'd been left behind. Next, he looked into a means of automating the application of adhesive to the cable tie bases.

"I thought the machine that affixed adhesive backing to the bases was a line of children at the kitchen table," my mother commented archly.

He purchased some aluminium strips which he drilled and screwed together into a chute. He could feed the bases down this chute and onto a long roll of adhesive, which could then be cut into individual strips. He invested £250 to have the necessary pieces made in steel, bought an old compressor, a pneumatic cylinder, and some tape. He was ready to go.

After a few trials, he needed to know his production capacity, so he decided to spend one whole day at the machine. "I stuck to the job all day until it was time to collect you," he tells me. I caught the train every day to my fancy school in Plymouth, but because our farmhouse was several miles out of town I had to be ferried to and from the station. "Victoria wanted to visit a friend in town, so we both jumped into the car. I dropped her in the market and rushed to the station, collected you, and in my panic to get on with production, I completely forgot her. It was about two hours later that I heard Brenda in the house enquiring, 'Has anyone seen Victoria?' 'Oh, no!' I thought to myself. 'What have I done?' "

He stuck thirty thousand bases that day—an unqualified success. Sometime later, he happened upon a man with a bowl feeder which would automate the process of feeding the bases into the chute. The farmer was using it as a door stop. His production capacity soon outstripped his sales and he was obliged to seek new customers. Of course, for him, being a salesman was the most difficult part of the whole enterprise. Somehow, he managed to find a few and survive, and from that cobbled-together chute and tape, he built a new, thriving company.

When I praise his success in building this business, he demurs. "Well, you first have to define success. I can see all my failures. I can see all the ways I should have succeeded and didn't, the opportunities I didn't take. That could be the depression, though, when you can see your failures more easily than your successes."

"Just supporting your family, keeping five people fed and clothed for twenty years, that qualifies as a success in my book," I say.

"Well, I suppose that last business was a success," he agrees begrudgingly. "I started it from nothing and sold it for a lot of money, so yes, that was a success."

All these idyllic locales are beginning to blend into one. We've skipped over several of the Lesser Antilles, that delicate arc of volcanic islands that defines the eastern boundary of the Caribbean Sea, in favour of the nation of Antigua and Barbuda. Admittedly, one major factor in Antigua's favour is its location as headquarters of LIAT, the Antilles' principal airline. From the capital, St. Johns, we bus to English Harbour, the site of a restored British naval base famous for being the home of Lord Horatio Nelson during his tour of duty in the Caribbean. We've missed Antigua Sailing Week by days, and what was recently a hive of racing and social activity is now comatose. On the upside, accommodation is bountiful, and we have a large dormitory all to ourselves.

English Harbour offers little entertainment beyond strolling up and down Dockyard Drive trying to spot the biggest superyacht, and sitting in the sun, reading. I almost persuade myself to hire a car and explore the island's many amazing beaches, but the devil's advocate talks me out of it. As revenge, I make him accompany me to nearby Galleon Beach. He doesn't swim, of course, and he refuses to hire a sun lounger or umbrella; instead, he opts to sit on a wall, then moves to a boulder when somebody dares sit next to him.

"Ugh," he gags when I ask him to apply sun cream to my back. "Have you got a rubber glove?"

His resurgent negativity drives me to seek solitude for the evening, I walk up to the lookout at Shirley Heights, an old gun battery from Britain's eighteenth century domination of the Caribbean, now refurbished as an expensive sunset restaurant. I sit on a bench and watch the calm waters and poky inlets of the town slowly imbued with the colour of burnished gold, the tall masts of the yachts marring the sheen like so many scratches on King Midas' dinner plate. It certainly is a view and a half. Not for the first time, I feel a longing for different company, specifically Gerda, as frolicking on a gorgeous stretch of sand in the warm Caribbean Sea would be right up her street. Until now, I've been pretty blasé about missing my wife, but I do. I miss her a lot, even more so lately because of how much she'd love it here. It's wasted on Dad.

The next morning, we visit our usual breakfast spot, a charming, two room wooden eatery called Grace's. Simply furnished but gaily painted, with a traditional and tasty menu of pork stew, baked chicken, rice, and roti, this place is a gem. Grace is a bright and beaming one-woman carnival who seems delighted to feed us her delicious meals and coax us back for more. The rear half of her café is up a short flight of steps, where we now take our seats. I sit facing the front of the café while Dad is across the small table with his back to the stairs.

We haven't even broached a topic of conversation when it happens. As his coffee arrives, he shuffles back a few centimetres to make room. As he opens his mouth to voice his thanks, a look of puzzlement appears on his creased features. In fascinating slow motion, that confusion becomes panic, his eyes widening grotesquely. At the same time, his face seems to retreat, before disappearing altogether, leaving me staring at the wall behind where he was sitting. It takes another fraction of a second to realise what has happened—on moving his chair, one foot has hovered briefly over empty space before slowly dipping down, pulling with it the other legs, body, and surprised occupant. Then comes the crash. Before my brain can jerk my muscles into action, he's hit the floor.

Grace and another customer reach him before I do. He's flat on his back at the foot of the stairs with his head underneath an empty table, limbs splayed. My mind screams wordlessly in a state of utter panic. This is no split emotion like when he took a dive in the hostel in Panama City. There's no trace of shame at his clumsiness now, only 100 percent terror that he's done some serious damage. Together, we pull him upright. He's shaken but, amazingly, unharmed.

"You cool, Pops?" asks Grace, her tone betraying the concern behind her nonchalant words.

He is, apparently, cool, with just a bruised hip to show for his mishap. I can't believe he's walking away from this with only a minor case of humiliation. What if the table had been an arm's length closer? What if there'd been a chair drawn up to it? It would have taken his head off! I'm literally shaking with relief.

"You didn't know I could fly, did you, son?" he says, trying to lighten the mood. I can't laugh; it's too soon.

Our frenzied island hopping culminates in a single night in the Dominican Republic. It's singularly embarrassing to me to disrespect a country so, but that's the way our complex schedule has come together. I normally aim to spend at least a week in any given country, preferably longer, but since the primary objective of this trip is quality time, I'll try not to let our brevity bother me. We at least have time for a walking tour around the handsome stone buildings of Santo Domingo, the country's ancient capital.

Founded in 1496 by Bartholomew Colombus, Christopher's brother, Santo Domingo was long thought to be the first European settlement in the new world and home to its oldest non-indigenous structures. In fact, that honour goes to the sod and wood dwellings at *L'Anse aux Meadows* on the northernmost tip of Newfoundland in Canada. Norse explorers, possibly led by Leif Eriksson, established a small settlement there in around 1000 CE, five hundred years before Santo Domingo.

We stroll through the *Zona Colonial,* the mature yet still beating heart of the city. Most of these buildings were constructed in the early sixteenth century from massive blocks of stone and have withstood, to varying degrees, invasions, hurricanes, earthquakes, and pirates. *Parque Colón*, a serene courtyard before the stately *Catedral Primada de América*, has as its centrepiece a statue of Christopher Columbus, father of two continents. Like an American Trafalgar Square, the statue's reverence is muted by the flock of disrespectful pigeons roosting on its outstretched arm, one finger raised as if pointing out what Christopher thought was going to be India.

The plaza is peaceful today, only a few tourists braving the grey skies, but its calm belies the violence that begot this nation. The indigenous people of Hispaniola, the name of the island shared by Dominican Republic and Haiti, were called the *Taíno*, which meant "friendly people" in their language. Of an estimated 400,000 residing on the island during the arrival of the conquistadors, barely five hundred were still alive fifty years later. Maybe friendliness wasn't the best policy. Freedom from the Spanish yoke in 1864 was only the excuse for a series of brutal and corrupt presidents that has continued almost to this day. Widespread repression, assassination, and embezzlement reminds us that, not only geographically but politically, we've turned a corner and begun our journey back towards Central America.

While the comfort of our relationship has grown exponentially since Tulum, today, Dad is continuing to get on my nerves. His consistently negative attitude to our surroundings is starting to grate as are the repetitive rants about the evils of modern society. I may agree with them but don't necessarily wish to hear them every day. It's his turn to draw cash from the ATM, but he's procrastinating, and I know exactly why—for such a short stay, the small amount of Dominican pesos we require means the bank's withdrawal fee will be disproportionately large, approximately 10 percent. I sympathise, but today my exasperation is roiling just beneath the surface. *Just draw the money, already!* I shout in my head.

He's also being infuriatingly picky about his coffee. He refuses to patronise a coffee shop that doesn't have 'caffè latte' printed on its menu, even though they all clearly have espresso machines and baristas capable of fulfilling his simple requirements. When we eventually find an acceptable cuppa, he initiates a debate we've already had several times about whether or not the government should be allowed to shut down food vendors due to health regulations. "All restaurants and businesses serving food should receive a health rating so that buyers can make their own decision," he maintains. "They could choose to remain unrated, for instance, in the case of street food stalls, but they shouldn't be forced to close. Wouldn't you agree with that?"

I would, but I offer only a grunt of acknowledgement before turning away and studiously examining a shop across the street. It's a waste of carefully choreographed body language as he seamlessly segues into the topic of the nanny state.

"Western governments try to shield foolish people from real life, basically saying, 'You're too stupid to look after yourself so we will protect you,' and compensating them when they have done something idiotic."

I understand how the combination of high mathematical-logical intelligence and low interpersonal intelligence might result in prejudice against the academically challenged, but he's being particularly blunt today, and it's rubbing me the wrong way. I stare at the muddy froth in his half-empty cup, willing him to gulp it down so we can change location and, with it, the subject matter. "I don't believe in compensation culture at all."

Neither do I, but his thinking is too black and white, and I'm drawn in, despite myself. "Governments have a duty to protect the less fortunate, the stupid even, from being exploited."

"Impossible," he huffs. "You can't legislate against stupidity. The rich will always exploit the poor and the clever the stupid."

I bristle, finally turning to face him, the better to defend my opinions. "It's not necessarily stupidity. It only takes a single act of carelessness and someone's life can be ruined." Aspergians are notoriously gullible. If I was a conman, I'd actively seek them out as their overly trusting nature would make them easy prey. "Are you happy to condemn the careless so easily?"

"Should people be responsible for their own actions, or not?" he challenges, a conversational ultimatum.

"Well, of course." My knuckles unconsciously grip the arms of the chair. "But that's not the point." I know there's a better rebuttal, but I can't think fast enough, and his calm deconstruction of my efforts increases my frustration. I have a Bachelor of Engineering and a Postgraduate diploma in Archaeology, but I'm not clever enough to win an argument with this man who left school at the age of fifteen. I'm not even in his league.

As the topic subsides, I wonder if I'm subconsciously holding back. Maybe I want to agree with him because he's my father and I admire him, even when our opinions differ so widely. Could internal conflict be diminishing my ability to produce a coherent counter argument? Whatever the reason, I've become nothing more than a helpless foil to his ranting protagonist. I glower at him until he drains his cup and starts patting his pockets for money. Why can't we just have a regular chat instead of an emotionally charged debate?

That evening I sneak away from our hotel without telling him and seek out a bar, where I sit alone in a corner, nursing my beer, and completely failing to talk to anyone.

Chapter 15

Tacenda

In some ways, these last eleven weeks have been just a prelude to one of the most fascinating countries on the planet. Culturally and politically, the Republic of Cuba is the jewel in the crown of our Caribbean odyssey. Since 1959, Fidel Castro has successfully led this island nation as a Unitary Marxist-Leninist One-Party Socialist Republic, officially one of only four hard-line socialist states remaining in the world. Though there were tough times for the people, mainly due to economic and trade sanctions imposed by the US and the Organisation of American States, he was generally well respected and often loved by them. He scourged his predecessor Batista's regime of corruption, organised crime, and foreign interests, and installed free health care, housing, education, and electricity. For fifty years, Castro protected and nurtured Cuba, during which time many people didn't realise the extent of their country's impoverishment. With the arrival of the internet and the resignation, five years ago, of Castro as president, dissatisfaction in Cuba's position in the world may be growing, but most Cubans will be forever thankful for El Fidel's guiding hand.[61]

Flying from the Dominican Republic, we land in the nation's most easterly city, *Santiago de Cuba*. It's hard to express how excited I am. My eyes cannot sit still in their sockets; they flicker around the airport, searching for any strange and unusual facet, drinking in every delicious detail, from the posters on the walls to the facial features of the

61 Castro died in 2016

immigration officers. I want to be immersed in 'Cubanity.' The city infrastructure forces us to take a taxi to our accommodation, a *casa particulare,* i.e., a room in a privately owned house. It's similar to a bed and breakfast, but guests are incorporated into the daily life of the family, so it's a wonderfully natural and immersive hosting experience.

Far from the classic American automobile portrayed in every television show about Cuba, ever, the airport taxi rank is populated by ageing Ladas sourced from Russia during the early days of Castro's reign. This practical, durable, and easily fixable model makes up a third of all cars in the country and, despite lacking the inherent beauty of the US models, are beloved by their owners. The one we load our bags into looks like it was lucky to make it to work this morning, or any morning for that matter. Its bodywork could charitably be described as minimalist, and the ghost of a dashboard is a tangle of projecting wires and dead gauges. Our driver is chatty, though, delighted to be the first to welcome us to his country as he careers down the steep streets into the heart of the city.

I peer out of the cracked window at the passing architecture—uniformly tall, square, buff-coloured buildings form an imposing street grid. Thankfully, the city has been spared the stark cubism of other communist regimes. Many of the grand Spanish colonial-era buildings are resplendent with arches, colonnades, and balconies, and tile roofs dominate the cityscape. My eye is drawn especially to the dilapidated yet majestic Imperial Hotel which dominates one massive street corner. Its crumbling and grimy stucco facade, built in 1916, is a reminder of past glories. While lacking the winding charm of naturally evolved European towns, there is a beauty in Santiago's orderliness, and though the city blocks look somehow forlorn, the roads and pavements are immaculately clean. The early evening streets bustle with playful children and commuting workers, their skin tones representing every shade of brown due to their heritage of European, African, and indigenous intermarriage.

We pull up outside an expanse of wall, peeling ochre paint swallowing the single wooden door at which we're welcomed enthusiastically by an elderly lady, the host of our *casa particulare.* Her and her husband's scrupulously neat and tidy apartment is an environment I've only seen in period television shows or old magazines and documentaries about the golden era of the US. We're shown to a sparse yet immaculate bedroom, followed by possibly the saddest looking dog in the whole world, a Basset Hound with lower eyelids so droopy I could use them to store my spare change. I love Cuba already.

The next couple of days are devoted to exploring Santiago and the Cuban way of life. We consider ourselves fortunate to be visiting one of the country's less glitzy cities first, where we can slowly absorb the distinctive atmosphere without being distracted by tourist kitsch.

Of course, alongside the Ladas are the sleek 1950s US vehicles ranging from gaily painted, lovingly maintained museum pieces to clapped-out, creaking wrecks, the recipients of numerous mechanical resurrections. The Buicks, Studebakers, and Chryslers vie for the transport peso with Bicitaxis—three-wheeled, pedal-powered rickshaws with a roof canopy and space for two passengers. The cracked and austere walls of the city, some of which are gutted shells held up only by long-forgotten scaffolding, are linked by webs of tangled overhead cables, a hideous mess of improvised electricity and communications. On the other hand, cute statues appear in random places, complemented by the elegant filigree ironwork on lampposts and balconies. Oh, how things were built in the first half of the twentieth century, before cost became more important than style! I'm drowning in anemoia—nostalgia for a time I never experienced.

The rhythm of day-to-day life is coupled with an awareness of constant background musicality, seeping from doorways or the quiet corners of outdoor spaces, where groups of friends tease beautiful melodies from their instruments. *Parque Céspedes*, the city's main plaza, forms a natural hub just a couple of blocks from our *casa*. It's surrounded by stately old buildings like the *Catedral de Nuestra Senora de la Asuncion,* one of Santiago's many churches, and the *Hotel Casa Granda*, where more salubrious holidaymakers stay. These edifices certainly have character, but I personally prefer the *Castillo de San Pedro de la Roca del Morro*, an impregnable citadel perched atop a promontory towering over the entrance to Santiago harbour, its stones steeped in history. This mouthful of a fort was designed in 1587 to protect the settlement, first from pirates then rival European powers, and is now a UNESCO World Heritage site.

The serene castle is a welcome refuge from the burning midday sun, but just a hundred kilometres away is Guantanamo Bay, the body of water on Cuba's south coast that is home to the famous US naval base and detention camp. Officially, the land has been leased from the Cuban government since 1903, although, since the revolution, Castro has insisted the agreement was imposed upon Cuba illegally. He refuses to accept the income from the lease, which has no expiration date. As for the detention camp, which houses terrorist suspects and captured combatants from recent US-led wars, it's widely accepted that torture of inmates, detained indefinitely without trial, occurs here. It amazes me that such atrocities can be so blatantly carried out in this day and age by a so-called civilised power with no noticeable condemnation from other world leaders.

It's only after a couple of days that I work out what's so refreshing about Cuba. It's been affecting me since our arrival, but I couldn't put my finger on it. What I initially noticed as blank walls and clean architecture now strikes me from a different perspective—a complete and utter absence of public advertising. The billboards, bus stops, posters, and hoardings that bombard us relentlessly in the rest of the world are missing here. Because the government owns and runs all retail stores, which stock a very limited range of goods, combined with the high expense of anything but the basic necessities, advertising is largely defunct.

The resultant urban space is filled by national flags, by the red, five-pointed star of communism, and by political slogans, mostly of gratitude to the heroes of the revolution. *"Por Cuba, Con Fidel—Revolución,"* shouts a two-storey poster of Castro, looking pensive and saintly. *"Patria o Muerte"*—Fatherland or Death, is another popular scrawl. The iconic image of Ernesto 'Che' Guevara is accompanied by his famous rallying cry *"Hasta La Victoria, Siempre"*—Ever Onward to Victory. Ignoring for a moment the other hardships of Cuban life, if given the choice between a) fewer consumer goods and no advertising, versus b) a thousand different types of orange juice and the hideous Technicolor marketing nightmare in which modern society now exists, I would 100 percent choose the former. Once I come to this realisation, I revel in it. I bathe in the lack of intrusive garishness, admiring anew the cleanliness of the streets, my eyes pain free for the first time in forty years.

We're often the focus of attention as we wander, mostly from citizens asking for money. Young and old, they are usually polite, sometimes insistent, and all poignant, but I admit to rarely giving money to street beggars. Right or wrong, the scale of the problem overpowers me; if one can't help them all, how to choose one over another? And how to pick the genuine needy from the panhandling chancer? I do my best to steer us away from such incidents.

"But what if they really are starving?" asks my father, concerned, as I lead him away from one young hopeful. Over the last few days, he's been muted again. If a stranger speaks to him, he'll look to me to translate. Sometimes he'll just point at me noiselessly, shunning speech altogether. I'm sure the soreness of his bladder arrangement is a contributing factor. He found blood in his urine bag this morning from the pipe chafing. Maybe we've been walking too much.

When I remind him we're meeting my friend Marcus in a few days, he claims to have forgotten I had company planned, and that he "isn't interested in being part of a threesome." He even grumbles something about leaving as soon as Marcus arrives, and I wonder if the efficacy of the sertraline is waning. In any case, despite my recent irritability, I fervently hope he isn't serious. We still have over a week before we must go our separate ways, he to Spain and I back to Australia.

Saturday, on a street near *Parque Céspedes*, we're drawn to the sounds of music and duck into a buzzing bar, its front windows open to the street. Inside is a five-piece band belting out *son*, a particularly Cuban musical genre related to rhumba and salsa, incorporating elements from both Hispanic and African roots. The stage that covers a good part of the small room hosts two guitarists, a double bass, bongos, and some maracas played soulfully by a tall black man with a startling white goatee and loud Hawaiian shirt. The walls are chock-a-block with black and white photographs and oil portraits of *son* and *trova*[62] legends, and a couple of rows of rickety wooden chairs support the meagre but eager audience. This is the *Casa de la Trova*.

The floor space before the stage is occupied by the shimmying of two very contrasting dancers. The first is an amazingly enthusiastic old dear, probably in her seventies, twisting and shaking, skinny arms raised up like she's thanking Jesus for the gift of music. She's an absolute delight to watch. The second is younger, sullen and obese, her body fat bouncing as she gyrates grotesquely, clearly on autopilot. Her mechanical dance and blank stare are explained when she approaches us for money; she's displaying herself as an object of ridicule in return for tips. Later we see her unashamedly urinating in the street, a clear indication of mental illness.

Apart from that, *Casa de la Trova* is fantastic. The listeners are mostly of the older generation and dressed in their weekend best—faded, ill-fitting suits and trilby hats, the clothing equivalent of their cars. We chat to a couple of them, complimenting their look and the band. Dad seems to be enjoying himself until the inevitable supplication begins; our companions request alcohol, even though they look like they haven't eaten in days. I take pity on one particularly sad-faced old gent and hand him a few pesos with the admonition: '*Para comer, no para tomar*'—for food, not drink. He nods obediently, eyes brimming with either gratitude or self-loathing, and leaves the bar. I can only hope he keeps his word and buys himself a decent meal.

I'm still digging the vibe, but Dad claims to be overheating and goes outside. I imagine he just wants to escape the overwhelming attention, and when a perfectly healthy and well-built young man virtually demands I buy him a drink, my patience is exhausted, and I also leave. I find Dad in the plaza, sitting on a kerb with his feet in the gutter and his head in his hands. My step falters at the sight of his hunched figure and I slow my pace, needing time to work out how to ask if he's okay. In the end, he beats me to it, raising his head at my footfall.

62 A musical genre embodied by a lone singer/songwriter with a guitar.

"I'm just resting my eyes," he says too quickly, as if caught misbehaving. It looks more like he's sliding back into, if not outright depression, then certainly unhappiness. I don't know what I can do about it. I pray this is just a blip on his recently upward trajectory.

"If you don't mind, I'd like to go out after dinner," I say the next evening, "on my own."

Today is my birthday, the big four-zero, and I do not intend to commemorate it by talking politics all night. It's taken me all day to summon the courage to deliver this offhand remark.

Dad doesn't really do birthday and Christmas presents. He prefers gifting for no reason. "Buying gifts on specific occasions is mostly copied behaviour combined with clever marketing," is his take. "When I was young, I don't recollect there being a Father's Day.[63] If greeting card manufacturers had their way, we'd have a Grandparents' Day, if we don't already, and a Second Cousin's Day. How about a Neighbour's Day? There's more stress than pleasure in obligated gift giving for both parties. The main winners are the traders. How much better is it to say, 'I'm giving this to you because I love you,' or, 'I got this for you because you need one or want one,' and for the recipient to know that it was not out of obligation?"

I'd say he's probably in the minority with that opinion. Maybe his dislike is rooted in the pre-Christmas tragedy of his mother's death—or perhaps he's just a miserable old git. I don't know, but most people get over the cultural obligation and still enjoy giving and receiving.

Although he's stauncher in his behaviour now, he had to conform when we were young. We did get gifts, both at traditional and random times. I remember the last Christmas he actively participated in. I was about twenty-four, and the whole brood was home for the holidays

63 He's half right. Father's Day was formally recognised in the US in 1966, and the UK followed suit, although the tradition has been strong in majority Catholic countries in Europe since the middle ages.

for the first time in years. He wrapped a couple of dozen presents without labels and made us take turns choosing one. All the items were non-specific—a flashlight, a Thermos flask, chocolates—so it didn't matter who received what. One offering was literally a wooden spoon, and when my sister unwrapped it, he laughed his head off. At the other end of the scale, I recently happened to mention how much I liked a particular set of very expensive noise-cancelling headphones, and the next time I saw him, he presented me with a pair.

"You must do what you want to do," he states after a short pause, giving nothing away.

"I'm sorry," I blurt. "I just need an evening with, y'know, some real people!" It's been almost two weeks since his return, and I've loved (almost) every minute, but sometimes a guy needs a break.

"Don't worry, you can't possibly hurt my feelings," he states, ridiculously.

"That's because you don't have any," I mutter under my breath. I don't believe him, anyway. He does have feelings, I know it, but how can I get him to admit it? "What if I committed mass murder and told the police I did it to spite you?"

"Okay," he says after another moment's thought. "Allow me to clarify that. There's nothing anyone could *say* to hurt my feelings, but some people could *do* things to disappoint me. Few people have the power to hurt me, but you are one of them." I guess I should take this as a compliment, but his confidence in his emotional shield is ludicrous. I'm sure I could say something that would cause him mental anguish, but pursuing this theory would only end badly.

I don't know if I'm doing the right thing here. Our time together is precious, and I already lost it once. Like a cancer patient in remission, I should grasp the gift of his company with both hands and talk his ear off every night, but at the same time, it's not unreasonable to desire regular company. It's only one night. His doleful mood doesn't help, although this is probably when I should stick to him like glue. He's still tiring early from the drugs anyway; he'll be asleep soon, I reason.

I wander up to the *Parque Céspedes*, bathed in orange from the incandescent streetlights, take a sip from my tin of Cristal beer, and wonder what the hell to do next. It isn't long before a curious young guy approaches, casually dressed in jeans and a t-shirt. Thankfully, Lazarus isn't after my money but genuinely wants to make friends and doesn't realise I'm more eager than him to do so. After wishing me "*Feliz compleaños*!" he invites me to a Mother's Day street party. There are food stalls, banners, cheap Cuba Libres, and a few rides, including a small Ferris wheel for children, a clanking structure of rotating rusty cages that resembles some sort of medieval punishment.

Lazarus's friends are hip twentysomethings with decent threads and cash for drinks. I don't know much about the Cuban social hierarchy, but they seem pretty middle class and welcome me into their circle. My Spanish is insufficient to keep abreast of the conversation, but that's not important—I'm happy just to sit there, fielding the occasional enquiry and glowing in the warmth of normal human companionship. I love Dad's company 99 percent of the time, but he does sometimes lack that natural unspoken affection, that almost imperceptible sensation that, when one feels it, confirms one is welcome in a person's presence. I may be borderline misanthropic, but I still require that from time to time, and despite only just meeting these young, happy Cubans, I feel it already. I can't imagine how difficult being his wife must have been without that emotional feedback.

Even after twenty-five years of marriage, Mum still didn't know how to communicate with her husband, how to make him understand what she wanted.

"He used to dress to upset me," she claimed during our last conversation, somewhat improbably. "He was very fond of what he called his lumberjack coat, a padded check shirt, which was alright for wearing around the house and yard but not to go out in. We'd be going to dinner, and I'd spend time getting nicely dressed and then he'd turn up in that bloody lumberjack coat! I'd say 'Are you going to change? I don't think that's smart enough,' and he'd get ever so defensive. He started doing it on purpose. I know he did. I put it every which way I could put it nicely—'That's not suitable' or 'I think we need to dress up a bit'—until one day, I just said, 'If that jacket's going out to dinner, I'm not!' He didn't argue. He went and changed, and it never happened again. And I thought: was it that easy? I'd been trying to put it nicely for a couple of years, and that's all it took."

This mirrors my experience with Paul on the boat through the Amazon. "Maybe he genuinely didn't understand what you wanted until you told him straight out?" I speculated. "You were being too subtle." His inability to read social signals and understand the subtleties of indirect language was clearly a major factor in the breakdown of their relationship.

"Yes, I wonder," she mused, casting her mind back to how everything could have been different had she just known how he functioned. Admittedly, sorting out their own problems would've been of low precedence during those years. Dad was a workaholic and Mum took care of three separate school runs, the housework, meals, and her chiropody clients. Any spare time was spent helping out in the factory. There was little time for luxuries and little inclination on his part.

"We were just coping at that point," she said. "Bumbling along on a wing and a prayer, with a gang of children whose lives you have to keep steady, fed and watered, and get to school on time in clean clothes with their lunch packed. That was my priority."

Money was still tight at that stage, and they were forced to sell the barn that had previously been the factory. Dad had pre-designed it for conversion into a residential dwelling, and he was able to run his base-sticking machines, and eventually base-moulding machines, from a smaller outhouse. That meant we acquired close neighbours, a retired couple living right across the yard, which was never part of the plan and must have been of some annoyance to Dad.

One day, he was chopping wood in the lean-to behind the kitchen. We had a lovely wood-burning Rayburn stove that filled a cavernous chimney in the kitchen, and we used to keep it alight all winter to prevent our extremities from freezing off. Chopping wood was far from a chore; it was an activity for relieving stress. I used to enjoy a good log-splitting session when I was frustrated, and I imagine he did too. He was hard at it when two strangers appeared. They were large, muscular types with close-cropped hair, and smartly dressed—intentionally intimidating. They were, in a word, thugs, and they'd come to invite him to settle his debt with a former employee.

Back when he was struggling with his staff in Birmingham, Dad had hit upon a plan to minimise his interaction with them in the hope of reducing his stress levels. He decided to subcontract all the work to them, an idea well ahead of its time. He would sell his employees the raw material, purchase from them the finished product, add on a percentage, then sell it to his customers. Everything went as planned until one of the men became greedy. Polycarbonate is a strong plastic, but in order to mould correctly, it must be thoroughly dried and contain only a small percentage of non-virgin material, i.e., ground-up sprues. The rogue employee deduced he could improve his profit margin by mixing in more reground material than advised. Similarly, he could speed up the process by not allowing sufficient drying time.

The product at that time, a metre-long folding rule, appeared to be adequate, but when printed and assembled, it cracked easily at the joints. The plastic was too weak. The customer was naturally dissatisfied and refused to pay, leaving Dad with a loss in excess of £23,000. He was consequently obliged to withhold payment of £12,000 from the employee, who denied any wrongdoing, while the dispute was settled in court.

Dad employed a lawyer in the belief that whoever was at fault, it couldn't possibly be him, as he was effectively only the distributor. He was wrong. The customer's lawyers were adept at prolonging the dispute, not allowing it to come to court, while the employee managed to successfully claim legal aid. This left Dad with a growing solicitor's bill and no end in sight. He was eventually obliged to withdraw, unable to recover any payment from the customer and unable to pay his employee. He discovered years later that his lawyer could have arranged to pass the debt directly onto the employee, excluding him from the process altogether, but that would have resulted in considerably less profit for the lawyer. But that's lawyers for you.

Now, the employee had sold his debt to these gangsters. They would have paid him something like half the money he was owed with the intention of recovering the full amount by means of intimidation. Spotting the men for what they were, Dad politely invited them into the house and explained the circumstances of the debt. Their response was one of subtle menace. One of them quickly took a photograph of him, an act designed to threaten future violence. Having delivered their terms, they left. They'd arrived on foot, obviously walking from the bottom of the long, winding lane that led to our property.

As soon as they'd turned the first corner, Dad called our new neighbour as a witness and drove with him down the lane, passing the two standover men on the way. At the bottom was a parked car with a third man at the wheel. They noted its registration number and returned home. Within a few days Dad received a phone call from his former employee explaining that these people were dangerous and he should worry about the safety of his family if he didn't pay them. This wasn't some friendly warning but another avenue of intimidation.

As a result of this incident, Dad applied for a shotgun licence and purchased a trained Alsatian for his personal protection. I remember being mightily surprised when he turned up at the house one day with this monstrous beast, for we'd always been a cat family. We still were, much to the shock of the cats! The dog was called Otto and was intelligent and mostly obedient. In fact, he was excellent in many respects except one—if a stranger entered the farmyard, the dog would run away. When one of our neighbours popped around, Otto was terrified. He whined and cowered, claws scraping at the slate floor to get away. I could tell Dad was embarrassed as he struggled to drag the hulking yet timorous creature to meet our visitor. The German Shepherd's voice was not so much a gruff bark as a craven yowl, for which I nicknamed him Otto von Misbark.[64] This wasn't ideal behaviour in a guard dog, and Dad eventually had to return him.

However, Mike had a friend who was married to a Birmingham police inspector. This man assured Dad that the people who practised this type of debt collection generally kept within the law and relied on intimidation to encourage payment. With the aid of the car

64 After Otto von Bismarck, the late 19th century German Chancellor.

registration number, he was able to identify the culprits and warn them off, solving the problem for good.

"I didn't think it likely the family would be harmed in any way, for two reasons," Dad says of the episode. "Firstly, operating from Birmingham, they'd have to go to a great deal of trouble to know where and when to locate you away from the house. Secondly, since I had the car registration number, they would be traceable and first suspects of any such action." He omits any mention of how he may have felt at the time, reporting the incident with as much emotion as he would a trip to the shops to buy milk. "The worst I anticipated was that they would return and threaten me with, or administer, a beating."

My parents' relationship began to deteriorate more rapidly after my brother and I moved out. I can't say exactly what happened, but there was a change. Dad began to cut himself off, physically and emotionally, from his wife. "I felt him withdrawing from me," she says. "I thought we'd be able to rub along together, but he absolutely withdrew his good will. That's the only way I can describe it. I felt very lonely. My best friend had shrunk away from me. He wasn't there anymore. We tried counselling once, but he got upset and refused to go again, which left me at a dead end."

It was then she started to think about autism. People born in the 1940s didn't have the opportunity to be AS or autistic because it hadn't been invented. It was only much later that child psychologists began looking at difficult children and found a pattern, and so everything was geared towards diagnosing and managing autism in children. She had a suspicion he was affected, but nobody was treating adults except Professor Simon Baron-Cohen in Cambridge, and there was something like a two-year waiting list for the research centre there. Cambridge is a long way from Cornwall, and he wouldn't have gone anyway, so she gave it up.

Around that time Mum took an Access to Education course for mature students, one day a week in Plymouth. From there, she applied to the University of St. Mark and St. John to read History and Development Studies. "I hadn't ever got a proper degree, only my diploma in Podiatric Medicine, and the government was funding it, so I thought, 'Why not?' " There were lots of easily obtainable grants flying about at the time. "I had more money going through my hands than I'd had in years."

The other reason for studying originally was to give Dad some space, but this somehow escalated into a full-blown separation when Mum decided to move to Plymouth for the duration of her degree. I still cringe when I remember her telling me the news. I was sitting in the farmhouse kitchen, eating breakfast. The early morning sun was blocked by the thick wooden window shutters but still succeeding in casting a dim glow around the room. The atmosphere was heavy, turbid, but I didn't know why. I was home from university for Easter, working in the factory, sticking bases, as ever. I was slaving like a madman to finance my forthcoming year in Australia, working ten to twelve hours a day.

Mum entered the room as I spooned cereal into my mouth. She was uncharacteristically quiet as she sat beside me. No "Good morning, darling" that day; she seemed pensive. She's never been one to sugarcoat the truth. When one of our beloved cats choked to death while we were at school, she broke it to us in the car on the way home. "Angie died today," she said, apropos of nothing. No preamble, no "I've got some bad news . . ." It was her way of ripping off the plaster, quick sharp. I suppose it worked as we didn't burst into tears, but I was shocked at the abruptness of it.

That day, she used the same method. "I'm moving to Plymouth," she said. At first, I didn't understand. It didn't make sense. Why would she do that? "I'm leaving your father. I still love him very much, but I can't live with him any longer."

I said nothing. I was taken aback. Where did this come from? Living in Birmingham, I'd been unaware of the stresses of the last couple of years and my parents growing estrangement, and if I had been, I would've ignored it. Silence remained my strategy. I stared glumly into the bowl, watching the floating remnants of soggy cornflakes drift around my spoon. I didn't know what to say anyway. If I didn't reply, maybe she'd just go away and this would be over.

She didn't, though. She explained her reasons—the distance, the coldness—as time stretched into the following week. It's the longest conversation I've ever had, if a conversation can be had by one person and a mute. I just wanted it to stop. I was an adult, old enough not to get upset. I understood: marriages break down all the time, so why should our family survive unscathed? But I *was* upset; I was ready to be devastated, but I was withholding that reaction until I had proof of her words, until she actually moved out. That way, I wouldn't waste my emotions if it never came to pass, if it was just talk. But I was angry, angry they couldn't work it out. I imagined one or both of them giving up too soon. I labelled them quitters, co-conspirators in a failed marriage. They'd failed *me*.

I stayed quiet until she finished her explanation and left me to process it. I don't remember most of what she said. I had to get to the factory. There was work to be done.

When I question her about it now, Mum cautiously admits she may have said the wrong thing to Dad. " 'Don't worry about considering we're married,' I said to him. 'We're just friends. Don't worry about the sex thing if that bothers you. Just consider we house share.' I thought that'd give him space. I always came back at the weekend. But he took that as a licence to do whatever he wanted."

"Well, yes," I have to tell her, gently. "So would I. If one takes the meaning of the words literally, which he would, and I would, it means it's over. You're free to do whatever you like."

She sighs. "Looking back, I didn't communicate well. I just wanted to take the pressure off him and not make the relationship any more than he could cope with, but I obviously expressed it wrong."

After her move, Dad confided in the neighbour across the farmyard. "Brenda says she doesn't want to live with me anymore. She's going to leave me and go and live in Plymouth." While this seems out of character, it just proves how very surprised he was. Relations between the two were not cordial during this period. Colin, semi-retired, was working part-time in our factory while concurrently lodging a complaint about the noise to the council. The building wasn't officially zoned for industrial use, so he certainly had a case, but its success would cost him his job. Strange behaviour until one understands the main complainant was actually his wife, who said the noise from the moulding machines kept her awake at night. Dad had to keep the machines running continuously, but spent much effort and money soundproofing the pneumatic system. He tried many different methods, but she always claimed to be able to hear the *pshhhht* of pressurised air escaping the valves.

One evening, he informed Colin he was trialling a new dampening method, and to ask his wife once more if she was disturbed during the night. The following morning, the answer was the same—she'd been kept awake by the hissing. At that point Dad revealed he'd shut off the equipment altogether and there'd been no sound to hear. It was an awkward victory but made no real difference, and eventually he was forced to move his entire premises to an industrial estate thirty kilometres away.

"Don't worry, you'll find someone else," consoled Colin.

"Who says I'm looking for someone else?" was Dad's reply. However, he reasoned there was no harm in having some female company, so he joined a dating organisation. He answered newspaper ads and even posted one or two. "I went on dates and regularly updated Brenda on my exploits," he tells me. "She was okay with it." Was she, though?

"Well, I certainly wasn't expecting that," she says, still in shock after twenty-three years.

"He took what you said literally," I remind her.

"Well, I didn't know about that then. I just wanted to reassure him and let him go his own way. I didn't think he'd go and join a singles club. I mean, doesn't he have enough trouble with women?" She's got a point.

He found that whereas he was looking for after dinner conversation, the ladies he met were mostly seeking second husbands or sexual partners. He had several offers of no-commitment sex, and one very attractive lady kept telling him what great chemistry existed between them. She plied him with her best whisky one night, late at her house, and he barely escaped with his honour intact. His policy was not to get involved. He'd spend the evening dining or dancing, escort the lucky lady to her car, shake her by the hand and watch her jaw drop as he wished her good evening and walked away.

One of his dates, Christine, didn't fall into either of the above categories. They'd meet up regularly and became good friends, until one day her estranged husband interfered. He'd invented a guitar bridge of some kind and was very protective of the design because he didn't yet have a patent. By coincidence, he'd unsuccessfully approached Mike sometime in the past with a view to manufacturing this bridge. When he heard about Christine's friendship with a Mr. Slater, he assumed Dad was Mike. He then jumped to the conclusion that Christine and Dad (or Mike) were conspiring to cheat him out of his invention.

"Whoever he thought he was dealing with, it was my telephone number he found, and I started to receive calls threatening what he would do to me should this betrayal occur," Dad's story goes. "He would not accept that I was not my brother, nor was I my brother's keeper. I cannot remember in detail the threats he made, but in the end, he attempted to arrange a contract for Christine." He's typically downplaying this part. In fact, the man travelled to Chard in Somerset, a town with a rough reputation and high regional crime rate and attempted to hire somebody to murder his wife. I believe he started by asking around one of the pubs. "Sadly for him, he ended up approaching a police officer to make the final arrangements and pay the fee, so the poor fellow ended up in jail." So, my father was involved in an attempted hit and could conceivably have been next on the list, yet he tells the story in the same tone as he would an anecdote about building materials.

"You say, 'sadly for him,' and 'the poor fellow,' " I point out. "Most people would've been pleased he got his comeuppance after trying to have their girlfriend killed. Why the sympathy?"

"I didn't feel sympathy," he disagrees. " 'Sadly for him' means it would have made him sad, which I believe to be true. 'The poor fellow' would apply to anyone incarcerated, in that they would be poor in liberty."

"Yes, logically, you are correct," I sigh, "but for ninety-nine percent of people, that would sound like you were sympathising."

"Well, there you have my difficulty in relating to the ninety-nine percent," he concludes obstinately.

After three years away, Mum graduated from her course in Plymouth and returned to the farmhouse, by which time my sister had also left home. Dad was partway through converting the remaining barn into a self-contained house, where he could live in splendid isolation, his own little hideaway from the world. And thus, their relationship continued, static and broken yet still alive.

I meet Markus in the cobblestoned streets of Trinidad, a picturesque colonial town exactly half the country away from Santiago. Originally from Vienna, Austria, Mucki is one of the friendliest guys I've ever met. He's quick with a smile and has a talent for putting people at ease. He's damn good looking too, and he knows it. We first crossed paths in Grenada, Nicaragua, where I was travelling with a Swedish guy I'd met in Honduras, and he with one of his friends from home. One morning in the hostel kitchen, I sat near the two Austrians while they were discussing their plans for the day—a boat trip on the lake. It sounded like fun, but I wasn't about to invite myself into the company of this pair of confident young bucks, no siree, so I half listened while reading my book. I must've looked like Billy No Mates because after finalising their arrangements, Mucki hooked a thumb in my direction and said loudly to his mate: "Shall we invite this lonely guy?" The cheeky bugger!

"Hey," I protested in mock outrage. "I have a friend! Josef's my friend." Secretly, though, I was stricken by that offhand and mischievous gesture of inclusivity, and I liked him straightaway. Josef and I joined them on the lake, along with some other stragglers, and over the following few days, the small group we formed became a self-perpetuating party machine. Mucki and I met a few more times on the route up through Central America, and many times since in all corners of the globe.

Mucki's smile is as wide as ever as he grips me in a bear hug, arms muscled beneath his trademark white t-shirt and board shorts, eyes doubtless twinkling behind his sunglasses. I swear he could charm a smile out of a gargoyle downspout, but I'm concerned his charisma may not work on my miserable father. I apologetically explain that my travelling companion isn't the friendliest of people, and that he hates the beach, which is where Mucki has announced the day's destination to be. He's spectacularly unfazed by my negativity as I guide him along the narrow alleys to our *casa particulare*.

We'd arrived very early that morning on a night bus from *Santiago de Cuba*, a long journey which had exhausted the old man. He seems brighter after a nap though and greets my friend warmly enough. Mucki immediately proposes a deal: if he can locate a taxi older than my Dad, the latter will have to accompany us for a ride in it. This isn't phrased as a question, more a statement of challenge Dad doesn't reject quickly enough. He looks ready to demur, but Mucki keeps up the patter, asking him all manner of questions as we're marched up Trinidad's main street.

Waiting there is an original 1929 Model A Ford, its driver ready to chauffeur us to *Playa Ancón*. It's a real beauty, I have to admit. The buff-coloured cabriolet comes complete with running boards, a gorgeous flying goose hood ornament, and a rumble seat—a rear bench which unfolds from the boot. Though neither of us are car enthusiasts, I can tell even Dad is secretly impressed as we trundle off, the wind in our hair, like a dysfunctional family in a silent movie.

Dad spends the whole day conversing with Mucki like an old friend. As with Dave, he's turned on the geniality to avoid alienating a friend of mine, but I can see he's also drawn in by Mucki's easy charisma. I sit and watch, impressed by the way my friend has put this curmudgeonly old misanthropist at ease. It's a masterclass in affability, a relentless charm offensive which nobody can resist. If anyone can drag a man from the sucking whirlpool of depression, it's Mucki.

"He's a nice guy, your friend, isn't he?" admits Dad back at our casa as we change for dinner. It's possibly the biggest compliment he's paid anybody in three months.

"Yes, and you seem very chatty given he's a complete stranger," I point out, subjecting various items of tatty clothing to the age-old sniff test.

"Actually, nowadays, I am perfectly comfortable speaking to people on a first occasion," he corrects, buttoning a fresh shirt. "My difficulty is in judging the depth of the relationship on a future basis. When you meet someone for the first time, you know there is no relationship, and you don't have to judge anything at all. You can go into a routine—'How do you do?' etc. The next time you meet them, and every time thereafter, you can't know exactly how they judge the relationship, so you don't know how to deal with them. This certainly wasn't true of me as a young person, of course. I wouldn't have dreamed of approaching anybody."

Despite this logical explanation, I find it hard to recognise my father throughout our evening meal. Gone is the brooding grump, jettisoned in favour of a talkative avuncular figure who laughs and converses like a practised socialite. He engages Mucki in his usual subject matter, which is responded to with lively debate, and tests his opinion on the voluntary food preparation ratings scheme. I don't think I've ever seen Dad so familiar; he may even have used the word "mate"! When he begins to tell his new favourite story, the eye-watering Colombian catheter incident, I walk away and leave them to it.

After dinner, in a bizarre nightclub located thirty metres beneath Trinidad, Mucki gives me his first impressions. "He seems quite normal to me," he shouts in his mangled US/Schwarzenegger accent, the product of learning English through the medium of Hollywood. We've deposited Dad home and ventured out for a nightcap. "We got along well. I thought him sharing his prostate story was a very personal thing. I liked that."

Discoteca Ayala is installed in a cave at the north end of town, accessed via a narrow gate and a steep staircase through the rock. Subtle lighting shows the way, the air eerily quiet until the final corner, around which you discover exactly what you're in for: blaring salsa and techno; huge, hanging television screens; and smartly dressed Trinitarians, their white clothes blinding under the neon lights.

"Without any background knowledge, I wouldn't have said he was in any way abnormal," he continues, as all four of our eyes follow some particularly nice curves on their way to the bar. The main cavern's rough limestone walls define its interior spaces, the ceiling out of sight above. Dark nooks are utilised for speakers, booths, even the bar, and ragged pinnacles jut from the floor as unexpected obstacles to drunken patrons. Bright splashes from coloured lights stain the walls. What can I say? He's fooled Mucki as he fooled Dave. Yes, if Mucki has displayed his talents of persuasion, Dad has responded with an Oscar-worthy acting performance.

"I love that you're doing this trip together," finishes Mucki, returning his attention to the topic at hand. "He seems completely unfussed at low budget travel or at being in Cuba. My father would hate it. He'd never travel this way. You're very lucky." We lapse into silence while the club's ridiculous floorshow gets underway—dancing girls and male hunks picking up tables with their teeth. It's not really my scene, but the location is fabulous, and further enhanced by knowing Disco Ayala's gruesome secret.

One Carlos "Coco" Ayala, a deserter from the Cuban war of independence, hid out in this cave in the late nineteenth century. Here he developed a career as a killer, kidnapping and murdering small children. Local whispers tally his victims at fifteen before being discovered and beheaded by a local mob. The facts are more conservative, however. In 1879, he was captured by police after abducting a local girl, whose half-buried body was found in this cave, along with the unidentifiable remains of two other victims. The twenty-nine-year-old was held for three years before his execution. That the nightclub, a state-run enterprise, should name itself after the killer is a tad provocative for small-town Cuba, but may be a result of the man's continuing legend. Even now, parents use his name to threaten their children into obedience: "Be good or Carlos Ayala will get you!"

I've scheduled another couple of stops before our big finish in Havana, but the evening before we're due to leave Trinidad, Dad announces he'll go straight to the capital and await us there. It's exactly what I've been afraid of. He claims he won't be able to keep up with us, but that's nonsense; he's carrying out his threat, refusing to be 'part of a threesome,' as he put it. I've felt him withdrawing from me of late, not in as damaging a way as he did with Mum, but harmlessly, gently, with a wave and a smile. His flight home from Cancún is a few days earlier than mine, a discrepancy that had seemed unimportant when we were booking our tickets, a few days here or there, but now those few days seem like a tragic loss. The night we reconvene in Havana will be our last.

I'm torn. My initial reaction is to argue, to persuade him to accompany us as planned, maximising our time together. Another part of me doesn't mind so much, relishing some time with my old mate Mucki and his madcap schemes for adventure. I remember him persuading me to go tubing in the Guatemalan Highlands, which sounds innocent enough, except it was night and the river was full of sharp, unseen rocks, and of course we were several beers the worse for wear. We were lucky to locate the exit point as we could easily have floated miles too far and ended up flailing over a waterfall in the dark. This is probably not something that would've happened travelling with a seventy-two-year-old depressive.

There's no sense in fighting, though; he's made his decision. At least we'll be parting by design, rather than having him rudely torn away from me like before. I feel myself start to relax, a sensation of comfort creeping over me, a freedom from the responsibility of chaperone.

"You're not off the hook yet!" he admonishes, as if interpreting my thoughts. "I'd like you to book me transport to Havana and a *casa particulare*." I do so, taking a photo of the *casa* name on his phone to show the taxi driver. I still worry he won't cope, that he'll get lost or mugged or just sit around being unhappy, and what then would I do?

"I'm not as decrepit as I make out, you know," he says, firm but gentle eye contact reinforcing his words. "I can get around by myself." In my heart, I know this to be true, but part of me would prefer it wasn't. That way I'd get to look after him for longer. I'll never have children, but I think I've caught a glimpse of the bittersweet melancholy that waits to reward fretful parents on the independence of their offspring.

The next morning, I walk him to his shared taxi. "Son," he says as the driver loads his pack into the boot. "I've really enjoyed not having any responsibility on this trip. Having someone to book everything, handle the cash, find out information, and above all, to worry about things—I feel like royalty. Thanks for everything you've done for me." I coolly shrug off his praise but appreciate it, nonetheless. However, I can't help interpreting these words as a farewell. As soon as the taxi rounds that cobbled corner, he'll disappear. "I still don't understand why you wanted to travel with me in the first place," he adds.

This time I give it to him straight, no ice. "When you die, I don't want to think I didn't spend enough time with you."

"You've already spent more time and given me more attention than I expected from you," he replies. I assume he means that as a compliment. "I appreciate it. You don't have to worry. I promise this is true."

He climbs into the backseat carefully, as though it's a spring-loaded trap that might clamp its jaws down on him, and shuffles around the upholstery looking for the sweet spot. The driver is still awaiting other passengers, so I don't linger to wave him off. I just fake a quick smile, although the mistiness of my eyes and horizontal line of my mouth could only deceive a mindblind person. By turning smartly and walking away, like a parent leaving a child on the first day of school, I manage to keep SAD[65] at bay. Will he wait for us in Havana? I honestly don't know. And if he doesn't, how long will it be before next we meet?

65 Separation Anxiety Disorder

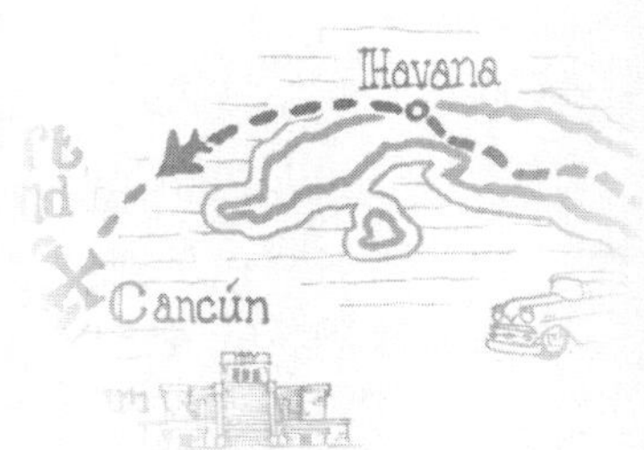

Chapter 16

Absquatulation

One can't really avoid prostitutes in Havana, not if one ventures into any remotely touristy area after dark, but it's not often I actually get propositioned, even less so when the offer includes one of my mates. We look at each other for half a second before bursting into laughter.

"We're married!" we shout in unison, by way of declining. After all, we wouldn't want to hurt her feelings—or each other's!

It's a gauntlet one must run in order to experience the *casas de musica*, the jazz bars and rumba clubs for which the city is famous. Fidel once proclaimed that Cubans didn't need to earn extra money by sleeping with foreign tourists, hence the women who did so were just having fun. They were called *jineteras*, after the word for 'jockey'—they rode the tourists for pleasure. Nowadays, the word more accurately translates as 'hustler,' and male *jineteros* also roam the streets trying to relieve gullible tourists of their money. Fidel also said that although Cuba has no prostitution, if it had, they'd be the best-educated prostitutes in the world!

We've spent a good portion of the evening lounging around the Malecón—the long, seafront promenade that runs east-west across the top of the city. Beyond the seawall lie the Straits of Florida, and the foundation of much of Cuba's economic frustration. Yet the US is also a source of income[66] and an object of desire for many, the

66 $2b was sent to Cuba from the US in 2013, mostly by expat Cubans

mythical land of milk and honey. On this Saturday night, we have our backs to that beast, perched on the wall with an arsenal of Cristal beer, just a couple of bodies in a long line of revellers that stretches away in both directions.

We'd wandered up after dark and easily befriended the people sitting either side of us. That's the Mucki Effect. They were curious, shy at first, but more talkative as time, and their own alcohol, wore on. We'd answered their questions and asked our own, and by the time we were assailed by the elegant sounds of the troubadours who wandered up and down the wall, busking for pennies, we readily jumped up to dance with our new pals. The atmosphere was electric and the mood joyous, illuminated by the fluorescent streetlights lining the road, until somebody got a little carried away. One of the young ladies offered to show us both a good time, as it were, simultaneously, in a more private setting. No lady of the night, she, just inquisitive and fun, a true *jinetera*. Needless to say, we made our excuses and left.

Beautiful in its dilapidation, Havana is a gem of a city. Wandering through the various districts, each bustling with its own unique demographic—workers, layabouts, foreigners, the elite—is far more rewarding to me than an itinerary of plazas, churches, and castles. Settled in the early sixteenth century, the city only came into its own three hundred years later as an important trading post between North and South America. Money began to flow in and many of the classic structures were erected at that time, prompting the city's nickname: The Paris of the Antilles.

Havana continued to flourish through independence in 1902, until its prosperity ended for good with the Revolution of 1959 and subsequent US embargo. Now, the once-grand buildings crumble, hiding behind peeling façades, but are all the more charming for it. Restoration of the most prestigious architecture has begun, but the process is slow and concentrated mainly in *Havana Vieja*. The freshness of this work has the strange effect of making the Old Quarter seem much newer than the more recent, and more derelict, areas of the city. There, rusty scaffolding pipes crawl over semi-collapsed buildings, studiously supporting their forlorn and empty frontages until some unknown future when they may be rescued from total oblivion.

By day, the Malecón hosts lines of fisherman hanging their rods against the backdrop of the *Castillo de los Tres Santos Reyes Magnos del Morro,* a vast fortress perched on the bare headland that guards the entrance to Havana Port. Where the swell laps against the rocky foundations of the sea wall, no shortage of teenagers congregate to gossip, sunbathe, and outdo each other's back flips, their faces alight with youthful vivacity. Uncovered by the mantle of night, modern hotel high-rises stand out between the colonial mansions, stark and ugly like a plastic vase on a shelf of earthenware jars.

For the past few days, we've explored the city, from the concrete wasteland of the *Plaza Revolución* with its hideous Che mural, to the tree-lined boulevard of the *Paseo del Prado*. We've counted thousands of Cuban flags—flying from lampposts, draped from balconies, and printed on almost every t-shirt worn beneath a white face. We've ridden in a 1955 Chevy Bel Air, eaten more delicious and addictive one dollar street pizzas than there are meals in a day, and dodged the gangs of proud yet intimidating trans-women who roam the streets around the *Capitolio Nacional*, a glorious 1920s dome that once housed Cuba's congress. My favourite activity, though, is to gaze at the elegant edifices, handsome in their decay: the flaking window shutter, the missing spindle of a balustrade, the masonry shadow left where a balcony has fallen completely off its wall.

Before Havana, Mucki and I had enjoyed our last few days of rural Cuba, stopping off in colonial Cienfuegos before heading to the beach town of *Playa Larga*. Parenthesising my trip in Scuba gear, *Cueva el Brinco* turned out to be one of the most stunning dive sites it's been my privilege to experience. The entrance was via a secret pool, hidden in a narrow crack in the earth at the end of a rough forest track. Beneath the surface, this apparently modest swimming hole opened out into a gigantic, flooded, rectilinear cavern. Following our DM, we slowly descended one vertical wall, the base of which lay far beyond the extent of our torchlight. We swam through the eerie halocline towards the furthest dark corner of the roughly formed chamber.

There, we fine-tuned our buoyancy, switched off our lights, and returned to the womb.

Black, silent, and weightless in a vast and remote sensory deprivation tank, I hung suspended with my thoughts. As in the Blue Hole months ago, the darkness brought to mind my father, but this time a shaft of positivity pierced the indigo depths. It wasn't just the antidepressants; something had happened to my attitude along the way. My initial frustration with his idiosyncrasies had evolved into tolerance and appreciation. Learning more fully of his struggle to fit in with society had brought us closer together, from my side at least. I didn't know if he felt that much closer to me, but I didn't mind. I felt sympathy, and love, and a patience that was no longer finite. The motivation for our trip was reconnection, and slowly but surely, almost imperceptibly at times, this had happened.

Insignificant specks lost in an inky abyss, Mucki and I turned back to the entrance just as the silhouettes of another group of divers were outlined against the greenish-blue light. Their torches twitched back and forth like searchlights roving the night for an escaped beast, the clarity of the water incredible. Suddenly, a needle of sunlight struck through the gloom like a schism in hell, except this was not hell; far from it.

From *Playa Larga*, we'd journeyed west to Viñales, a quiet town adjacent to a large national park famous for its limestone mountains, caves, and traditional agriculture. We initially arranged a guide to explore the park by foot, but when he didn't show up, we set off on our own. Of course, half an hour later, we were scratching our heads at a confluence of muddy tracks, the route not quite as obvious as it appeared on our map. As we were wondering whether to persevere in a random direction or turn back, up trotted a cowboy, ten-gallon hat, spurs and all, who asked what on earth we were doing there, on foot, alone.

After some preamble the man offered to take us pony trekking for a reasonable sum, touring the park's highlights: the painted rocks, the cave, the lookout. At the cigar ranch, Mucki fulfilled his dream of puffing on a Cuban stogie that'd been expertly rolled and trimmed before his eyes, not on a virgin's thighs but on a wooden table by a nimble-fingered young man with a pile of dried leaves and some heavy steel scissors. Possibly the most overriding memory of that day is our lack of suitable horse-riding attire—thin board shorts are not well-known for adequately protecting a chap's *cojones* from a hard leather saddle. To add to our discomfort, Rosario and Negro had competition issues. Both steeds preferred the lead, with the result being that most of the ride was a stop-start race between the two. Any slight widening of the trail was an opportunity for a spurt from the trailing beast, regardless of whatever bush, branch, or jutting rock was to pass over its head and into its rider's face.

The evening was well advanced when we reached Havana the following day. It took a while longer to find some accommodation and navigate to Dad's *casa*, so 11:00 p.m. was chiming as we rocked up. I felt unexpectedly wobbly as I mounted the stairs. My breath rasped in my chest. Was I that unfit, or was I scared the door would be opened by a blank-faced stranger with a room to let? Thankfully, we were ushered into the living room where Dad sat on the sofa, his body in the awkward, unrelaxed posture of a formal visitor in a stranger's house.

Obviously awaiting our rescue committee, he jumped up, and I forced him into a hug. He introduced us to Rosa, his hostess: "*Es mi hijo!*" he beamed, his chest puffing out slightly with pride. "This is my son!" She'd apparently forced him to accompany her and her whole extended family out to dinner on his first night, not taking no for an answer. Despite sounding like a recipe for instant trauma all around, it seems like he secretly enjoyed it.

Dog-tired by then, I was all for going straight to bed and reconvening in the morning, but he was adamant we find somewhere for a nightcap. And so, we ventured out into the dark streets of this strange city, its broken beauty transformed into creepy shadows by night, looking for somewhere, anywhere that was open. It was sad to think we'd come to the end of our grand adventure. Arriving in Havana meant our circuit of the Caribbean Sea was virtually complete, the circle closing, the snake's jaws approaching its own tail. Dad cut a piteous figure as he shuffled along the pavement. His life hasn't been easy, and despite his recent sunny disposition, I fear its heavy burden has lain too long on his shoulders.

He and my mother continued their bizarre, estranged existence for another five years. I manage to piece together an image of this period after questioning them about it separately.

"When she'd left, I'd been relieved I wasn't in that relationship anymore," he states, frank as ever. "It had never sat well with me. And so I made it perfectly clear on her return from Plymouth that we would be housemates only. There was no way I would consider going back into the marriage."

He moved into the newly refurbished barn, content and still dating, while she lived in the main house, unemployed and unhappy. Divorce was mooted, but being born in the 1940s, neither could stand the perceived disgrace and self-loathing that would follow. "I believe when two people stand and say 'Til death us do part' then death is what ends the marriage, nothing else," is Dad's forthright opinion, with which I absolutely agree. "I'm appalled at people who get married time after time and stand there and say 'Til death us do part.' What a load of blinking liars they are. You say it, you keep it."

Dad had employed a local lady in the factory, Pauline, who shared his love of Willie Nelson. Having recently left her husband, she moved into a standalone bedsit attached to the main farmhouse.

"I never saw it coming," says Mum of the event which finally did for their marriage. "When it was suggested Pauline live in the granny flat, I was all for it," she continues sadly. "I thought it'd be nice having a woman next door. I used to take her post round, thinking I'd stay for a chat, but I always got the impression she wanted rid of me. She was uncomfortable and didn't want me in there chatting. I thought it strange then, but it's obvious now that she knew what she was after. Once when Jean came to stay, she took me to one side and said, 'I don't like how that Pauline is with your Peter.' 'Well,' I thought, 'he works all day with her.' I knew they were friends, but I still didn't see it."

Dad is adamant she had nothing to be shocked at. "It was never a secret," he argues. "Brenda and I were separated, and Pauline and I went to singles nights in town. I had been out dating other women the whole time, just for something to do, and I'd even introduced her to these other women if they were visiting, and she'd been perfectly civil and accepting. What was I supposed to think?

"Okay, so at some point, Brenda unilaterally decided she wanted me back," he admits. "There was never any discussion. It may be partially my fault because I treated her extremely well. I lent her a car, bought her some new clothes, and didn't push her for the rent. I bought investment properties and allowed her to manage them. As far as I was concerned, she was a friend in need, so I helped her out. We were being pleasant to each other, and maybe she took that to mean we were back together, but I hadn't ever agreed to that. I was much happier in this loose relationship where we could be nice to each other voluntarily, as opposed to a marriage where you are obliged to behave in a certain way. I had no indication of trouble until one New Year's Eve when all three of us went to the singles club party. I mean, we were all single! And that's when the whole thing exploded."

I dare not delve too deeply into the details of that night for fear of upsetting either party; suffice it to say, that was the beginning of the very end.

"I looked across the table at them, chatting and laughing," I remember Mum saying at the time. "And suddenly, I realised they were a couple, and I was the third wheel. I was taken aback. I thought he was with me, not her!" How two intelligent people could somehow come to such a gross misunderstanding boggles the mind. That is until one considers the AS factor: one person recognises explicitly the words that are spoken and the other the meaning that's conveyed or intended to be conveyed.

"And then it was: 'I insist you give this woman up!'" Dad continues. "What? 'It's not for you to insist,' I told her. 'I refuse.' I knew that giving Pauline up would mean I was back in the marriage, so I was hanging on to her like crazy because she was my evidence that I wasn't. It was difficult to believe that suddenly Brenda thought we were married again. I'd made every effort to live in a separate accommodation, and had given no verbal indication that I was going along that road, but she'd been back long enough to convince herself that was the case."

By this time Mum had apparently forgotten she ever left Dad in the first place, hence her outrage. "His line was: 'I'm not going to let you tell me who I can go out with.' To say it wasn't my place to ask him not to take Pauline out is so beyond reasonable that it left me speechless!" She proceeded to go out of her head with grief and anger, resulting in her own lengthy bout of depression. "During our arguments he often said: 'Too much, too much, I can't take it all in at once. You talk too fast, too many words, too many ideas.' I realised then I must give him time to think about things. I mustn't pound him with questions and thoughts. I have to let him process one thing at a time.[67] This is also when he said 'For years I've being trying to be a person I'm not, and I won't do it anymore!' That gave me something to think about; I knew nothing of this! So, when he's finally decided he can't go on any longer, then he gives me some clue as to what's going on? Of course, by then it was too late.

"I was very upset on every level about losing him. He was, still is, the love of my life. I was hurt, depressed, and knotted up. It was a dreadful, dreadful time. I was under so much strain. I remember driving around Newquay in the small hours of the morning, just screaming. A policeman stopped me and asked if I was alright. 'Yes, thank you,' I told him, before shutting the window and driving on, still screaming."

Mum was clearly distraught at losing her life partner, but Dad couldn't reconcile her behaviour with that loss. "Her conduct was, in my opinion, totally unreasonable," he states. "Suddenly she's going crazy, raving and shouting and in great distress, and I'm looking for a reason for this behaviour because this wasn't the person I knew. She had recently started hormone replacement therapy, so I thought we should look at that because something had happened to turn her into a totally

67 Difficulty processing many ideas at once is a common symptom of AS.

different person to the one I'd known for forty years. I insisted she speak to the doctor about it." He simply could not believe her hysterics were the result of heartbreak, and still can't. "How can it be? She'd told me she was leaving me nearly ten years before!" he exclaims in disbelief.

After two years of this pain, she finally insisted on a divorce. "I felt I was already being disgraced because he was around town with her, taking her to places we used to go together. My only way to retain any dignity was to cut myself off. I was ashamed of divorce and viewed it as a failure, but I felt forced into it because he was making a fool of me."

" 'Brenda, I don't think you should divorce me,' he said to me. 'It's a very bad idea.' But I couldn't help myself. Starting the process, I never really imagined it would actually happen. All along he was saying he didn't want to get divorced, and that I was his oldest and best friend. I hoped all along that he wouldn't go through with it, but after a while he said: 'If you want a divorce and I don't, I suppose there's nothing I can do about it.' "

"I endured all the hard times," she says coldly, "living with him while he built the business. I'd be on my own most of the time, and he didn't spend any money on the house or on holidays. It all went back into the factory. Retirement was supposed to be the fun bit. But it's *her* who gets to enjoy that, spending every day with him and going on holidays to nice places. That was supposed to be me, not her!"

"But you said you were leaving him!" I say, in a final attempt to draw a line under this tragedy forever.

"I was trying to take the pressure off. I never really wanted to be finished with him," she says. "But what you say is what he hears. Women expect men to read between the lines, as other women do, but they are very poor at it, and some, like him, can't do it at all."

When I explain to Dad for the last time that, although she said she was leaving him, that didn't mean it was what she really wanted, he doesn't respond.

"What people say and what they think aren't always the same thing," I summarise.

"Well, they are to us Aspergians. We have to listen to the words."

He knows what I say is true, though, because he's intelligent, but knowing it doesn't make it easier for him to recognise when it happens. He'll forever be at a loss when faced with non-verbal communication. And this is the nub of AS relationships: if one party doesn't realise the traits of the other, miscommunication will be rife. Without AS behavioural knowledge, it's a wonder my parents stayed married a few months, never mind thirty-three years. Looking now at the chain of misunderstandings that turned their relationship, loving on the one side and very amicable on the other, into one of vitriol and betrayal, I want to weep with frustration.

In the courtroom, at the finalisation of the divorce, when all was done and dusted, Mum looked to the judge and asked: "Can I cancel it now? I've changed my mind. Can we not do it?" It was too late, though, and that's one of the saddest things about the whole affair. She never wanted to lose him—she loved him still—but didn't realise that mind games and psychological warfare don't work on Aspergians. He was gone. A few years later, he sold his business and retired to Spain with Pauline, after which I didn't see him until my wedding, which is where the crazy idea for this trip was hatched.

"You're opening the box," is Dad's last word on the subject, his voice weak and entreating. "I've got all this shut in a box so I can deal with Brenda civilly. I have it locked away securely, but when I get it out, I start to lose sleep. I lie in bed, and all the things she said, all the things she denied, go over and over in my head. Our previous conversations have picked at the edge of it and caused it to be exposed. It was a distressing period, and I don't like to get it out."

"We shouldn't get it out then," I immediately agree. I'm done asking questions. Case closed.

"You're right, we shouldn't. It's a little bit out now, so let's put it back again. It's easier to shut, as time goes on, than hitherto."

Now I know the whole story of confusion and misunderstanding, I can no longer view my parents' marriage as a failure. It would be melodramatic to say it was doomed from the start, but it certainly required a much fuller understanding of the nature of AS to have had any chance of success. Some of the defining symptoms of the condition seem to be deliberately designed to sabotage marriages: the absence of emotional recognition or support, the self-centredness, depression, and tactile sensitivity. Coming from the era of the 1940s and '50s, my mother, although inexperienced with men, would've had reasonable expectations of how her marriage would turn out. She would've anticipated regular expressions of love, and living with an antisocial, uncommunicative workaholic was a disappointment. She was lonely and suffered affection deprivation, leading to low self-esteem and depression.

Professor Tony Attwood agrees the most common problem for the non-AS partner is loneliness. "Conversations may be few and—the person with AS—may not notice, recall, or want to talk about information of emotional significance to their partner."[68] In a survey of the mental and physical health of couples where the male partner in the relationship had AS, his results were that "men stated that their mental and physical health had greatly improved due to the relationship. This was in contrast to their partners, who reported that their mental health had deteriorated due to the relationship. They described feeling emotionally neglected and physically exhausted and depressed."[69]

Mum moved to another Cornish village to live alone, a sad old cat lady.

"I was very regretful that house and home was broken up," she laments. "It was very hard at the beginning, with the house in such a state and him concentrating on the business, but I did like living there eventually." Twenty years later, her situation has improved. She now lives next door to my sister and her grandchildren in Australia, enjoying watching them grow up from the peace of her verandah, surrounded by her beautiful garden. She's never remarried or even dated. She still carries a photo of him in her purse. Her heart, once confused, now beats true. It knows what it wants, what it wanted all along—the thing it can never have again.

68 Attwood, *Relationship Problems of People with Asperger's Syndrome*, 6.

69 Attwood, *Relationship Problems of People with Asperger's Syndrome*, 7.

Midnight, and we're still wandering through dodgy suburban Havana. Three- and four-story buildings loom above the pavement, blocking out the moonlight, and municipal street lighting is somewhat lacking. We must watch our step, in more ways than one. Eventually we stumble into a posh hotel bar, the sort that has me feeling like I'm betraying my backpacker roots and making a mockery of the local people's financial situation.

"Can we afford this place?" asks Dad as we walk in. He's down to his last few pesos, which he'll need in order to catch a taxi to the airport in the morning.

"Probably," I reply, wrinkling my nose, "but it is my worst nightmare."

"Worst nightmare, right," he repeats, as if processing important new information, "Aye, aye, Captain." With that, he does an about face and walks out. Bless him. The conversation seems a little stilted tonight, anyway, as if the comfortable silence Dad and I have learned to share is fighting the chatty vibe of my Austrian friend with no clear winner. Unspoken words ring louder than verbalised ones. I, for one, can't think of anything to say about Dad's impending departure. Any step in that direction would eventually lead to talk of our next meeting, but there lies a dead end. In any case, no words seem adequate to portray the gratitude I feel for his company in the first place, even more so for his surprise return, and the overwhelming satisfaction I have for this trip which I will never, ever forget.

I'm exceedingly fortunate to have discovered so much about his life, and his way of life, that I never knew. I've observed his idiosyncrasies with amusement and, sometimes, frustration, and I've come to the realisation that I admire him now even more than I did three months ago. If I'm his genetic shadow, I won't complain. If nothing else, if I'm still travelling the world at seventy-two, I'll be delighted with the genes he's bequeathed me. As for his Asperger's, I've seen more of it than ever before. I'm no longer a child, and he no longer feels the need to act normal in front of me, for which I'm grateful. It's fascinating to learn the changes that have occurred in his behaviour over time. Many of the characteristics he displays are in no way negative, just unusual. Some are even commendable and inspire emulation.

"It was quite late in my life that I discovered AS and read the books and got this revelation that explained how I felt about things," he'd said during one of our discussions. "Reading about it enabled me to deal with it a lot better and to behave like other people, because I could see where I was lacking and what I had to work on. Although I have all the acknowledged symptoms, I don't know whether I have them to the degree that I would actually be diagnosed with Asperger's Syndrome. I believe I could have had them worse."

"I don't agree you do have all the traits," I'd argued, defensive to the end.

"Yes, but I've been learning how to hide them for sixty years. I've been working at it. We all have to work at it to fit into society. We change and get better, so you can't judge now who I was as a child, which was a person who avoided speaking to pretty much anybody. I've continued to improve throughout my life as far as dealing with emotions and situations and people, even quite recently."

This is certainly not true of all Aspergians. Since autism, and by extraction AS, only began to be identified regularly in the 1970s, there have been no long-term studies on how Aspergians' behaviour may change over the course of their lifetimes. Of course, this will vary between individuals, sometimes to a high degree, but according to Rebecca Ann Charlton, a senior lecturer in psychology at Goldsmiths University, London, age and severity of autism are linked.

"As age increases, so does the severity of autism traits in social situations, communication and flexible thinking (such as coping with change or generating new ideas or solutions). We also found that older people with autism are more likely than younger people to extract rules from situations or prefer structure (for example, wanting to know how committees are organized or always following the same routine during a task)." The subjects in her ongoing study "all had cognitive abilities in the normal range and did not receive a diagnosis in childhood when autism is most often recognized. Despite this, older people in the study showed more severe features of autism. This might suggest that autism features become more severe with age."[70] I'm very fortunate that isn't the case with Dad, and I'm tempted to mark the positive changes down to brute willpower, although it's surely more complex than that.

The psychologist Devon MacEachron writes, "Neurodiversity is the concept that neurological differences among people should be recognised and respected. The genes for autism and ADHD are not errors but rather the result of variations in the human genome that have and will continue to have advantages for society. Genes associated with autism . . . go back more than 10,000 years. Research suggests that genetic variants linked to autism might have been positively selected during human evolution because they contributed to exceptional memory skills, heightened perception in vision, taste and smell, a precise eye for detail, and an enhanced understanding of systems such as animal behaviour. These characteristics likely remain in the gene pool today because they are still advantageous."[71]

My brother puts it more bluntly: "Asperger's is not a *thing* which people should struggle to understand," he explains. "It is just a word which tries to describe a set of atypical behaviours, and as such, everyone understands it differently. They get confused when the *thing* they are looking for is elusive. The issue of what it is and how to diagnose it, and whether it needs treatment, and with what drugs or what therapies, is very political in the medical profession. They need a *thing* they can agree on in order to make policy, find commercial solutions, and make money. At the moment, there is a very real danger of wrong diagnoses of ADD, AS, and things like that leading to harmful treatments."

He sounds like a guest author in one of Professor Baron-Cohen's books. "It is clear to me that Asperger's, whatever it is, is well within the range of normal human phenomena. By making it a *thing,* we tend to exclude those people as 'not like us' and problematic, thus narrowing our idea of what is healthy and normal. What we should be

70 Charlton, "Autism in Old Age."
71 NowThis News, "Human Neurodiversity."

doing, rather than diagnosing and 'othering,'[72] is accept there is a different mix of Asperger, gender confusion, and manic depressive in all of us, and allow that everyone is special and everyone is normal. If some people are unhappy, or make other people unhappy, then help should be available which doesn't encumber them with too many medical prejudices.

"As Asperger's becomes better known, hopefully people will become more conscious of the unspoken rules, less offended by gauche conversations, more appreciative of engineers creating more soft spaces for people who don't like over-stimulation. Instead of treating Asperger's differently, hopefully society will learn to broaden their idea of what is normal, as it does with the other politically correct categories."

While never a bully, I confess to having veered away from the eccentrics, the shufflers, and the nerds. Just like Dad described himself way back in Belize: "I was always perceived as the 'weirdo,' that guy you speak to once and, from his responses, you know to move on." I plead guilty, your Honour. I'll try to be more patient from now on. I'll look out for the overly detailed, one-sided conversations, the lack of eye contact, the awkwardness, the look of panic before an inappropriate response. I'll realise the cause and make allowances, engage the speaker differently. In the words of Thich Nhat Hanh, Vietnamese Buddhist monk and peace activist: "When you plant lettuce, if it does not grow well, you don't blame the lettuce. You look for reasons it is not doing well. It may need fertilizer, or more water, or less sun. You never blame the lettuce. Yet if we have problems with our friends or family, we blame the other person."[73]Above all, I will understand.

We walk Dad back to his *casa*, the shortness of our strides revealing a shared exhaustion. Due to the iniquities of her neighbourhood, Rosa was particular that we bring him right to her door. She seems very fond

72 John A. Powell and Stephen Menendian, *The Problem with Othering: Towards Inclusiveness and Belonging.* According to the Othering and Belonging Forum, othering is "*a set of dynamics, processes, and structures that engender marginality and persistent inequality across any of the full range of human differences based on group identities.*"

73 Guided Mind, "9 Life Lessons."

of him. Having seen him safely home, we arrange to meet for breakfast before he departs for the airport. I bid him a swift goodnight, still relieved he didn't pull another eccentricity, ditching us and flying home without saying goodbye. That would've been just like him.

It's a quiet afternoon; sensible Mexicans are hiding from the glare of the sun. The streets are dusty but clean, and a faint breeze, combined with the awning shadows outside the little convenience stores, provide the only respite from the shrivelling heat. It's a few days later, and I'm strolling around the same small Cancún plaza where we ate on our first night. The melancholy of ending my travels is seeping away, replaced by the agreeable prospect of returning home. Tomorrow I'll be reunited with Gerda, and I can't wait. She's planned a huge belated birthday party in a local craft brewery with a Caribbean theme, no less, and invited all our friends. It's going to be a great night. She's a legend. I'm a very lucky man.

That first evening, the square was busy with promenading families: an ensemble played acoustic numbers in the bandstand, fathers pulled their young ones around on plastic carts, brightly coloured stalls sold ice cream and enchiladas and beer. We watched the people enjoying life and discussed our future trip. It turned out quite different to how I'd imagined.

I'm still touched by what happened in Havana. Mucki and I returned bright and early the next morning to Dad's *casa,* with plenty of time for breakfast before seeing him into a taxi. The trouble was . . . he wasn't there. When Rosa opened the door, her bright and smiling face fell, and she ushered us inside, where she explained in broken English.

"He go," she said, apologetically. "He say me, say you, he no like say goodbye."

He'd gone, just like that, lit out early for the airport, not because he was anxious about missing his flight but because he intentionally wanted to avoid us. He'd done a smokebomb, disappeared back out of my life without a final word.

When I realised I'd been stood up, part of me couldn't have been less surprised, but another part couldn't quite believe it. It's fair to say I was disappointed.

"I avoid goodbyes," he'd told me. "It's an emotional thing, and I never understood it. If we go out to a bar and Pauline goes around saying goodbye to everyone, I leave first." I have to admit doing the same thing with Gerda, but a quick hug and a "see ya later" would've been nice. I wasn't angry with him, of course, just saddened. I know he's reticent to deal with other, peripheral people, but me—his blood, his *hijo*? Maybe that signifies that I mean more to him than those from whom he can more easily take his leave? Maybe.

Rosa made me understand that she'd been asked to give me a big kiss and a hug in his place, and she did. I embraced her tightly, closing my eyes and imagining him in my grasp. I sucked in my belly to make room for his, felt his bristles on my cheek, and buried my face in his tatty fishing vest, all the while remembering our amazing, enlightening, reaffirming, disjointed, painful, emotional, and overall precious circumnavigation of the Caribbean. It helped, a little.

And now, back at our starting point, afternoon has faded to evening. The bandstand is dark and quiet, and the food stalls all closed. I stand against a shadowed wall, breathing in the salty air tinged with diesel fumes, and opening my ears to the night for the last time. Between the backfiring exhausts, overused car horns, and clamouring of hustlers, I can discern another, more pleasant sound—the soothing yet dramatic notes of a mariachi trio. The guitar, violin, and trumpet knit into a musical rope which encircles and tugs me from my hiding place. I'm pulled along a side street into a larger, busier plaza, where I find the musicians playing to a table of uninterested diners.

I've no idea what they're singing about—although it's bound to be love, revenge, or heroism—but that doesn't matter. The music transports me three months back in time to that warm, dusty night in Tulum. Back then, having just learnt the depressing truth about my father that would colour the whole of our journey, the notes conveyed sadness, longing, and failure. Now, the violin is singing, the guitar strident, and the trumpet soulful. I feel a surge of positivity. I practically float across to the three men, their cheesy black and silver outfits twinkling under the streetlights. They give me their full attention, delighted to be performing for an attentive *gringo*, even one with a strange, faraway look in his eyes. I listen a while longer before tossing them a handful of pesos, then I wander away, smiling.

Epilogue

Kairosclerosis

Two months later, I'm working at the desk in our spare room when the telephone rings. It's Dad, and his tone is upbeat.

"I wanted to tell you that two wonderful things have resulted from our Caribbean odyssey, quite apart from the time we spent together."

"Go on," I say. I'm intrigued, rising to pace the room as is my habit when taking a call. I can picture him doing the same. He has a similar custom when knocking on peoples' front doors—he'll go for a short stroll while he waits for someone to answer, inevitably ending up with his back to them when they do.

"Firstly," he says, "my prostate operation has been successful. For the first time in years, I am comfortable with urination, and I no longer have the worry of the medical procedure hanging over my head." This is the news I've been waiting for, and I make congratulatory noises into the mouthpiece. "The incident on the yacht was a traumatic and painful experience, but it was more than worth it."

"Secondly, I'm still happy! The sertraline has made an incredible difference." This is something I hadn't really thought about since Cuba, having returned to my working life and its attendant distractions. Now that I hear it, though, my face creases up, and I can feel the slight burn of salt water as my tear ducts dilate in involuntary sympathy. I can't think of anything I'd rather have heard today—or any other day. "Were it not for our travel plans I would not have sought it out and would have remained in a state of depression." He goes on to explain how he and Pauline are now the centre of their social circle. They hold dinner parties and karaoke evenings. Elvis is his speciality.

When I describe the person he was during the early part of the trip, he has difficulty recognising himself.

"I wasn't that bad, was I?" he contests.

Yes, you were.

I ring off, delighted to think such a difference could have come from our little sojourn. I'm still on a high when I relate the call to Gerda that evening.

"You've saved his life," she says, squeezing me tightly.

Well, I don't know about that, but it feels really good.

To view photos of Dan & Peter's trip, go to the link:
www.thisisnotaholiday.com/blackdogpix

Appendix I

Further Notes on Asperger Syndrome

This book represents one person's journey (literal and figurative) to understand his father and his father's experience of living with Asperger's and depression. I don't pretend to have expert knowledge on the issues herein but have read widely on the topic to better comprehend the man, his life, and my relationship with him.

Scientists have tried to describe the differing functions of the brain in many ways. An early theory was called Hemispheric Dominance, or the Left Brain vs. Right Brain model, which claimed the left side of the brain dealt with logic and processes while the right side was used more for intuition and emotion. While brain imaging has since debunked this premise, the division of the organ into these two categories led to a more popular hypothesis—the controversial Male Brain vs. Female Brain theory, as presented by leading autism expert Professor Simon Baron-Cohen of Cambridge University.

The "extreme male behaviour" theory may partially explain the uneven gender weighting in, for instance, engineering and IT jobs where systemising is paramount (more males), and the caring professions in which empathy is essential (more females). Of course, many other explanations can be offered for this imbalance, not least the continued existence of societal gender-inequality issues.

At the time of writing, the terms "neurotypical" (NT), describing someone who is not on the autistic spectrum, and "atypical" (AT) (or "neuroatypical"), describing someone who is on the spectrum or is suffering from other mental or behavioural disorders, have gained popularity. The use of NT and AT thus removes to some extent the dangers associated with Baron-Cohen's gender-based terms. Nevertheless, throughout this book I have used the term Asperger Syndrome, or Asperger's or AS for short, as this is the one with which most people are familiar.

If AS does present as "extreme male" behaviour, then males are inherently closer to the condition than females, so it follows that AS would probably be more prevalent in males. In fact, a 2017 report by the American Academy of Child and Adolescent Psychiatry concluded a ratio of 3:1.[74] Women with AS are less easily diagnosed because their behaviour is closer to that of a regular male, and so they stand out less in society. Assuming the existence of the "extreme male brain," it is natural to postulate the existence of the opposite, an "extreme female brain," although examples of this have so far not been identified, maybe because being "systemblind" ("Argh, bloody computers never do what I tell them!") is more acceptable in society than being "mind-blind" ("A busload of school kids just drove off a bridge? So what?").

Diagnosing autism is not an exact science but is based on behavioural profiles in the *American Psychiatric Association's Diagnostic and Statistical Manual of Mental Disorders* (DSM). In 2013, Asperger Syndrome was removed from the DSM in favour of the term Autism Spectrum Disorder (ASD), which takes into account a broader group of developmental disorders. Instead of the DSM, UK doctors tend to refer to the World Health Organisation's *International Classification of Diseases* (ICD). No change has been made to this manual, so UK doctors continue to diagnose Asperger Syndrome.

It's hard to say how prevalent AS is today due to the unspecific nature of the spectrum and the large number of cases going undiagnosed. Previous estimates have ranged from 1 person in 150 to 1 in 250. Since AS has been absorbed into ASD, which covers a larger

74 Loomes et al, "*What is the male-to-female ratio in Autism Spectrum Disorder? A systematic review and meta-analysis,*" 466-474.

range of symptoms, evaluation has been further confused. In 2016, the US Centers for Disease Control Autism and Developmental Disabilities Monitoring Network published a figure of 1 in 54 children identified as being ASD.[75]

Professor Simon Baron-Cohen's book about male vs. female brain theory, *The Essential Difference* (2003), is still considered an important volume in AS research. Throughout this book, I have referred to many suppositions based on his studies. Unless otherwise identified, all commonly held beliefs about AS should be attributed to Baron-Cohen.

The newest *Diagnostic and Statistical Manual of Mental Disorders* (DSM–5) from the American Psychiatric Association now includes three levels of autism based on necessary levels of support. People with Level One autism need the least support, while people with Level Three autism need the most. Some people still use the terms high- and low-functioning autism to describe relative positions on the spectrum, but Lisa Jo Rudy, autism advocate, parent, and author, argues against this:

"Despite problems inherent in the terms high- and low-functioning autism, they are in common use, usually by people who are not autistic. And they are used to describe the degree to which someone on the spectrum is (or appears to be) similar to people who are *not* on the spectrum. In other words, autistic people who are or appear to be closer to "normal" are considered to be high functioning. Thus, for example:

- High-functioning people use spoken language to communicate. Low-functioning people are more likely to use technology or picture boards and may have limited or no spoken language.
- High-functioning people are more likely to be able to manage the expectations of an academic setting. This is often a result of having a better handle on spoken language and a greater awareness of the expectations of others.

75 Centers for Disease Control, *"Data and statistics on Autism Spectrum Disorder."*

- High-functioning people are usually more aware of social conventions. For example, they are more likely to use tools and utensils typically, greet others appropriately, etc.
- Low-functioning people generally look and sound very different from their typical peers. In other words, their disability is more visually and aurally obvious to the casual observer. High functioning people are more likely to appear typical (until some event or conversation makes their autism more obvious).
- Low-functioning people are less likely to be included in typical classes or activities and are more likely to be in a "substantially separate" academic setting. High-functioning people are more likely to be included—with or without support—in general classrooms and out-of-school programs.

All of these distinctions, however, are artificial, and they are by no means absolute. That's because autistic people behave differently in different situations, and every individual has a range of strengths and challenges."[76]

76 Rudy, "What's the difference between high and low functioning autism."

Appendix II

Intelligence

The nine types of intelligence identified by Professor Gardner, and summarised by the Association for Supervision and Curriculum Development, are:

- Linguistic intelligence–the ability to think in words and to use language to express and appreciate complex meanings.
- Logical-Mathematic intelligence–the ability to calculate, quantify, consider propositions and hypotheses, and carry out complete mathematical operations.
- Spatial intelligence–the ability to think in three dimensions.
- Musical intelligence–the capacity to discern pitch, rhythm, timbre, and tone.
- Bodily-Kinaesthetic intelligence–the capacity to manipulate objects and use a variety of physical skills.
- Interpersonal intelligence–the ability to understand and interact effectively with others.
- Intrapersonal intelligence–the capacity to understand oneself and one's thoughts and feelings.
- Existential intelligence–the ability to tackle deep questions about human existence, such as the meaning of life.
- Naturalist intelligence–the ability to discriminate among living things.

Gardner's theory has not been widely embraced by the scientific community due to the impossibility of proving or disproving it, but still, it displays a useful rough categorisation of thought functions, if not necessarily "intelligences."

Appendix III

Temple Grandin

Temple Grandin relates love in her life to a sense of achievement, which she titles "I Am What I Do."

"For me," she writes, "emotional complexity is replaced with intellectual complexity. My greatest satisfaction in life comes from doing things. My best social interactions always involved activities with others with whom I shared a common interest. My career gives my life meaning."

On the need to be perfect, she writes: "People with autism and AS tend towards black-and-white thinking. They see themselves and the world around them in polar opposites, and this tendency feeds their need to be perfect. Even the tiniest mistakes and mishaps can seem like monumental failures to them, creating high levels of anxiety when their efforts of the events around them do not measure up to this all-or-nothing scale."

While Dad disputes this need to be perfect, it can be seen in his behaviour. He demands very high standards from himself. As an adult, he took numerous open university courses and needed to get at least 98 percent to be satisfied. It was the same with any hobby he tried, from macro photography to Indian cooking. In the latter, he insisted on making his own garam masala from scratch.

At one stage, he concluded the most important question regarding how to live and structure one's life was whether or not there was a god and an afterlife with punishment or reward. "If there is a god, then one should surely abide by his instructions. Most folk, I believe, live their lives on the basis that maybe there is a god. They try not do anything terrible and hope they are forgiven when judgement time comes." Too vague, he thought, so he decided to study the subject intently. He bought a multitude of books; he read the Bible and the Koran from cover to cover, both in their original languages with direct page-by-page translation. In the end, he concluded that both seemed to be written by men to control men.

Appendix IV

Deep and Shallow Empathy

Baron-Cohen's bold statements in *The Essential Difference* are not accepted wholesale by the psychology community. Steve Taylor, PhD, a psychology lecturer in the UK, is among those questioning Baron-Cohen's initial assumption. He argues that it is incorrect to define autism and AS as empathy disorders, and that the kind of empathy Aspergians do not display is only "shallow" or "cognitive" empathy. This is "the cognitive ability to put yourself in another person's shoes, or to gain an inkling of how they are feeling based on their behaviour, facial expressions, and speech. This is the kind of empathy that is 'measured' in tests where people are asked to look at pictures of faces or eyes and guess what emotion they are expressing." There is also "deep" or "emotional" empathy, which is "the ability not just to imagine but also to actually *feel* what other people are experiencing. It's the ability to actually enter the 'mind space' of another person, so that you can sense their feelings and emotions . . . Deep empathy is the source of compassion and often leads to altruistic behaviour, which is rooted in the desire to alleviate the suffering we can sense in others."

MRI studies on neural systems have shown that different parts of the brain are engaged when each of the empathies are activated, and to some extent, they can be seen as independent. A person can display strong cognitive empathy yet little emotional empathy, and vice versa. In Steve Taylor's example, "A successful politician may have a high level of shallow empathy, in the sense that they can read the emotional atmosphere, know instinctively how to respond to situations or body language, and tell people what they want to hear. But they may also have a low level of deep empathy, which makes it possible for them to behave ruthlessly, by exploiting and maltreating others in order to achieve their ambitions. (Exploitative behaviour is only possible if there is absence of deep empathy, which means you can't sense the suffering you inflict on others.) And it may be that for people on the autistic spectrum, this equation is reversed: They may not be good at shallow empathy, but may be not at all impaired in terms of deep empathy."[77]

77 Taylor, "Is Autism Really an 'Empathy Disorder'?"

Glossary

Introduction: Monochopsis –the subtle but persistent feeling of being out of place.

Chapter 1: Dysphoria–a state of unease or generalised dissatisfaction with life.
Chapter 2: Farouche–sullen or shy in company.
Chapter 3: Alexithymia–the inability to express one's feelings in words.
Chapter 4: Sophronise–to imbue with sound moral principles.
Chapter 5: Aflunters–in a state of disorder
Chapter 6: Atrabilious–given to or marked by melancholy.
Chapter 7: Myötähäpeä–embarrassment one feels on someone else's behalf.
Chapter 8: Begrutten–showing the effects of much weeping.
Chapter 9: Sillage–the impression left in a room after someone has been and gone.
Chapter 10: Jouska–a hypothetical conversation compulsively played out in the head.
Chapter 11: Dromomania–an uncontrollable impulse or desire to wander or travel.
Chapter 12: Retrouvailles–the joy of reuniting with someone after a long separation.
Chapter 13: Thelemite–one who does as he pleases.
Chapter 14: Ergophile–a person who loves to work.
Chapter 15: Tacenda–things that are better left unsaid.
Chapter 16: Absquatulate–to leave suddenly without saying goodbye.

Epilogue: Kairosclerosis–the moment you realise you're currently happy.

Citations

4. John Elder Robinson, *Look Me in the Eye* (New York: Crown Publishers, 2008), 5.
5. Simon Baron-Cohen, *The Essential Difference* (London: Penguin | Allen Lane, 2003).
6. Simon Baron-Cohen, *The Essential Difference* (London: Penguin | Allen Lane, 2003), 7.
8. Simon Baron-Cohen, S, *The Essential Difference* (London: Penguin | Allen Lane, 2003), 141.
9. Simon Baron-Cohen, S, *The Essential Difference* (London: Penguin | Allen Lane, 2003), 45.
10. Simon Baron-Cohen, S, *The Essential Difference* (London: Penguin | Allen Lane, 2003), 147.
11. Temple Grandin, *The Way I See It* (Arlington, Texas: Future Horizons, 2008), 225.
13. Temple Grandin, *The Way I See It* (Arlington, Texas: Future Horizons, 2008), 167.
14. John Elder Robison, *Look Me in the Eye* (New York: Crown Publishers, 2008), 31.
16. Temple Grandin, *The Way I See It* (Arlington, Texas: Future Horizons, 2008), 191.
21. Simon Baron-Cohen, *The Essential Difference* (London: Penguin | Allen Lane, 2003), 137.
24. Simon Baron-Cohen, *The Essential Difference* (London: Penguin | Allen Lane, 2003), 123.

26. Simon Baron-Cohen, *The Essential Difference* (London: Penguin | Allen Lane, 2003), 141.
27. Sarah Cassidy et al, "Suicidal Ideation and Suicide Plans or Attempts in Adults with Asperger's Syndrome Attending a Specialist Diagnostic Clinic: A Clinical Cohort Study," *The Lancet Psychiatry* 1, no. 2 (July 2014): 142–147.
30. Ann Thwaite, "Daddy Dearest," *The Guardian*, November 1, 2002, https://www.theguardian.com/books/2002/nov/02/featuresreviews.guardianreview35.
31. "Norway Gasoline Prices," Trading Economics, accessed March 24, 2020, https://tradingeconomics.com/norway/gasoline-prices.
32. Kenneth Roberson, "What Causes Asperger's Syndrome?" *Kenneth Roberson, Ph.D.* (blog), accessed March 24, 2020, https://www.kennethrobersonphd.com/what-causes-aspergers-syndrome.
33. Simon Baron-Cohen, *The Essential Difference* (London: Penguin | Allen Lane, 2003), 23–27.
39. Tony Attwood, *Relationship Problems of People with Asperger's Syndrome* (London: Jessica Kingsley Publishers, 2012), 10.
40. John Elder Robison, *Look Me in the Eye* (New York: Crown Publishers, 2008), 221.
41. Hazel Muir, "Einstein and Newton Showed Signs of Autism," *New Scientist,* April 30, 2003, https://www.newscientist.com/article/dn3676-einstein-and-newton-showed-signs-of-autism.
43. Arthur Conan Doyle, *The Lost World* (Oxford: Oxford University Press, 1995), 92.
46. "Downloadable Tests," Autism Research Centre, accessed March 24, 2020, https://www.autismresearchcentre.com/arc_tests.
47. Simon Baron-Cohen, *The Essential Difference* (London: Penguin | Allen Lane, 2003), 163.
48. Henri Charrière, *Papillon,* Translated by June P. Wilson and Walker B. Michaels. (London: HarperCollins, 2012).
49. Henri Charrière, *Papillon,* Translated by June P. Wilson and Walker B. Michaels. (London: HarperCollins, 2012), 252.
50. Henri Charrière, *Papillon,* Translated by June P. Wilson and Walker B. Michaels. (London: HarperCollins, 2012), 227.

51. Franklin J. Schnaffner, dir., *Papillon* (1973; Culver City, CA: Columbia Pictures)
52. Gérard de Villiers, *Papillon Épinglé* (Paris: Presses de la Cité, 1970)
56. "Pitch Drop Experiment," The University of Queensland, accessed July 8, 2020, https://smp.uq.edu.au/pitch-drop-experiment
57. Herbert Abraham, *Asphalts and Allied Substances* (New York: D. Van Nostrand Company, 1938), 42.
68. Tony Attwood, *Relationship Problems of People with Asperger's Syndrome* (London: Jessica Kingsley Publishers, 2012), 6.
69. Tony Attwood, *Relationship Problems of People with Asperger's Syndrome* (London: Jessica Kingsley Publishers, 2012), 7.
70. Rebecca Ann Charlton, "Autism Features May Be More Severe in Old Age," *Spectrum News*, October 18, 2016, https://www.spectrumnews.org/opinion/autism-features-may-be-more-severe-in-old-age.
71. NowThis News, "Human Neurodiversity Should Be Celebrated, Not Treated as a Disorder," YouTube video, 3:15, July 23, 2018, https://www.youtube.com/watch?v=aWxmEv7fOFY.
73. "9 Life Lessons from Thich Nhat Hanh," *Guided Mind* (blog), accessed March 24, 2020, https://www.guidedmind.com/blog/9-life-lessons-from-thich-nhat-hanh.
74. Rachel Loomes et al, "What is the male-to-female ratio in Autism Spectrum Disorder? A systematic review and meta-analysis," *Journal of the American Academy of Adolescent and Child Psychiatry* 55, issue 6 (June 2017): 466-474.
75. Centers for Disease Control and Prevention, "Data and statistics on Autism Spectrum Disorder," accessed July 22, 2020, https://www.cdc.gov/ncbddd/autism/data.html.
76. Lisa Jo Rudy, "What's the difference between high and low functioning autism," *Verywell Health*, November 19, 2019, https://www.verywellhealth.com/high-and-low-functioning-autism-260599.
77. Steve Taylor, "Is Autism Really an 'Empathy Disorder'?" *Psychology Today*, May 20, 2017, https://www.psychologytoday.com/au/blog/out-the-darkness/201705/is-autism-really-empathy-disorder.